# A Darling of the Twenties

## Madge Bellamy

# A Darling of the Twenties

## Madge Bellamy

### by Madge Bellamy

### Introduction by Kevin Brownlow

**Filmography by William M. Drew**

The Vestal Press Ltd.
Vestal, New York

**Library of Congress Cataloging-in-Publication Data**

Bellamy, Madge, 1899–
  A darling of the twenties.

  "Filmography": p.
  1. Bellamy, Madge, 1899–     . 2. Motion picture
actors and actresses—United States—Biography.
I. Title.
PN2287.B416A3  1989     791.43′028′092[B] 89-22587
ISBN 0-911572-85-6 (alk. paper)
ISBN 0-911572-75-9 (pbk. : alk. paper)

The illustration reproduced on the front cover is taken from
*Picture Play* magazine, August, 1928.

The Vestal Press, Ltd.
PO Box 97
Vestal, NY 13851-0097

# *Contents*

# *Acknowledgements*

Although the major work of writing has been Miss Bellamy's and the majority of photographs come from her personal collection, individuals and organizations who have given additional assistance need to be recognized for their contributions in enhancing the presentation of her materials. Among those individuals are Margaret D. Lemke, Robert S. Birchard, the late Stephen Jochsberger, William M. Drew, and Q. David Bowers; organizations include the National Film Archive, London; the Wisconsin Center for Film & Theater Research, and the Larry Edmunds Bookshop. Thank you.

The Publisher

# A Darling of the Twenties

## Madge Bellamy

# Introduction

Somehow the image is wrong. You don't associate the virginal image of the typical silent screen heroine with a woman shooting at a recalcitrant lover. But what about *Sunset Boulevard*? Didn't Gloria Swanson do precisely that? Yes, but that was only a movie. This is real life. And as one of Swanson's contemporaries is supposed to have said, "None of us floozies was that nuts."

Madge Bellamy is revealing her turbulent life not simply to warm the embers of memory in her old age. She is trying to confront the strange and willful personality that was hers—sixty years ago.

You may not have heard of Madge Bellamy. That's not her fault. Her films have mostly disappeared, and the handful that survive are seldom revived. But she was an important Hollywood star of the twenties. She also had the reputation of being hard to handle. She was unconventional, impulsive, and extremely beautiful; it's surprising that no one has made a film about her. Once this book is out, maybe they will.

Madge Bellamy—her real name is Margaret Philpott—was born in the last year of the nineteenth century. By then, the moving picture, only a few years older, had found a humble home in amusement arcades. It seemed destined to be swept away as a passing fad. Madge had little interest; she can barely recall the first films she ever saw. She reserved her admiration for the stage and the dance.

By the time she was old enough to appear in public, the moving picture had made a remarkable transformation. The nickelodeon craze had seized the cities, and every small town had a theatre. Those who ran the business came mostly from the stage—vaudeville—and they knew all about stars, their temperamental ways, and the staggering salaries they had to be paid. These producers were determined to avoid all that. Some of them tried an experiment: advertising the company, but not the players, in the hope that the public would want to see, for example, Biograph films, and not grow curious about the fetching blonde who played in them.

It was too much to hope. The fetching blonde became known as The Biograph Girl, and that fame was enough for her to be stolen by rivals and advertised under her real name: Florence Lawrence. The next Biograph Girl didn't last long either. She became considerably better known as Mary Pickford, and considerably better off, working for producer Adolph Zukor.

Zukor had long believed in the drawing power of great names. He felt the nickelodeon era was over and advocated high-class films with high-class names to attract the carriage trade. He began at the top, importing a French version of *Queen Elizabeth* starring Sarah Bernhardt to inaugurate his new company: Famous Players in Famous Plays.

He saw a future in which stars would step, ready-made, from stage to screen. So did many other producers, including Samuel Goldwyn, responsible for many of the films featuring the great opera star Geraldine Farrar with whom Madge Bellamy made her first appearance.

But the film-going public—still largely working class and ignorant of the theatre—was unimpressed by such high-toned entertainment. They preferred Mary Pickford. In this, they showed remarkably good

Evans Studio
L. A.

taste; while the players from the stage were remote and exaggerated in their acting, Mary Pickford was remarkably direct and natural. She was an extremely attractive girl from a poor background in Toronto, Canada. She was phenomenally gifted: she could play children or adults, tragedy or comedy with heart-catching realism. She quickly learned the intricacies of film-making and had an astonishing head for business. She married one of the most popular players of the time—Douglas Fairbanks—and lived in style in Beverly Hills.

And yet with all of her advantages, her career failed to survive much past the end of the silent era. Her most prolific years were around the First World War. Then, of course, her mother, Charlotte, was at her elbow, and the power of movie mothers should never be underestimated. Had Madge Bellamy's mother been a better businesswoman, undoubtedly Madge would have had an even more successful career. (Her career, it must be stressed, was highly successful by most standards; film-struck girls would have given anything to experience a week of it.)

The mothers were the *eminences grises* of the early industry, approving or rejecting scenarios, salaries, and prospective husbands with the same intensity. Studio heads realized that stars were a necessary evil, that the public was going to part with huge sums of money to gaze at them, and there was absolutely nothing they could do about it. While a steelworker earned, at best, $25.00 a week in 1916, Mary Pickford received $10,000. And that was only her drawing account; the benefits remained a secret.

A few years later, when Madge Bellamy entered pictures, the star system was in place and ready to bring her similar fame and fortune, provided she cooperated, or ready to wreck her if she proved rebellious. The star system was a collusion between producers and exhibitors, aided and abetted by the press, which stood to gain millions from advertising. Its benefits were obvious: dedicated technicians and a sophisticated distributing system helped stars appeal to the widest audiences. A vital element was promotion; how Madge Bellamy became famous before the public ever saw her on the screen can be read about in this book.

The trouble was that human beings tended to be regarded as merchandise by this system. Press agents knew that no lie was too blatant if it sold tickets. No trick was too despicable if it benefited the producers.

Producers in the silent days had little to do with the creative side of picture-making. They were content to make money and let the directors make the pictures. Madge Bellamy's first producer, Tom Ince, was an exception; he had been a director, so he worked at his studio and exercised control over its creative output. But the rest of the producers were money men. Most of the big names operated from New York—3,000 miles away from the studios in Los Angeles. They dealt with the banks and delegated virtually all other affairs—except those with chorus girls—to secondary figures like Winfield Sheehan or Sol Wurtzel. If the New York men were the dictators, these were the *gauleiters*—working at the studios, hiring and firing, immensely powerful, but largely uncreative. Few of them even understood how to make a picture. But they knew the star system because they operated it. Most sinister of all, they knew each other, met frequently over poker games, and ran a blacklist. If an actor or actress failed the system in any way—well, read what happened to Madge Bellamy.

Mind you, when Madge fell foul of the system, there was little surprise. If anyone asked for it, she did. But that is one of the reasons she wrote this book—to try to understand her own behavior.

What sort of actress was she? The trouble is that so few Bellamy films survive that she is hard to judge. Mary Pickford thought highly of her; she cast her opposite her beloved brother, Jack, in *Garrison's Finish* (1923), and Mary had excellent taste.

I have seen *Lorna Doone* (1922), and I have to admit that while it was directed by a man for whom I have the highest admiration (the Frenchman Maurice Tourneur), the picture is a sad disappointment. It came early in Madge Bellamy's career when she admits she was more interested in looking beautiful than in portraying a character. And she undoubtedly succeeded.

Beauty, remember, was new to the screen. The early players had been filmed on stages open to the sky with harsh sunlight diffused by muslin scrims. This flatness had been replaced by exquisite lighting enhanced by gauze to soften facial features.

Madge poses through the film as if being painted, and she looks very impressive. Although she loved the novel and empathized with the character, none of that comes through in the film. Tourneur betrayed the story in a way that shows he was more interested in form than content. For example, he filmed a long-shot for the wedding scene without Madge because the clouds were right and she arrived at the set late. Tourneur gave her little helpful direction, and she ended up being what she termed "a sugar-water heroine."

She is far better in *Lazybones*, but she clashed with its director, Frank Borzage, because he wanted her to dirty her fingernails. Thus she lost the biggest opportunity of her career: the lead in *Seventh Heaven*, which went to Janet Gaynor. Borzage refused her, even though the head of the studio wanted her and had arranged for her to be filmed on the battlefields of France during her trip to Europe. Borzage was one of the studio's top directors, but even so, he must have had a fight with studio brass. How Madge regretted her commitment to "beauty!"

But we cannot blame her. The fan magazines were obsessed with beauty. The star system depended on it. And though she did not consider herself a beauty, Penrhyn Stanlaws, the artist (and later film director), considered Madge to be the most beautiful young girl he had ever seen.

"If I am beautiful," she said, "it was just due to the fact that I thought myself into being beautiful."

This engrossment with beauty did not sit too well with directors who hoped for more human behavior before the cameras. And that is how she won the reputation of being hard to handle.

"You were the hardest dame to handle in all Hollywood," Harry Carr told her. "Either you were crying or the director was crying most of the time" (*Screen Secrets*, May 1929, p. 99).

"It was a matter of upbringing," Madge explained. "It is very hard for a girl brought up in the South, as I had been, to be so ordered, to be told to stand up while they looked her over like a horse."

She admitted, too, that she found it hard to let herself go. She was always self-conscious. Yet she screened, as Tom Ince put it, "like a million dollars." This made it hard for the producers to cast her aside—as they did very casually with scores of others. Their investment in Madge was too great. Hadn't her first publicity acclaimed her as "Someone Extraordinary"?

"The torch of dramatic genius is truly alight in this little girl," declared *Motion Picture Classic* (January 1921, p. 46).

They gave her a slogan: "The most sensitive face on the screen." They built her up as a Bernhardt and then cast her in comedies she hated.

"Tragediennes are supposed to suffer," she said, "and so I suffer—in comedies."

What sort of person was Madge Bellamy in the twenties? One hard-bitten journalist called her "a conversational bootlegger":

> I don't know whether she will like my saying it or not, but she can peddle more conversation in a minute than any other cinema sister in Hollywood can get off her chest in an hour. She scintillates, coruscates —and I would say enervates, if she were not so brilliant with it all. I have never heard so much talk all at once from one small girl in my life. (*Motion Picture Classic*, March 1922, p. 36).

He thought she had a 40-year-old mind in a nineteen-year-old body (Madge was shedding years from her age even at this early stage).

"And for the life of me, I couldn't tell you what it is that makes you want to hug her all the time you are talking to her. Even Mary Pickford never affected me that way."

MADGE BELLAMY
in
"The Man in Blue"

(National Film Archive, London)

Press agents did not have to write dialogue for her. She spoke of her work with rare intelligence.

"I don't believe in seltzer-water acting," she told journalist Myrtle Gebhart. "An old French axiom has it that 'to suggest is to create, to state is to destroy.' I don't want to be too positive, too blatant—for that destroys illusion. I want to suggest a thing subtly, just strongly enough to make the people go home and *think* about it" (*Picture Play*, August 1922, p. 58).

How much she put her ideas into practice we will not be able to tell unless or until her missing films reappear. It is possible that some of her playing was *too* quiet, for she won a reputaton for being "beautiful, but dumb."

"Madge Bellamy is sure that she is stupid," reported Agnes Smith in *Photoplay*. "She is just as certain of her stupidity as most people are of their cleverness. For years, the critics have elected Madge as the prize scholar in the 'beautiful, but dumb' class. And, like the rest of us, Madge believes anything she sees in print" (October 1926, p. 31).

"'Sometimes,' says Madge, 'I feel so discouraged that I'd like to take my money—I've made plenty of it—and retire. Sometimes I feel that nobody likes me and I'd like to quit and live among people who will love me.'"

If being stupid means making a firm place for yourself on the screen and putting away a nice little pile of money, wouldn't it be great to be dumb?

And yet, in *Sandy*, Madge came out of her shell, giving a lively and sparkling flapper performance. She bobbed her hair, dyed it blonde, and cut loose from the soulful-eyes stuff. Madge had her little fling and surprised 'em all.

Alas, Allan Dwan, her director for another comedy, *Summer Bachelors*, said that her blonde hair made her look dumber than ever. But once again, her conversation was scarcely that of an idiot.

"I know that I've been wrong about a lot of things," she told Agnes Smith.

"Acting, for instance. I always thought that acting was a question of emotions—that you felt a scene and played it as you felt it.

"Well, I was wrong about that. Acting is a matter of intelligence and observation. You don't have to feel an emotion to portray it. You must observe how other people express their emotions.

"Mr. Dwan and I had an interesting conversation on the set this morning. I had been playing a sad scene and when I finished, Mr. Dwan asked me what I had been thinking about. And I told him I had been thinking about something sad. 'Well,' said Mr. Dwan, 'you should have been thinking of the muscles of your face.

"Now I see what has been wrong with me. I have been trying to feel emotions and express them. I have never thought much about the technique; I simply wanted to be sincere. That was a mistake.

"So I have been sitting here practicing with the muscles of my face. Look!" And Miss Bellamy drew her eyebrows. Instantly, the tears slowly rose to her eyes.

"See, I am crying and yet, I am not thinking of anything sad. It's just a muscular reaction."(*Photoplay*, October 1927, p. 31)

The "beautiful, but dumb" slogan caused controversy. Norbert Lusk, the reporter whom she met upon her arrival in Hollywood, came to her defence in *Picture Play* in an article headed "She is NOT Dumb!":

Madge Bellamy is one of the most intelligent girls I know. She is a rare instance of pure beauty combined with intellect. . . .

"What do you mean by intelligence in her case?" unbelievers have asked. "Does she know whether it's raining, and don't you have to tell her?" Patiently, I have moved over to another line of defense.

For one thing, Miss Bellamy writes very well. She thinks clearly and puts her thoughts on paper likewise. She has style, too, a delicate wit and quaint, somewhat old-fashioned phrasing which makes you think a rather elderly person is writing. . . .

When I told her that *Sandy* had put her across with some of her most severe critics instead of preening herself on a victory, she said, "It was a flashy part. If it was a success, then it only proves what I've lately discovered: naturalness doesn't make itself felt on the screen nearly so much as artful imitation" (November 1926, p. 16).

Of course, her public decided she WAS Sandy, a wild-living flapper with a hip-flask under her rolled stockings. Surviving members of this unofficial fan club will be fascinated to see how right they were—and how wrong.

"To say that Madge Bellamy longs to create some film character deeper, more true than those she has already created, and created well, is putting it tritely," wrote Peter Milnes. "Just at present the screen seems to be in the rather embarrassing position of treating one of its assets a little shabbily" (*Motion Picture Classic*, April 1927, p. 87).

The screen finally gave her that coveted role . . . as Sally Quail in Fox's talking picture version of Edna Ferber's *Mother Knows Best* (1928). It was tailor-made for Madge Bellamy because it portrays an ambitious, stage-made mother (Louise Dresser) who robs the till in her husband's drugstore to pay for singing and dancing lessons for her daughter. As the girl grows up, her career is manipulated until she bursts onto the Broadway stage. But the mother dictates even her romantic life, and no boy is allowed to come near her daughter for long.

"The most effective sequence," said *Motion Picture Magazine*, "is the final scene where the mother is finally convinced that her efforts to thwart natural emotional impulses in her daughter have almost robbed the girl of life itself" (December 1928, p. 68).

The Movietone sound track enabled Madge Bellamy to demonstrate her versatility—she did impressions of Harry Lauder, Anna Held, and Al Jolson—and she won the finest notices of her career.

"The acting is positively superb," said *Motion Picture Magazine*. "Madge Bellamy proves herself a real star" (December 1928, p.68).

It was the high point of her career. And it was virtually the end of it. She walked out of her contract; and although she did a few pictures after that, she never returned to full employment at a studio.

We can deplore the waste of talent and the loss it represents to us. But none of us can do more than guess at the emotional strains of stardom and how such stress affected her behavior. Could any of us have survived the withering glare of publicity, the ceaseless demands on our time and energy, the vultures who surround anyone of great wealth, and—more simply and most significantly—the lack of fulfillment?

We look back on the silent era as a period of astonishing achievement, but the Hollywood star system had its victims. This is the dramatic and touching case history of one of them.

*Kevin Brownlow*

Madge's star on Hollywood Boulevard.

# Chapter One

It was 1917; America had entered the World War. Our closest friend's son was sent home in a box, and I attended the first funeral in my life. During the drive to the cemetery, his older brother held my hand in a cold, vise-like grip as if he were holding on to life itself.

About this time, Mama and I went to Kansas City because we did not have enough money to go to New York City. Mama got a job as a saleslady in a department store right away, and an agent teamed me with a pimply-faced boy to sing and dance.

Our performance at an Elk's Club affair met with mild success. Then the agent sent me and Mama to a "tab" (short for "tabloid") show, which was a small musical, and I was engaged to travel with it.

There were four chorus girls, the manager's wife, me, and two other girls who were the loveliest, most fragile blondes whom I had ever seen. The manager, who was the comedian, did "blackouts" (short charades with a surprise or naughty ending) with several of the girls. I did a toe dance in a white tarlatan ballet dress. At the first performance, I was politely, if coolly, received. These were dirty, howling, gum-chomping, tobacco-spitting, smoking, rowdy audiences.

We travelled over Kansas and Oklahoma. I admired the blonde girls; they could build out their eyelashes with hot wax until they were an inch long. At night, men stood in line outside their hotel door, Mama told me.

When we came to Oklahoma City, a bigger tab company was playing there. It was burlesque, and the famous comedian Jim Barton was the star. We went to see their manager, and he hired Mama to be a chorus girl and me to do two solo toe dances. There were about fifty chorus girls and several comedians. We travelled on up to Canada. A staircase was built for me to run down on my toes as I made my entrance on stage. Several times I fell, but the audiences were kind and applauded when I got up and carried on.

It may be hard to believe, but I heard few dirty words in the time that I was with these companies except once from Mama when she told a chorus girl, "You kiss my ass." The girl smiled sweetly and said, "I will, dearie, if you'll wash it."

The sadness and isolation of this lifestyle was brought home to me when the girl who dressed next to me was seized with an epileptic attack. She clutched the mirror and shook it before she fell. No friends came to console her during her illness, and I realized how much sadness and loneliness these girls suffered.

At night, in the cheap hotel rooms, Mother and I read aloud to each other. She said, "There is no pleasure like the pleasure of a good mind. Art is mankind saying, 'I will bring order and meaning out of the chaos of mind and heart. . . .'"

Annie-mama, as I called her, had the delicate shadowed face of a madonna. Her name was Anne Margaret Derden Philpott; she thought her maiden name, Derden, was Chinese, but the Derdens were from England. An estate called Derden Manor was the home of Lord Byron.

Someone said of her, "She may not seem the most beautiful, but when she smiles, she is." She had a gay, flashing smile. Her almost black hair was parted in the middle, and the curls about her neck looked like clusters of

Madge Bellamy (Margaret Philpott) and her mother, Anne "Annie" Margaret Derden Philpott.

Malaga grapes and were always tied into a psyche knot. Dimples surrounded her mouth, and her voice and laugh were as musical as the Chopin that she played so well. Even now, for me to go on living without her seems an almost sinister and macabre thing to do. The remembrance of her dark eyes dims the world's lights for me. When I was young, Mother said that I treated her more like a lover than a child. I adored her and was so jealous that I once cried when I found a man's picture among her things.

Daddy taught English for twenty years at Texas A & M University, first as an assistant professor and then as head of his department. He also coached the Texas Aggies' football team. The last three years that he was there, he never lost a game. Naturally, he was famous and is still remembered today.

William Bledsoe Philpott was tall and thin; he had lost his auburn hair before I was born. When I was little, he wore whiskers and looked very stern. Before he died, he resembled Eisenhower, which made me love the General. Daddy called himself a Jeffersonian Democrat and considered me to be dogmatic.

He was polite and gallant with women, a fine orator and in demand as a speaker and visionary. His wonderful schemes failed because he trusted other men and often was betrayed. Yet he started *Fad*, a magazine that became the successful *Munsey's*. He built and marketed a home cabinet steam bath and worked several years on a plan to use a dirigible to carry produce from the West Coast to the East Coast. He was the first realtor to bus customers out to land tracts, feeding and lecturing them on the way. He tried to sell the Fox Company a color motion picture camera years before color motion pictures were standard. This camera worked; he photographed me many times with it. Fox considered buying new cameras but rejected the idea as too expensive.

The Philpotts, my father's family, came from England but were of Welsh origin. The name is said to be of Greek derivation and means "Lover of Water."

We lived in New York, New Mexico, and Colorado. I attended Miss Hazel Wallack's school in Denver where about twelve of us danced and exercised with bars from nine in the morning until supper time. For lunch, we ate crackers and milk. I often spent the night there in a room next to Miss Wallack's room where I could hear her sobbing, Mama said, because her father had died. She was a tall, stiff-backed young lady. She was a good teacher, but although I soon could stand on my toes and do everything, my back was never supple. I blame her for this because she was my example.

Within four weeks, I was head of the class. My *pas de chat* was sensational. I could leap higher than anyone, perhaps because I had square toes and very bony, hard, little feet—excellent for toe dancing.

One of the students was Ted Shawn, who was past twenty years of age and just learning to toe-dance. (I have never heard of a male toe dancer—before or since). Later, he married Ruth St. Denis and started "Denishawn," the famous dancing school and company. At the time when he was studying with Miss Wallack, he was madly in love with her.

A touring opera company playing *Aïda* came along and needed a slave dancer. I was chosen. In burnt cork, with cymbals, I had my first professional engagement, which lasted one week.

A few weeks later, I became premier dancer in the Electric Show. The Denver paper printed a cartoon of me wearing black tights with great spangled wings. They also ran photographs and praised me.

Then I danced at Elitch's Garden in pink, white, and yellow ballet dresses, all spangled by Mama. This led to our being called before the famous Judge Ben Lindsey's child labor court. When Mama explained that I was not paid for my dancing, the case was dismissed.

When I was nine years old, Mother bought a season theatre ticket for me—second row, on the aisle—and I learned to love the theatre at the matinees that I attended. I saw Maude Adams in *Chanticleer* and was thrilled to be close enough to hear her breathe and see the saliva fly from her mouth. The play itself

William Bledsoe Philpott, Madge's father. "Head of English Department, Texas A & M for twenty years; football coach for three years during which time not one game was lost by the team."

was silly, I thought. Margaret Illington appeared in *Kindling*, a play about poverty. I adored Pavlova and was fascinated by Robert Mantell's Shakespearean repertoire company.

I suppose these plays led to my first appearance on the boards as Cordelia in *King Lear*, performed in my twelve-year-old neighbor's barn theater. He played King Lear. Our first and only public performance was ruined when the king was unable to lift the dead Cordelia, and I had to walk off the stage.

We moved to San Antonio, Texas, and were very poor. My mother did manage to continue my dancing lessons, and I attended St. Mary's Hall, a junior college affiliated with Vassar. My father, who had left Texas A & M University, where he had been a professor of English for 20 years, sold used cars.

Because I was ashamed of our home, I refused to make friends and spent most of my time at the public library. I read Plutarch's *Lives* and enjoyed books by French writers, especially Balzac. I read all that I could find on art and artists, and books about the opera.

I still have the scrapbooks that I kept at that time that contain pictures of a few film stars—mostly Mary Pickford—and all of the new and older opera stars.

This is one of the many esoteric and strange poems that I wrote at that time:

> There is an unsung song some where
> That none may sing alone. Upon a silent harp
> Its harmony will fill the air
> When once its music's known.
>
> From each the note, the needed note
> That swells in him from earth's full throat!
>
> Come all that dwell in gardens
> Open the scarlet gates!
> Sing out brave sounds! All the world awaits!

I was much impressed with an experience Daddy had in 1914 at the Ludlow Massacre when the Rockefeller Company police fired on strikers and burned their tent city, killing many people. Daddy was there on business for a copper company. The company police took him by the collar and made him get back on the train and out of town. This story made me aware of the working man's struggle, and ever afterwards, I longed for a society without the big contrast between a few wealthy and so many poor.

As far back as I can remember, we had socialist papers and magazines in the house. Mother's favorite saying was, "It's all economic"—meaning what people were, what they did, and what they thought depended upon how they obtained their bread and butter. She believed that if everyone had enough of the necessities, enough to eat, and a little security, there would be no crime, no wars. All my life, I have believed in a socialist society. How things are done in Russia or China has had no effect on my belief in one world without nationalism and with equality, regardless of race; without religion, or any mystical beliefs—just plain brotherhood on earth.

Finally, Mama and I landed in New York with no job and little of anything. We got a room in a brownstone and started out walking, armed with my toe-slippers, down Broadway. Oh, what joy! It was the happiest day of my life. As we walked through the grand canyons of the streets, we looked for theaters or agents or the sound of music. As if drawn by a Pied Piper, we came to Tin Pan Alley, 32nd Street, where music is written and sold, where all the halls are rehearsal halls.

"Listen," I said. "There is music coming from upstairs."

We climbed some old, dusty steps and, sure enough, we came upon a dancing troupe, madly whirling and jumping to the accompaniment of an out-of-tune piano and a woman shouting strident instructions.

There was a pause and we asked, "Could you use another dancer?"

"Ja," the lady said, introducing herself as the touring ballerina Albertina Rasch. "Let me see vat you can do."

I danced for her for a few minutes.

"All right," she said. "You may join us if you vish."

I was about to accept joyfully when Mama whispered, "Come here a minute." She led me towards the door, saying, "Let's don't be too

Poster for "The Love Mill," at the Brady Theater—Madge's first play on Broadway (note that her last name is not spelled correctly).

hasty. I hear music upstairs. Why don't we go up there before we decide?"

Upstairs, a large company was rehearsing. We stood in the doorway and watched dancers, singers, and actors. A man came to us and inquired about our business.

"I dance," I told him. "Could you use another dancer?"

"As a matter of fact," he replied, "we could. Clear the stage, everyone," he called out. "What would you like played?"

"Delibes' *Les Sylphides*," I told him. The company retired to sit around the hall and I danced.

After I finished, the man took me to an elderly gentleman.

"This is Mr. Andreas Dippel," he said, "the producer of this play, *The Love Mill*. We open on Broadway in three weeks at The Brady Theater. Mr. Dippel, I believe the young lady is satisfactory. Do you agree?"

Mr. Dippel smiled benignly at me. "I quite agree, Miss . . . Miss . . ."

"Philpott."

"Come to my office tomorrow morning and sign your run-of-the-play contract."

Mama whispered in my ear, "Andreas Dippel is a famous opera singer."

"Oh, Mr. Dippel, are you going to sing in this show?"

"No, my child," he laughed. "I only croak now."

The man who had introduced me to Mr. Dippel was the stage manager. He suggested that I begin rehearsing at once. Without further ado, I became a member of a Broadway company at the age of seventeen.

I was to do three dances with another girl: a riding dance in which lights flickered off and on above us to give the illusion of fast movement, an innovation at that time; a Grecian dance in a blue light among marble columns; and a traditional toe-dance in a long tarlatan ballet skirt.

While we rehearsed, Mama went to symphony concerts, lectures, and plays.

Madge: "My only proof I was a toe dancer."

I don't know why it was so easy for me to get started. I think my mother's cultural background had something to do with it. I think my love of paintings of beautiful women helped me to grow pretty. I studied portraits by Greuze, Romney, Gainsborough, and Turner. Who can say that by some kind of osmosis the pictures gave carriage to my head, a turn to my shoulder, and position to my arms and torso? Mama used to call me her "little Greuze." She thought I resembled his portraits.

One day, the landlady at our rooming house told us, "Since you are an actress, you must meet another roomer of mine." She led the way down the hall to her dining room.

"His name is Sydney Greenstreet, an Englishman . . . a Shakespearean actor."

Mr. Greenstreet was sitting before a great leg of lamb.

"You must join me, my dears," he insisted at once, and we sat down to a gargantuan and welcome meal. We had been living off coffee cake with sugar crumbs on top, purchased every day from a nearby bakery.

Mr. Greenstreet was a very expansive person in more ways than one. He gave me autographed pictures of himself as Falstaff, Mercurio, and Touchstone; read us parts from the plays of the Bard; forced second helpings upon us; said that he would teach me the heroine roles of Shakespeare; and told me that he'd take me in the morning to see his agent. He did so, and the agent got me work posing for photographers of candy-box covers to augment our income while I rehearsed. Producers did not have to pay actors before the opening.

Mr. Greenstreet also kept his first promise: to teach me Shakespeare's heroine roles. At that time, he was about forty years old and had the ebullience of youth. He seemed stuffed with ale and pork pies, goose grease, rich blood, good will, and a real Shakespearean gusto for life. In those days, he had hair, bright brown eyes, rosy cheeks, and of course, the same rich-fleshed lips that panted and sputtered and expressed more than most actors' whole bodies. Those fat lips could register surprise, greed, gluttony, sensuality, and throw saliva on you at the same time. Twenty years later, he became a success in movies like *The Maltese Falcon*.

My first lessons in Shakespearean roles began as Audrey, a country wench, in *As You Like It*. Sidney was Touchstone, a clown. This was good lesson material because Audrey has a small part, and Sidney taught me how to make the most of it—in other words, to make a small part into a big part.

When Touchstone asks Audrey, "Doth my simple features content you?", her reply is, "Your features? Lord warrant us! What features?" Simple lines, but I was taught to speak them with great unction.

When the clown says, "Truly, I would the gods had made thee poetical", Sidney taught me to take a burr out of my shoe, a louse out of my hair, and then to pick my nose as Audrey replies, "I do not know what 'poetical' is." That is how scenes are stolen, even from Touchstone.

Sidney had only recently arrived from London* and was appearing in a Broadway production. He had been a member of the famous Abbey Players, playing all the clowns, knaves, and kings of Shakespeare. He worked on the part of Juliet with me, and later on, I was given the opportunity to play the part, although for only one matineé. I owe that small brush with Shakespeare to my fellow boarder in the New York brownstone.

Sidney introduced Mama and me to his fianceé, a sweet young woman from a wealthy New York family. They took us on picnics when Sidney would dance the role of Touch-stone with a basket full of fried chicken, ham steaks, and quarts of Jell-o while I would play Audrey with a chicken leg in either hand. Oh, wonderful, happy days! Thank you, Sidney.

While I worked on Shakespeare at night with Mr. Greenstreet and rehearsed the play by day, we still had time to walk the streets. Once we saw Olive Thomas, the famous showgirl, emerging from her car. She wore a black satin dress and a purple picture hat. Mama thought that she was the most beautiful person she had ever seen.

As we stared at her, Mama heard her say about me, "What a lovely girl!" But I missed that.

One day, Mama noticed a picture on the back of the *Saturday Evening Post* of a straw-berry-blonde girl wearing a yellow sweater and a toboggan cap like mine.

"I know it's a picture of you!" she exclaim-ed. "Let's go ask the artist!"

He was Penrhyn Stanlaws,** a famous "cover" artist. It was, indeed, a likeness of me that he had painted one day after seeing me in Central Park. From then on, he painted a number of pictures of me. Often, he knelt at my feet, declaring that he felt like Conrad in quest of his youth or like the Chevalier des Grieux in his passion for Manon. I rewarded his devotion by naming the dog that he gave to me "Manon."

Later, many artists painted me. They said that I was interesting to paint because my face varied so much at different angles. For instance, front view, oval; chin up, square;

chin down, heart-shaped. Stanlaws said that he could paint dozens of pictures of me and that no two of them would be the same.

Mary Pickford once told me that she thought half of her fame came from her hair and that two-thirds of a woman's beauty was in her hair. I know my hair was greatly admired. Someone who did not like me said that she had never seen me without a brush in my hand.

Mama washed my hair in rain water, if possible, and always with Spratts Dog Soap. First, she rubbed my scalp with castor oil. Then, as my slightly curly hair dried, Mama worked on it, shaping it, twisting it, and brushing it until I had a mass of bronze curls with an overall halo effect achieved by the fluff of tiny tendrils that hung down to the middle of my back. Once I looked at hairs from my head through a microscope. Some were black, some were red, and some were gold. Artists have painted me with all three shades, accord-ing to the light shining on my hair. In movies, it photographed dark in the shade and blonde in the sun, but that was before the studio had me bob it and dye it.

We opened at the Brady in *The Love Mill*. On opening night, an important critic took notice of me.

"Good dancing by Margaret Philpott," he wrote. On the next night, my name was added to the names in front of the theater. I was so proud to see it that I bought a Brownie camera and photographed the sign.

A few days after our opening, Al Jolson invited us to a party. Held on the roof of a theater, it was the biggest party that I had ever seen. Champagne flowed, and I was separated from Mama. At my side was Count Czechy, one of the world's richest men. He was Brulatour's partner in the Eastman agency, the celluloid monopoly distributing film upon which moving pictures were made. Somehow, he manoeuvered me into a private room and asked me if I was a virgin. I did not slap him, but I did run away. He was small, dark, plump, and middle-aged, so I deserve no moral approbation for running.

Later, he sent me gifts, some that Mama

---

*He was born at Sandwich in Kent.

**later a silent film director

Madge (seated left) with Daniel Frohman (seated center), Lois Wilson, (seated right) and stage actress Frances Starr (standing center).

With Daniel Frohman, owner of the Belasco and Lyceum Theaters, and on the board of Paramount Pictures.

would not let me see. I did glimpse a large, dark mink coat. Mama returned them all, and I never saw the count again.

When our play was near its closing (it ran only eight weeks), Daniel Frohman came to see it and then came backstage to meet me. He told me that he had chosen me as one of the players whom he was inviting from each company to appear in the Actors' Fund Benefit, which he headed. At that time, Mr. Frohman was sole owner of the Frohman Company; his brother Charles had died in the *Titanic* disaster. He owned part of the Famous Players Film Company and also two New York theaters—the Lyceum Theater and the Empire Theater. He was, at that time, about sixty-five years old and a most cultured man.

I adored him at once. He was tall and ramrod straight. His thin, grizzled hair fringed a bald spot and his beard was sparse. His large eyes, brown and prominent behind heavy glasses, had the sadness of the ages in them. I learned later that he was hurt by the anti-Semitic slights and insults inflicted upon him by New York's exclusive circles. He, more than anyone else, taught me to love art and artists.

On the night of the benefit, he was waiting in the wings for me.

"Miss Philgreen," he said, getting my name wrong, "I think you should be an actress rather than a dancer. Bring your mother and come to see me in the morning at the Lyceum Theater."

His office, above the Lyceum Theater, was a fairyland for any stage-struck girl. From an outer office, we entered a large room lined with portraits of the great actors and actresses of the past. There were Sarah Bernhardt, Elenora Duse, Ada Rehan, Margaret Illington, Maude Adams, and pictures and momentos from the great dramatists like Sardou and Pinero. Set into the wall near the floor of the next room was a viewbox with a siding panel. When the panel was moved, we had a splendid view of the play going on down in the theater below. "D. F.," as he was known, lived here with a Philipino servant. What wonderful times I was to have in this place with him and his famous guests!

"Miss Philgreen," Mr. Frohman said, handing me a letter, "this is an introduction to George Tyler recommending you for the role of Pollyanna in his next production. Now shall I write on this 'Madge Bellamy' or 'Madge Gwynn'?" he smiled. "You see, I have named or renamed the actresses who have worked for me, including Billie Burke, Marie Doro, and Margaret Illington. Which name do you choose?"

"How did you decide on these names?" I asked.

"Well, 'Madge'," he explained, "was the name of my favorite actress long ago, the first I managed. Her name was Madge Kendall. Now the 'Gwynn' is for Nell Gwynn, the actress loved by King Charles II of England. 'Bellamy'—just because it looks and sounds good beside 'Madge.'"

"I'll take 'Madge Bellamy.'" I decided.

Mr. Tyler was willing to sign me at once to the road company. Again, Mama and I hesitated. My agent had another offer, and he took me to see Arthur Hopkins at his theater. He was putting on Maeterlinck's *Betrothal*. Mr. Hopkins was, perhaps, the most distinguished producer on Broadway at that time, and I was thrilled to meet him.

He took Mama and me; and his assistant, Guthrie McClintic (who became a fine producer himself), downstairs to his now-dark theater. There is nothing so mystical as a dark theater. It is as if all the life of the world has ended in its empty seats, its drafty stage, its damp and musty odors. It's like being one of the gods and knowing that at eight-thirty, life will resume.

They gave me the script to read, put one lone spotlight on the empty stage, and I acted out the part as best I could.

Mama heard Mr. Hopkins say to Mr. McClintic, "She'll be all right. Even her whisper carries."

Back in Mr. McClintic's office, the producer's assistant told us, "Mr. Hopkins says you are to be given the part." We read the contract. It said that I was to be paid twenty dollars a week. How our faces fell!

"But my daughter has been offered one hundred dollars a week to play Pollyanna on the road!"

"Pooh!" McClintic scoffed. "Do you understand that hundreds of girls, good actresses, would pay to play this part?"

We turned down the Maeterlinck play. I have always thought that this was a big mistake. I might have become a Broadway star overnight if I had taken this part. However, one hundred dollars looked big to us, and I was under the spell of Mr. Frohman. He wanted me to do *Pollyanna*, so I began rehearsals at once.

From the first, only the leading man spoke to us. The rest of the company wrapped themselves in silent animosity, and this treatment continued through the whole twenty weeks on tour. At that time, I did not understand this. I do now. They were all seasoned actors with many brilliant memories, supporting an upstart who had never spoken a line on stage, but who was treated like a star in the press. I wouldn't have spoken to me either.

We opened in Pittsburgh and played there to big business at the Duquesne Theatre for eight weeks. On the opening night, the old stage manager, whose wife played my aunt, came to my dressing room door.

"I just came to tell you that while you may have a star on your door, you're not a star!" With this happy news, I went on stage.

Hatred for me seeped down even to the stagehands, and for all twenty weeks of the tour, I had cuts and bruises because they would let the trapdoor by which I entered fall too soon.

My notices in the papers were absurdly laudatory. My fellow workers grew colder, as did the weather. In Pittsburgh, I had the pleasure of meeting Lillian Russell.

We were introduced to each other in our hotel lobby, and she exclaimed, "What a beautiful girl!" Her blonde hair was pressed to her forehead and cheeks in little curls. Her long, blue eyes were still beautiful, and her features were almost perfectly regular. She was very tall, and though now distinctly large of hip and bust, she had kept her hourglass figure.

Eleanor Porter, who wrote *Pollyanna*, came to Pittsburgh to see me. She said that she would write a play for me to be called *Alice in Blunderland*, but I did not hear of this idea again.

The tour continued, weeks at one place, days at another. We were harassed by timetables and drenched by cold rain at roofless stations, waiting all night, sometimes, for trains that did not arrive.

Far more distressing were the war casualties that we saw. Neighborhood boys whom I knew in San Antonio went to war, but I didn't fully realize the ghastly horror of it until I saw great lines of soldiers' coffins stacked along the railroad tracks. At this time, too, a terrible influenza epidemic spread through the country. Only five states escaped it, and there were 127,000 cases in our army camps.

We performed with only a few hours of sleep in drafty barns that would have killed a cow. Yet, I could recite Pollyanna's creed, a very long speech, before a fake window with a fake sun pouring in with joy and conviction every night, for I was a true believer that "everything is for the best."

I got thinner and thinner; my voice became weaker every day, but my applause grew. One morning, my neck was so stiff that I could not turn my head. I went on that night anyway, but the next morning, I could not speak at all. Mama called the doctor, who said that I had an abcessed throat. We left for New York that night. Every member of the company signed an affidavit that I had not been ill at all—they said my notices in the paper proved that I had performed well.

In New York, the doctor operated, and I was ill for about three weeks. It cost me my coloratura voice. Never again could I sing above high C. This illness also almost cost me my career.

When I was well enough, I went to Mr. Frohman's office. He showed me a document sent to him and all of the producers in New York which claimed that I was unreliable. I was broken-hearted at the injustice of it; however, Mr. Frohman was convinced that I had been ill and cast me at once as the dream girl opposite William Gillette in Sir James Barrie's *Dear Brutus*. I replaced Helen Hayes. Another member of the distinguised cast was Judith Anderson.

On opening night, the second act, in which Mr. Gillette and I were the sole actors, received sixteen curtain calls. Mr. Hayman, the manager of Frohman productions, came backstage at the Empire Theater on Broadway and presented me with an apple, the customary reward for a good first-night performance.

We played there for three wonderful months. Mama and I took an apartment in Greenwich Village in Washington Square, and I wonder if the person who wrote *My Sister*

*Eileen* knew us because we led the same improbable life. Incredible people knocked on our basement windows when they came a-calling.

Mr Frohman, or "D. F." as everybody called him, invited me to the home of the president of the New York Conservatory of Music, Alexander Lambert. He was the composer of *Lambert's Piano Method*, a system studied by many young people. And I, too, had worked on these compositions with Mama during the many years that she tried to teach me to play the piano. Alas, I would not practice. Now I played these diminutive, simple pieces as duets with Mr. Lambert to his and my delight.

When I was invited to a party at Mr. Lambert's apartment and realized that I had no evening dress, Mama went right to work. She bought a white lace curtain at Gimbels' (I made only a hundred dollars a week in *Pollyanna*; this was so inadequate that Daddy had to send us money in order for us to get by). Now I was making two hundred a week, but only for a short time. Mama cut up her prized possession—a brown fur muff—and outlined the drop-shoulder dress with the fur. It was the prettiest dress that I'd ever had.

At Mr. Lambert's, I met Matzenhauer, the Wagnerian contralto, and many other singers. At this first party, Mr. Frohman said that I should leave at ten o'clock because later, a banquet was to be held for the great Paderewski, and I had not been invited to this. I went to the dressing room and got my coat at about nine-thirty, ready to go home. As I came into the reception room, the white-haired pianist was standing facing me.

"This is the most exquisite vision I have seen!" he exclaimed in a loud voice. Everyone turned to look at me. "I insist this lovely creature sit on my side at dinner." He came to me, gave me his arm, took me to the piano, asked me to sit on the bench beside him, and played, now and again glancing at me. Well, I was his dinner partner that night, the partner of my happiest memory.

Mother greatly admired the writer Frank Harris, who wrote *The Life and Loves of Shakespeare*. His later, very salacious book, *My Life and Loves*, was banned in America. We knew that he lived on Washington Square, found the address, and visited him. In his apartment hung many pictures given to him by great artists, but what impressed me the most was the sound slap he gave me on my bottom as we were leaving, and Mama was *not* looking.

He returned the call, and soon he was coming nearly every evening. Our basement apartment had windows about a foot high onto the sidewalk, and it seemed that Mr. Harris' cane was always tapping on our window.

An Englishman, Mr. Harris had been the editor of the *London Saturday Review* for years. He was about seventy-five years old; knew Whistler, Guy de Maupassant, Newman, and Carlyle; and was a close friend of Oscar Wilde and George Bernard Shaw. We made tea for Mr. Harris, and he drank it all evening, entrancing us with tales of his literary friends. He once told my mother, when I was not present, that she should let me have a baby and not ask where it came from.

We went to the odd, dark, little cafés in the Village where we picked up a few more friends, poets, writers, painters, and sculptors. I began to make sculptures, and Mr. Harris greatly admired my "Janus-Faced Woman." But I gave it to D. F., who put it on his mantle. I understand that it was given, along with his other effects (including a painting of me), to the Museum of Modern Art in New York City.

Among all of these friends, there were bound to be some odd ones. One night, we went to a black and foreboding little den. In the candlelight, a woman drew near and spoke to me.

She said, "I have just written a poem to you." We asked her to sit down and read it. She did, and we thought it quite good. For some reason, she came home with us and decided to spend the night. Our accommodations were limited, so I slept with our guest, a homely, middle-aged woman.

To my astonishment, in the middle of the night, she arose, turned on the lamp, disrobed, posed for me, and whispered, "Don't you feel the spirit of Oscar Wilde?"

"No, I don't," I said and slept the rest of the night with Mama.

Our apartment was an oddity to me, although I suppose the Village had many like it. It was below the street but on the ground floor. Through the front window, we could see only the feet of the people passing by. In the rear, we had a lovely little garden. The rooms were panelled in the 18th-century French manner, and set in the gold-framed panels were floor-length mirrors.

Of all the people whom I met, I enjoyed the musicians the most. Since actors are their own art, they seem egocentric and offensive in their self-concern while writers are often nervous and irritable. Musicians have an uninhibited delight in themselves and their art.

Mr. Lambert (called "Alec") and D. F. were my escorts to plays and concerts: two old men in evening clothes and a young girl all agog with the wonders that they showed her.

Mr. Frohman corrected any bad habits that I acquired. He taught me to say "uncanny" with a short "a" instead of the long, southern "a." He stopped me from pointing when I saw an actress, singer, or celebrity. Also, he was against the use of makeup. Surreptitiously, I put burnt cork on my eyelashes, and strong red pepper on my cheeks and lips. Once, I kissed him on the mouth and saw wonder in his eyes at the stinging on his lips.

I am afraid that I became a little false to myself at this time. D. F. had another protégée: a girl who was a year younger than I, but twice as big. She was exuberant, more beautiful than I, and enthusiastic about everything. I am ashamed to say that I tried to copy her. She shrieked, and jumped up and down at an invitation to dinner. When I saw how he loved this, I, too, squealed with delight and raved about everything in his august presence.

Some of the most wonderful times that we had were walks at the Lewissohn Estate in the violet-bedecked woods along the Hudson River; the fresh, wet smell of the foliage; the soft, leaf-padded ground beneath our feet; gold in the sky; gold in the river; and gold glimmering on the dewdrops.

## Chapter Two

At last we went on tour. First to Chicago. There my incipient love for Mr. Gillette suffered a setback. In front of the Illinois Theater was a large picture of me beside a portrait of him. He promptly ordered my picture and name removed. His picture, his name reigned supreme, and I did not speak to him for weeks.

We toured for three months and at first, Mama did not come along. But when I told her that I had so much money that I did not know what to do with it, that I was scared in hotels and slept with my hairbrush handy as a weapon, and that I was reading Mr. Gillette to sleep every night, she joined the company.

In Chicago, I was asked to name a zebra that had just arrived at the zoo. The zebra was alone in a small pen and, having no key because the keeper hadn't arrived, the photographer and I climbed over the fence. I posed, kissing the zebra, but as I crawled onto its back, it became restless. We ran for the fence. The zookeeper came running toward us.

"My God!" he cried. "Did you go in there? I wouldn't for a million bucks!"

At last I was allowed to choose my wardrobe, and I was never well-dressed again. In Ontario, Mama did not say a word when I bought a leopard-skin coat, a white fox fur, and a ten-gallon brown velvet hat with two-foot pheasant feathers. I wore all three purchases at the same time.

In Baltimore, I went with Mama to the theater to rehearse *Romeo and Juliet*, a play which I had been working on with Marie Wainwright, a great English actress who was in our company. I was surprised when Mama asked me to wear the white chiffon costume that she had made for me and the little jewelled Juliet cap. When we arrived at the theater, I found that the stage was set with a balcony. Miss Wainwright was in costume, too. I was put upon the balcony, the lights went on, the curtains went up, and we did the entire balcony scene impromptu. Mr. Gillette had arranged a special matinee with me as Juliet for a select audience out front.

The next day, Rennold Wolf, leading critic of a New York paper, wrote, "This is the first time that an actress playing the 14-year old Juliet is actually fourteen years old." (I was nineteen.)

In Cleveland, Mama, using Sterno to heat her curling iron, was dressing at five o'clock in the morning when she turned over the lighted Sterno can and set a curtain afire.

I leaned out of the window and screamed, "Fire!"

Mama screamed, "Fire!" into the telephone. Fortunately, between us, we were able to put out the fire with one of Mama's best coats because, believe it or not, nobody came to help us.

When we returned to New York, I was asked to play Geraldine Farrar's daughter in a film. I adored her and was glad to accept. Every morning, I rode to Fort Lee and worked all day.

Miss Farrar said, "Tres jolie" when I was introduced to her. I believe this was one of the last pictures that she made, and it was the first and only time that she spoke to me.

She was still beautiful, surprisingly short for one who could appear so tall; her eyes, though not large, sparkled; and her smile was generous. She had the same exuberant nature of other opera stars whom I have known:

Madge and Earle Fox (second couple from left) in Monte Bell's Stock Company, Washington, D.C., before her Hollywood days.

Mary McCormick, Galli-Curci, and Lucrecia Bori. I thought this was the result of proper breathing. She had the habit of patting the flesh under her chin with the back of her hand. When her husband, Lou Tellegen, came on the set, she rose from her chair to greet him, put both arms around his long neck, and kissed him like a woman languishing in love.

Accidentally, I flooded the second story of the hotel where we were staying by leaving the bathtub tap on. Mr. Gillette personally paid the bill for the damages, a mark of great affection for me because Mr. Gillette was rather stingy. He ate only in his hotel rooms, and then mostly corn flakes. He told me that he sent his corn flakes back if the hotel charged him more than fifty cents since he could get boxes of them at a store for that price. He was a very cynical man.

When I begged him to tell me about his life and his wife, who had died, he said, "I don't remember. It was too long ago." How different from Mr. Frohman, who kept the picture of his first love under a cloth and always kissed it good-night.

I prevailed upon Mr. Gillette, who was also a playwright, to read my first play. He read the first act and refused to read further.

"I don't have to," he said. "You have enough happening in the first act for a whole play."

Riding to the Fort Lee studio every morning

at about five o'clock and working all day, I began to show a lack of energy. I slept going to work on the subway, and I slept in my dressing room.

When I complained to Mr. Frohman about being tired, he said, "You can sleep when you are old."

He also said that the bad thing about being old was that you needed only about four hours of sleep while everybody else needed eight, and those four hours were very lonely.

Mr. Frohman said that he was arranging for me to appear in *The Prince and the Pauper* by Mark Twain with William Faversham as my co-star. I met Mr. Faversham and his wife. She told D. F. that I looked like something one dreamed of but never expected to see, but that I misquoted Shakespeare.

As it was now summer and since rehearsals for the play would not begin for some time, I took an engagement as star of the Bell Stock Company in Washington, D.C. Our first play was *Peg O' My Heart*. It was lucky for me that George Marion, the old master of dialects, was playing in Washington because I got him to coach my Irish brogue. My notices were great; and our audiences, dressed in evening clothes, were senators and congressmen. We did a new play every week while rehearsing the next one.

Mama stayed up many times all night with young actors or actresses who had trouble learning their lines or suffered from stage fright. One night, Mama stayed up all night with me, and my tears flowed as I said the long speeches over and over again.

I was called back to New York to make a screen test for the Thomas Ince Corporation in Hollywood. Twelve of us made the test. John H. Blackwood, a sweet, kindly man, represented the company; and a young publicity man, Norbert Lusk, had charge of us. He herded us all into one limousine. We were to pick up three Follies beauties at the Ziegfeld Theater.

"Now for our Ziegfeld Girls and some real glamour!" said Mr. Lusk. None of us could help giggling when the three beauties showed up in gingham dresses and wearing no make-

up. Poor Mr. Lusk's face was filled with surprise and disappointment, but we began our tests on a merry note.

Two of these twelve girls became my friends in Hollywood. Neither was an actress, but both were Follies girls. One of them* married the ex-husband of Mary Pickford, Owen Moore. The other girl married one of the funniest comedians in the world—Walter Catlett.

I won the test, I think, because the camera diffused the darkness of my eyes and, as someone said, "made them look as big as dollars." Mama bought me a plain navy-blue wool dress and a small brick-colored hat, and we left for Hollywood. D. F. told me good-bye in anger.

He said, "I was going to put on Schiller's *Mary Stuart* with you as the queen. Mady Christians was to have played Elizabeth. You are making a big mistake." Perhaps, but after the disappointment of our not doing *The Prince and the Pauper*, I wanted to try Hollywood.

We were met at the station in Hollywood by a young writer who suggested that Mama go to our hotel while I took a ride around the city with him. In the excitement and confusion, we agreed to this arrangement; but when I did not show up at the hotel for several hours, Mama notified the studio. And when evening came and I still did not appear, everyone became alarmed.

Nothing was really amiss. Our young writer showed me every hill in Hollywood, every residential and industrial district, plus the Los Angeles stockyard. Hollywood was a crying disappointment, an affront. Built by advertising, newsprint, pictures, and word-of-mouth into a place of glamour, Hollywood Boulevard really looked like Main Street back home. After New York, the nondescript small stores looked to me as if their tops had been blown off. They crawled on all fours, and their lower halves were buried in the cement. I had never been so disillusioned since I had found out that there was no Santa Claus. Hollywood was just a name. All that it stood for was in the back lots of the movie studios.

The Thomas H. Ince Studio was the most

*Kathryn Perry

imposing and beautiful studio in Hollywood, and it still is. After Ince's death, it became the Selznick Studio. It looked then, and now, like Mount Vernon—a great white mansion with columns from the porch to the third story. It was used in *Gone With the Wind*. Like Tara, it has survived all of the motion picture civil wars.

I arrived at the studio late and alone, gave my name, sat down, and in a few seconds, an excited young man arrived. I soon discovered that he felt an excruciating sense of admiration for himself.

"Come with me," he said as he ushered me into his office. "You have been sent as a Christmas present to me. Do sit down, Miss Bellamy. Let me introduce myself. I am Douglas MacLean."

"A Christmas present to *you*, did you say?" I asked.

"That's right." He smiled broadly, then frowned. "But I must say that you are a little thin."

That did it. I got up.

"Mr. MacLean," I said, "I have never heard of you, and I did not come out here as a Christmas present to you. If I did, I'm leaving."

At that point, despite his attempt to explain that I was to be his leading lady, I marched right out of the office, through the hall, and out the front door. As I hurried down the gravel driveway, there was a crunching of pebbles behind me, and several people came running up.

"I'm Tom Ince," said one man. "I'm your boss. Come back and talk. This guy, Mac-Lean," he pointed to the puffing actor, "doesn't know what he is talking about. I promise that you are not going to be in any picture with him."

I can still see the look of amusement in Mr. Ince's steely grey eyes. He liked to say that people could tell which of his eyes was the glass one—it looked kindly. He did not have a glass eye, but I often thought his eyes looked mean.

He was a short, stocky, light-haired man about forty years old. He had a pinkish complexion, and his eyes were very light. He had a good sense of humor, and he certainly knew the motion picture business. That evening, he was dressed as always—in pastel knickers, cashmere sweater, and cap.

Despite Mr. Ince's promise, my first picture at the Ince Studio was with the ubiquitous Douglas MacLean. It was called *Passing Thru*.

Mama and I had taken a small house, and she drove me to work. I put on my own make-up, using Max Factor's stick, which was greasy and discolored the powder with which I covered it. As the day progressed, it darkened around the mouth and nose. I did my own hair, curling it around my fingers. For mascara, I used wax heated in a small pan as we did on the stage. Applied to the lashes, this looked good at first, but was vulnerable to tears or wind, and often dropped, speck by speck, during the heat of the drama, to my cheeks.

We had not read my Ince contract carefully. The small print said that I was to furnish my own wardrobe, so Mama made the dresses that I wore in this picture. It was a comedy that was photographed mostly outdoors. Silver boards were used as reflectors that invariably made me squint. One small camera on a tripod weighed about 140 pounds and was carried about by the assistant cameraman.

All that I remember of this opus is that I was offended at the language of the director (William A. Seiter) and his references to "my fanny." After my experience on the stage and in burlesque, I don't understand why I was so squeamish.

I also resented Mr. MacLean's standing by the cameraman during my close-ups and warning him, "Don't make her look too pretty. It distracts from comedy."

Mr. Hobart Bosworth was in the next picture, and he behaved nicely to me. Late one night, he came to our house uninvited, unexpected, and wearing muddy boots. He stayed for some time and seemed inexplicably absent-minded. The next morning, we read in the papers that Mr. Bosworth had eloped with a young actress on the previous evening. He never called on us again nor explained his

In *Passing Thru* (1921) with Douglas MacLean (National Film Archive, London).

Madge and Tom Ince.

visit. He seemed to be very happily married.

My director, Rowland V. Lee, was a nice, blond, young man obsessed with thumbs. He believed that a person's personality was revealed by the way in which he or she held his or her thumbs—and I held mine incorrectly, i.e., close to the other fingers. He said that this meant that I was a close and stingy person. As I was playing the part of a Caucasian girl mistaken for a Chinese, I should have had an open thumb. All through the picture, I had difficulty holding my thumbs out.

There was another complaint about me, and I was sent to the head office and Mr. Ince.

He admonished me, "You are not being sociable enough about the set; you read a book between your takes, and people are talking about it. They don't like it."

Mr. Ince had a peculiar way of selecting titles that often had little relevance to the picture. After our picture was finished, he invited me to his office on the top floor of the studio to have lunch and to help name the picture. He took down a big book with hundreds of titles pasted in it from which we selected the name *The Cup of Life* (already used for an Ince drama in 1915 with a different story).

When he tried to kiss me, I pushed him off in no uncertain manner. He never held a grudge against me for resisting him. Although he was married, he had a sweetheart on the

With Niles Welch in *The Cup of Life* (1921).

lot who was liked by everyone. She went around the studio crying most of the time and wearing diamond bracelets from her wrist halfway to her elbow. She was the first girl I ever knew to wear falsies. They were made of rubber and filled with water that sloshed around as she moved.

Syd Chaplin, Charlie's brother, took me to my first party in Hollywood at Sam Goldwyn's beach house. There were about twenty people present, including Charlie, Goldwyn, and a well-known writer named Herman Mankiewicz.

We had a quiet dinner, formally served, after which Charlie did his balloon dance for us. While he danced rather intricate steps, he attempted to keep a balloon at strategic places for modesty's sake, the spectators having to assume that he was nude. It was made hysterically comical by Chaplin's dexterity in keeping the balloon moving.

Then he did his midget impersonation. A table was brought out and put between two curtains in a doorway. Chaplin reversed his coat, put his shoes on his hands, and danced as a midget on the table.

Afterwards, I was having a most interesting conversation about Nietzsche with Mr. Mankiewicz when the doorbell rang. Mama had come for me and was waiting in the car.

It seems that after I left for the party, Mr. Blackwood, the agent for Ince, called to see us.

In *The Cup of Life* (1921) with Hobart Bosworth and Tully Marshall.

Mama told him, "Madge has gone to her first Hollywood party at the beach."

"My God!" Mr. Blackwood cried. "You have no idea what goes on at those beach parties! Everyone gets raped. Get in your car at once, and we will go after her, and thank heaven if she is the same as when she went there!"

They piled into the car and raced to the scene. Mama said that she had never ridden so fast in all her life.

Of course, I had to leave the party.

As Mr. Goldwyn saw me to the door, he said, "I'll never, never speak to you again." And he didn't, for I never saw him again.

Years later, Charlie Chaplin said to my friend Neil Vanderbilt, "She could have been Mrs. Goldwyn if she'd wanted to be."

I was put in a picture called *Hail The Woman* with beautiful Florence Vidor, King Vidor's wife. The director on this picture was a little man named John Griffith Wray, who could shout louder through a megaphone than anyone on earth except Mr. Ince himself. He was a good director, and in proof of it, I gave

With Tully Marshall in *Hail the Woman* (1921) (National Film Archive, London).

my best performance in this role of a poor girl raped by a young preacher. She turns to street-walking to care for her baby and dies in the effort.

For this picture, Mr. Ince himself came from his office to direct the big scenes.

He sat cross-legged under the camera tripod and screamed through his megaphone, "You are broken-hearted! Cry! Cry! For God's sake, cry! Go on—sob! You are ill! You are in misery! Your baby is hungry!" Yet, he was not more than five feet away from me.

I did a picture with Hobart Bosworth called *Blind Hearts*. Then I did *Love Never Dies*, directed by King Vidor, who became one of the greatest of all directors. He was a very kind and gentle director, whispering what he wanted in my ear. The assistant director was Lewis Milestone, who became equally famous. I saw this picture recently. Its love scenes have a fresh, innocent beauty that I find very touching.

We bought a home in Beverly Hills on Beverly Drive that was small compared to the

(Above and right) In *Blind Hearts* (1921) with Hobart Bosworth and Bobby Herron.

With her mother in front of their Beverly Hills home at 517 Beverly Drive.

houses around it. On this street were (and still are) the tallest rows of palm trees anywhere. Directly across the street was a white Colonial house where Pola Negri was to live later. It all looks almost the same to this day.*

Mama bought me a Knabe grand piano on which I often played a song called *Faded Old Love Letters*. The words made me cry, even though I had no faded old love letters.

Mama also bought me a beautiful automobile, a National. It was grey with red leather upholstery and included thirty lights in its luxurious equipment. Lights lit as you stepped on the fender and lit as you sat down. It cost $10,000.

*Pola Negri's house has been demolished.

I say, "Mama bought"; this was true. I never selected, bought, or chose anything—neither homes, hats, nor dresses. And why didn't I? Was I indifferent to material possessions? Or too busy?

This beautiful car was almost immediately ruined. I was cast in a farce called *The Hotten-tot*. My car was parked for nearly three months at the racetrack where a scene for the picture was being filmed. The director, James Horne, insisted that my car remain there, sunk in the mud. It rained constantly and my distress was acute. Since I was not paid for the use of my car, my distress is still acute.

Although I had never met him, I was in love

with a young, handsome Irish director named Mickey Neilan. And not only I, but several other young actresses were deeply enamoured of him.

One evening, two other actresses and I took a wild ride around Hollywood in a big black limousine searching for the place where he was having a rendevous with his new *inamorata*. One of my companions was a Ziegfeld Follies beauty whom I had met in New York. She, too, was madly in love with Neilan and suspected that he was being unfaithful to her.

The search led to Gloria Swanson's driveway where we found his parked car. As we sadly drove away, my Follies beauty was in tears.

She turned her anger on me. "Oh, you don't know what it's all about," she said.

Of this photo from *The Hottentot* (1922) with Douglas MacLean, Madge comments: "Notice that neither of us is looking at the other."

About this time, I met the most eligible young millionaire in America, and I muffed it. He was Cliff Durant, the young heir to General Motors, who often came to my new home bringing along his violin, which he played extremely well. As a gift, he gave me a thoroughbred horse trained to do numerous tricks—untying a handkerchief blindfolded, shaking his head, etc.

Cliff's face was large and red, and he was not handsome. One day, I told him that I did not love him. Why I told him this, I don't remember, but I do remember that we were in my bedroom. I must have been teasing him, for he fell down on my bed sobbing, his face redder than ever. After this, he didn't come around much any more, and since I was too busy to ride, I sent his horse back to him.

When I was not working, I spent my afternoons dancing at the Old Biltmore Hotel where they had *thé dansants* with big bands providing the music. We did the foxtrot, two-step, tango, and the maxicheta. Once a week, we went to the Pantages Theatre where Edward Everett Horton played leading roles in a stock company for a long time. Then we often took in the vaudeville at the Orpheum.

It was "the thing" to go to boxing matches at the Vernon Country Club. Mama liked boxing, and I met most of the promising boxers.

Madge with her gift horse from Cliff Durant (under the hat) of General Motors.

I went to Ciros and the Macambo night clubs, and I attended my first premiere with a British director named Maurice Elvey. We arrived on time, at eight-thirty, before anyone else and were sent away to arrive later.

I attended parties where I was Charlie Chaplin's favorite partner in charades. In one of them, I was the Virgin Mary and he was Jesus.

Several of the parties which I attended were hosted by the two wildest bachelors in Hollywood: Lew Cody and Norman Kerry. At these hectic parties, everyone was either chasing someone or being chased because everyone was either angry at someone who had played

a joke on him, or he was planning to play a joke on someone.

The "progressive parties" were the strangest—beginning at one home, going on to others, and often ending up with an entirely different group of guests.

I met many writers—Carey Wilson, Joseph Hergesheimer, Sadakichi Hartmann, and many others. They came to my house bringing their scripts to read to me. I suppose that I was a non-challenging sounding board.

Then I was given the prize part of Lorna Doone. The English novel had been a favorite book of my childhood, and I had a picture of the fictitious Lorna Doone in my bedroom.

Madge as "Lorna Doone."

*Lorna Doone* (1922)

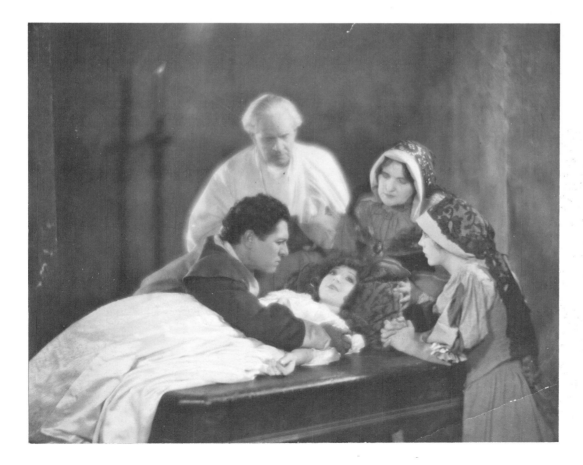

*Lorna Doone* (1922), with "stage actor Frank Keenan, patriarch of all the Keenans."

Madge with Jack Pickford in *Garrison's Finish* (1923) (National Film Archive, London).

Maurice Tourneur was the director—a Frenchman who spoke good English. An artist himself, he had worked with Puvis de Chavanne, the French painter. Tourneur was a big man with heavy shoulders that he carried hunched as if bearing too great a load.

Unless we annoyed him, he hardly noticed us actors. If we did annoy him, his temper broke and shook us like an earthquake. He did not yell at me, but his treatment of extra people almost ruined my nervous system.

Once I was late on the set; Mr. Tourneur would wait no longer, and he shot my wedding scene without me.

"How could you?" I asked him.

"I had to," he replied. "The clouds were exactly right." If you look closely at the march to the church in *Lorna Doone*, you will not see me—the bride.

In one scene, I was supposed to be kidnapped. Mr. Tourneur made it realistic by not telling me what they were going to do or having any rehearsal of it. As I arrived on the set and the Klieg lights came on, actors dressed as ruffians seized me, threw me on a bed, pummelled me, and then hung me by my hands on a door.

After the take, Mr. Tourneur called, "Cut!" and I was cut down—in a fainting condition, I might add. When I recovered from this ordeal, I went to my dressing room and refused to work for three days.

Madge's boss, Thomas H. Ince, had her learn to use the Bell and Howell camera.

John Griffith Wray directed one scene in *Lorna Doone*. He did not trust my ability to express surprise either. As I looked out of a window in a scene where I was supposed to see a dreadful sight, he fired a pistol behind my back. I jumped and overreacted in a way marvelous to behold. Not long ago, I saw *Lorna Doone* here in Los Angeles. The audience laughed at this scene at the window. Even in the darkness of the theater, I blushed.

In the development of the story, *Lorna Doone* is a failure, but it succeeds like a poem in capturing the mood of the novel. Tourneur was a pictorial artist. Later, he became a disillusioned, cynical man who saw the beauty of the world, but found no meaning in it. The narrative, to him, expressed nothing. He probably did not believe in man and woman relationships, nor mankind in general. *Lorna Doone*, to him, was sentimental and childish. He cared nothing for it. He was a typical elitist with no message to give or receive.

Next, I was lent to Mary Pickford for a picture—*Garrison's Finish*. She was not in it, but it starred her brother, Jack. I liked him. He always called me "Pretty Girl."

Mary fixed my hair a few times to show me how to do it. Two kid curlers for each curl. One rolled from the scalp, the other from the end. Two curlers on each strand of hair makes for poor sleeping, and I told Mary so.

"Oh, I can't sleep very well either unless I hold my hand under the curlers. See, this is how I do it," and she showed me.

She was the most beautiful person I have ever seen. I worshipped her and was dumbfounded when she let me wear her old dresses in the picture, getting down on the floor herself to let down the hems. She didn't seem to have any vanity.

When I told her how beautiful I thought she was, she said, "Oh, you are prettier than I am!"

She also advised me on beauty care.

"Don't buy all those expensive cosmetics—just get a big can of anhydrous raw lanolin. Pat it on your face every night; it's sticky, but it works." To this day, I've been sticky every night.

While making this picture, I spent all the time that I could on the nearby sets where her husband, Doug Fairbanks, was making *The Mark of Zorro*. When anyone visited his set, he would put on extra sword play for their amusement.

Then I was to go on tour to advertise *Lorna Doone*. It was being exploited to the sky. *Lorna Doone*—the Madge Bellamy edition, biscuits, hats, everything. I started out with a fanfare with Mama, a business agent, and a cameraman. We were to go to every state with my gold-plated camera (which I found difficult to use) to photograph each governor and invite him to California for our celebration of the California Centennial.

First, I was entertained at the White House where Mrs. Harding served tea in the Blue Room. She asked me if I knew how she could appear as young as the President in the newsreels, and I suggested a very light make-up. I took pictures of the handsome, genial, corrupt President. Mrs. Harding said that they planned to come to Los Angeles soon, but the President died before their trip. I also have pictures taken at the White House with General Pershing.

The governor whom I most admired was Pinchot. He played basketball with me in the state house.

Mr. Ince seeing Madge off on her tour of the States.

I met Al Smith in New York; he told me that he had three daughters and that I looked like the pretty one. When I went to his office, I wore a brown chiffon dress with a slight train and a picture hat as big as a coffee table, with plumes.

Our agent was nearly always intoxicated on this tour, and it resulted in funny mixups. I would make appearances in theatres that did not play Ince pictures. We went to Massachusetts when we were expected in Connecticut. It seemed that I was always at the wrong place at the right time, and at the right place at the wrong time.

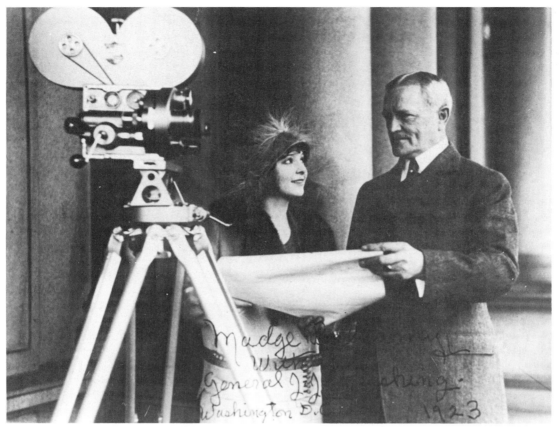

Madge with General John J. "Black Jack" Pershing at the White House.

With Governor Al Smith.

I wrote to Mr. Ince that we were coming home, but he wrote back "Please don't. The bankers are turning on me; don't you join them."

Somebody snitched on me and wrote to Mr. Ince that I was over-dressing on tour, wearing feathers and spangles. He wired me to get a plain serge suit and an untrimmed small sailor. This I did, the "plain serge" costing one hundred dollars.

As we arrived in each town, the newspapers would be alerted to greet me, although because I was still unknown, there were no "fans." But a crowd gathered when they saw five or six cameramen shooting pictures of someone being presented with the customary bouquet of roses (paid for by the studio).

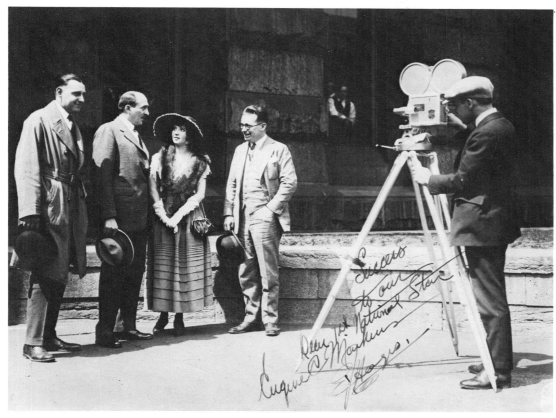

Madge and various theater operators.

With John Hyland,
mayor of New York City.

Madge with Motion Picture Exhibitors of America in Atlantic City.

On one occasion, Mama was presented with the bunch of roses and photographed from all angles before she could explain that she was not the would-be Movie Star; Madge Bellamy was the small person in the plain blue suit.

I got another wire from Mr. Ince: "Go back to the feathers."

I was also sent to Atlantic City to meet five hundred exhibitors gathered there for a convention.

In my speech, I said, "I don't know why I was sent here to meet you." It was the dumbest thing that I ever said, but it got a good laugh.

I think that this personal appearance tour around the USA, more than my films, made me famous.

When I returned home, Mr. Ince had announced that I would do Eugene O'Neill's *Anna Christie*. However, the newspaper critics derided the idea of my playing the Swedish prostitute: "This is like casting Jackie Coogan in the *Hairy Ape*" (another somber O'Neill play). So I lost this great opportunity as I was to lose so many others. Blanche Sweet played this silent version.

Instead, I was given a picture called *The Soul of the Beast* with the same director, John Griffith Wray. It was a merry, childish, fairy tale about a poor girl forced to play in a circus and

With Anna May in *Soul of the Beast* (1923).

double as a trick rider on an elephant. The elephant loved her dearly, and they ran away together to live in the forest.

As we made the film, we travelled with a regular circus for three days, and I was given lessons by the elephant trainer on how to put the beast, called Anna May, through her tricks: bowing, rearing, and lying down in a squat over my prone body.

The circus performance was to be photographed with a regular paying audience. On opening night in Oakland, California, we had a very large crowd. I rode in on Anna May's head. Now, an elephant's head is covered with bristles about an inch long, which makes

sitting there uncomfortable. Although an elephant seems to move slowly, it turns its head with incredible speed.

As the act began, I noticed that the elephant trainer was drunk. He could hardly stand or shout the orders to Anna May. At last, in our finale, I lay down, and Anna May started to fall on me—not in the squatting position, but broadside! Quickly, with her trunk, she grabbed me by the neck and dragged me into the clear as she fell. She saved my life.

This scene, which newspapermen claimed was the most miraculous episode that they had ever seen, had not been filmed. Mr. Wray disclosed that there had been no film in the

Making John Griffith Wray's *Soul of the Beast* (1923).

Madge with scientists after giving a lecture on elephants at the Museum of Natural History.

camera by his order because it was only a rehearsal and that we were to do it again on the next night. I refused to risk the elephant fall a second time.

During this picture, Mr. Wray succeeded in ruining my hair. He would take handfuls of cockle-burrs and rub them into my scalp every morning. In the eight weeks of shooting, my hair was shortened by twelve inches.

A nice thing that happened during the filming of the picture was the bond estab-lished between the elephant, Anna May, and me. Whenever I visited her thereafter in the Los Angeles Zoo, she seemed to know when I entered the grounds and would begin to trumpet.

When I worked for Pickford, Mary taught me something about lighting. I found that I looked best if I had a "baby" spot behind my right shoulder, a strong light on my right side, and a slight shadow on my left. Mr. Ince had no "baby" spots, and I ordered twenty of them and also some gauzes for the camera.

Mr. Ince called me to the front office.

"Are you running this studio or am I?" he asked. "And another thing," he went on, "the fire department allows only five cars on the lot. Since you keep yours next to the dressing rooms, I have to keep mine out. Could I please have my car on my own lot?"

Then Mr. Ince began lending me out to other studios; I think that he was still having trouble with the banks. I was sent to MGM to meet Mr. Thalberg, unaware that he was

With Jack Holt in *Call of the North* (1921) (National Film Archive, London).

Madge in *His Forgotten Wife* (1924) (National Film Archive, London).

With Tom Forman's company; Forman directed *Are You a Failure?* (1923).

Madge with Lloyd Hughes in *Are You a Failure?* (1923) (National Film Archive, London).

considered a great genius. He was a very polite, small, handsome, dark-haired young man.

"We have chosen you," he told me, "to be the leading lady in our production of *Ben Hur*."

"Thank you very much," I retorted, "but I don't want to do it. It will just be a lot of horses." I am astonished to this day that I could have been so stupid.

After the *Beast* picture, I made *His Forgotten Wife* with Warner Baxter, who later became a big star. I then went to Paramount to make *Call of the North* with Jack Holt.

At this studio, Cecil B. DeMille introduced himself to me. If I had been more aware of his importance and shown more deference, he might have had me in one of his pictures, but I admired only stage, not movie, producers.

After this, I made a movie for Schulberg called *Are You a Failure?* I liked him very much.

While I was making it, Louis B. Mayer sent for me to talk about my making a picture for him. At that time, his office was on the same lot, and as I entered his office, he did not rise, nor did he take his feet off his desk.

"I'm thinking about using you in a picture," he said, slowly eyeing me as he took the cigar out of his mouth.

"Well, I don't care about being in it," I snapped and walked out. Mr. Schulberg

*The White Sin* (1924) (Courtesy of Robert S. Birchard).

Hal Cooley, Francelia Billington, and Madge in *The White Sin* (1924) (Courtesy of Robert S. Birchard).

*The White Sin* (1924) (Larry Edmunds Bookshop).

In *No More Women* (1924) with Matt Moore (National Film Archive, London).

happened to be in the other office and was astonished to see me come out of Mayer's office so quickly. He was to produce the Mayer picture and had asked for me.

"I won't work for a man who won't get up when I enter a room," I told him. I had acquired delusions of grandeur by this time.

Instead of doing the Mayer picture, I was lent to Universal for two pictures. How I loved that studio! It seemed that nearly everybody in it was a cousin of the president, "Uncle" Carl Laemmle, and I was made a cousin, too. My new cousins took me to parties where many of the guests were musicians. Dr. Alfred Hertz, the director of the Hollywood Bowl Symphony Orchestra, played "The Star-Spangled Banner" on the piano with his nose; another beat out Beethoven on a drum, and we had to guess which symphony it was. Sometimes, everyone played a different piece on an instrument at once. What happy, loud fun; and there was no drinking, no jealousy, no pretense. Luncheon at the studio with Carl Laemmle was a banquet. I never heard a cross word at that studio, and I believe it was because of the ardent warmth of the old patriarch's personality.

I was lent out for twelve pictures to as many studios. Fox borrowed me for John Ford's *The Iron Horse,* and we went by train to the Arizona desert with ox carts, tents, Indians, Chinese, hundreds of cowboys, electricians, cowgirls, horses, cattle, actors and actresses— it was a real migration. For almost four months in this microcosm, everything happened just as it would have happened sixty years before when the great railroads really were being built. We had one natural

On "The Iron Horse" from the movie of the same name made by Jack Ford.

death, several accidental ones, fights, and many romances.

Mother and I were housed in the train in the observation and sitting-room section. Normally, the director would have taken this for himself, but not Jack Ford, who slept in an upper berth with the extra people. Every weekend, a real gambling train came to the location, and the extras lost most of their money.

Mama became enamored of one of these gamblers. He was a raw-boned, coarse-looking, middle-aged man. I could hear her and this man making love at night in the observation section next to my stateroom. This disturbed me out of all proportion, although I said nothing to her about it. To write about it

now seems a betrayal of my mother, but I cannot write the truth about myself without including the impact this man had on my life and my mother's for the next six years. I think it influenced much of what I did later.

As far as I know, only one doctor was assigned to care for the several hundred people at this location while making *The Iron Horse*. He was a handsome young blond man, and I prevailed upon him to take me to dinner in Reno, which was about two hours from our encampment. I may have wanted to seduce him. While we were gone, a man broke his arm, and my doctor was in trouble. Although we hurried back, he was in danger of being barred from his profession. I telephoned Sol Wurtzel, our production manager, and tried to

With George O'Brien in *The Iron Horse* (1924) (Courtesy of Robert S. Birchard).

take the blame. I'm sure that everyone thought that we were having an affair. I am quite sure that we would never have taken that trip if I hadn't overheard Mama and the gambler.

From the window of my stateroom at daybreak, I could see George O'Brien jogging and preparing for the day's work. He was dedicated to doing a good job with one of his first big parts and the start of a fine career.

When we returned to the studio to do the interior scenes, a dark man came up to me one day and asked, "How do you like your part in this picture, young lady?"

"I don't like it at all," I replied. "I'm angry all through the picture and don't know what in the world I'm so angry about."

After he was gone, I asked someone, "Who was that?"

"That," the person told me, "was your boss, William Fox."

People ask me about John Ford's genius. I don't think it lay in his direction of individual scenes; it lay in his panoramic view of the whole picture—his ability to achieve artistic unity. The timing, the emphasis, his grasp of the whole drama constituted his art.

My part in *The Iron Horse* was so extraneous that if I had been left out of the picture entirely, I would not have been missed. But I am glad that I appeared in such a classic film and that I got to know Jack Ford.

Mama and I attended many parties at his home where his sense of fun and hatred of pretense were evident. Once he grabbed a megaphone and shouted over the telephone to a pompous director, "Get off that high horse! You are just like the rest of us!" That was his philosophy.

I can see him now—sitting high on his platform, relaying his directions through his brother, Eddie O'Fearna, a white handkerchief on which he chewed in the big scenes hanging from his mouth.

"Now the horses! Now the Indians!" The rider falls, and "Cut!"

Returning to Mr. Ince, we made an insignificant picture called *Love's Whirlpool* with Lila Lee and her husband, James Kirkwood.

During my four-year contract, which only had a few months to go, I had made nearly seven pictures a year. There was talk that Mr. Ince was going over to the First National Pictures, taking me along as his star, but all this seemed to have fallen through. I met Mr. Ince on the stairs in front of the studio and complained bitterly that I was not put in an important picture.

He stared at me, hardly listening, as if he were thinking, "How little you know, or understand." His kind eye looked into my eyes reproachfully; his mean eye squinted at me.

"I've got too many troubles of my own," he said, "to worry about yours."

I heard before it was public that Mr. Ince had died on William Randolph Hearst's yacht during a big party. It was a terrific scandal and the wildest tales were told: that Hearst had shot him, that Marion Davies had shot him, that Chaplin had killed him. Years later, I asked Mickey Neilan about it; he said Mr. Ince had died of a stomachache.

I spent four years with the Ince company, making 21 pictures altogether, although only six were made directly for Ince. I had spent nights with wind machines blowing me speechless; days up to my neck in mud. I had been half blinded by Klieg lights and driven automobiles 80 miles an hour down Hollywood Boulevard with cameramen hanging onto the fenders. I had lost hair and temper, and I was getting insomnia. Mama drove me around at night while I tried to sleep on the back seat. I was still a virgin, and I was getting tired of that, too.

# HOLLYWOOD MOVIE FAN

DECEMBER, 1924

Cover of *Hollywood Movie Fan* magazine for December 1924, featuring Madge Bellamy.

DEDICATED TO MOTION PICTURE PATRONS

| NEWS * FEATURE STORIES THEATER REVIEWS | —The— **Movie Fan** | EDITORIALS AND COMMENTS BY WELL KNOWN WRITERS |

Leonard C. Boyd, Editor

# The Girl on the Cover

The girl on the cover, Madge Bellamy, film star and famous beauty, came to the moving picture world from the speaking stage, where she had played "Pollyanna," "Peg O' My Heart" and opposite William Gillette in James Barrie's "Dear Brutus." She was billed as the most beautiful girl on Broadway and often referred to as the "unforgetable girl."

Penhryn Stanlaws, artist of international fame, proclaimed her the most beautiful young girl in America, and later such authorities, on beauty, as Antoinette Donnelly and Neysa McNein, both included her in their selections of most beautiful women in the United States. Almost every prominent art photographer in Los Angeles has pronounced her the most beautiful girl in pictures.

Thos. H. Ince, the producer, said of her: "Hers is the most sensitive, volatile little face I have ever seen. Expressions quiver all over it. Her eyes are large and dark, with heavy lids, which she droops over them in the most disconcerting manner."

Harry Carr, noted critic and feature writer, recently wrote of her in The Los Angeles Times: "Madge Bellamy is the most beautiful girl I ever saw. I defy anybody—man, woman or child—to remember what he is talking about if Madge Bellamy suddenly looks at him in the middle of a sentence. That's just how beautiful she is. She is absolutely devastatingly overwhelming."

Madge Bellamy was born in Texas, her mother an accomplished musician, and her father a college professor of English. She lived only a few years in her native state, the family moving to New York City soon after her birth.

Her stage successes attracted the attention of Thos. H. Ince, who signed a three-year contract with her. She has played in many screen successes, including William Fox's magnificent production, "The Iron Horse," which has been playing continuously for over four months at the Lyric Theare in New York.

Letters to her should be addressed to 6318 Hollywood Boulevard, Hollywood, Calif.

**MADGE BELLAMY**

## TO MADGE BELLAMY

Once I fell in love with you, oh, years and
    years ago;
    You wore a child's short-waisted frock, a
    butterfly hair-bow,
Black "Mary-Janes," and short, white socks,
    and brown curls fairly shouting
    That they had felt no curling iron; a wist-
    ful mouth, half pouting.

But oh, the questioning dear eyes, with all
    the dreams of years,
    Grave eyes, that held a lurking smile, and
    just a hint of tears.
I tore it from the magazine (I who had
    laughed to scorn
    The foolish mortals who would thus their
    bedroom walls adorn.)

Where I have gone, it, too, has gone, and
    hung in many a place,
    And lighted many a sombre wall, that
    glowing pictured face,
But it is scarred with pin-pricks now—its
    jaunty charm is frayed,
    And I would like so much to have another
    shadow maid;

One that would fit into a frame to hang upon
    the wall,
    Reminding me eternally that years pass
    not at all;
That this illusive bit of youth will never
    change or die,
    That it holds fast the changing years for
    mortals such as I.

I have no way of getting one—please won't
    you, if you can,
    Bestow another "Dream Child" on a plead-
    ing                BETTY ANN.

Grace L. Houghton,          April 17th
President                              1989
The Vestal Press Ltd.
P. O Box 97
1320 N. Jensen Road.
Vestal. N.Y. 13850

Dear Mrs. Houghton:
    Can't find a Bellamy
hat picture, but 
this is what I recall it looked like.
                    good
There was one ^ thing about it.
It was $3.50 plus postage, as
advertized in the fan magazines.

Madge was a fashion trendsetter, popularizing a "Lorna Doone Cape" and a "Madge Bellamy Cap." Miss Bellamy recalls seeing herself advertising the cape in posters on the walls of the New York subway. In response to a request for a picture of the "Madge Bellamy Cap," Miss Bellamy provided the drawing above. The hat she wears in the photograph to the right, she says, is the hat in question. (Wisconsin Center for Film and Theater Research).

(Wisconsin Center for Film and Theater Research).

*Love and Glory* (1924) with Madge and Charles De Roche, a French actor.

With Gibson Gowland in *Love and Glory* (1924) (National Film Archive, London).

Madge in *The Reckless Sex* (1925) with Buster Collier (National Film Archive, London).

# Chapter Three

*Peter Pan* was to be made at Paramount, and setting my heart on playing Peter, I pestered Herbert Brenon, who was to direct it. He said that I could have the part of Wendy, but I was just too feminine-looking to play Peter.

Then he began to pester me. I don't think that he was in love with me—he acted too mean—but he certainly was infatuated. He would not let me alone and sat outside our house in his car honking for me to come out. Then he'd leave and soon after, the phone would ring. Daddy would beat me to it, and he and Daddy would call each other names and threaten bodily harm. After a few weeks, both men were in a furious state.

After a few hectic weeks, I decided that I should find out what it was all about. I was convinced that I was loved by a most unsuitable subject: a married man, middle-aged, grey, homely, and irascible. However, I was twenty-two years old and beginning to fear that life, or love, was passing me by. Since there was no one else, I decided that I loved him and went to his house, ready to give my all. Alas, as in the movies of the time, he would not deflower a maiden. After a very embarrassing scene which I haven't the stamina to describe, I left just as pure (or almost) as when I had come.

But my father must have sensed that something had taken place. That night, he went to Brenon's house and fired two shots through his front door.

The shots had the power that words did not, and the love-mad director left town. But he did not give up on me. It had become a game to win against my father. He phoned me nearly every night from New York and said

dreadful things to me, such as my being a "no-good, second-rate actress" and that he hated me. He never wanted to see me again, and if I didn't come to him in New York at once, it would be all the worse for me. Since he was safely away, and yet would not let me forget him, I decided that he was the love of my life.

Alas, he was the classic type—married with an invalid wife whom he could not divorce. This was a perfect set-up for a born mooner, and I mooned over him until at last, I went to him in New York—but that was three years later.

I don't know what charm this man had for me. Perhaps it was because he was Irish—sharp to hurt, and soft and tender to deceive.

The Fox company knew my contract with Ince was over. Mr. Winfield Sheehan, the vice-president, phoned me and said that they wished to offer me a contract. I invited him to dinner, and he said that he would bring along the terms of the contract. On our tablecloth after dinner, he sketched the terms. They were wonderful, much more than I had ever hoped to earn, so I signed the contract on the next day for four years with yearly options.

My first picture for Fox was *Wings of Youth*, directed by Emmett Flynn. The lovely Ethel Clayton was in it.

Next was *Lazybones* with Frank Borzage as the director. Frank and I did not get along. This was to prove a great disaster for me as he refused to have me for the role played by Janet Gaynor in *Seventh Heaven*, even though William Fox himself said that he had chosen me.

Borzage and I quarreled over the little matter of my fingernails. In the picture, I

Madge with Emmet Flynn's Company for *Wings of Youth* (1925).

*Lightnin'* (1925) (National Film Archive, London).

Madge with Buck Jones in *Lazybones* (1925) (National Film Archive, London).

With Arthur Houseman in Victor Schertzinger's picture *Thunder Mountain* (1925).

With Jack Mulhall in *The Dixie Merchant* (1926) (National Film Archive, London).

played a poor white-trash girl. Every morning, he would inspect my nails to see if they were dirty enough. They never were, so he had mud rubbed in them. I did not think that the camera was close enough to catch this detail and took it as an insult. Of course, in retrospect, I wonder how I could have been so uncooperative.

I failed to get along with several big directors: Borzage, Tourneur, John Griffith Wray, and one other whose name I have forgotten; but I remember that I threw a shoe at him. I adored Jack Ford, Schertzinger, Harry Beaumont, Roy Neill, Frank O'Connor, Lewis Milestone when he was assistant director, and John Blystone. I liked Allan Dwan, Victor Halperin, James Tinling, and Arthur Rosson.

Next, we did a picture called *Havoc* from the play; then we did *The Dancers*, *The Golden Strain*, *Thunder Mountain*, and another with Borzage—*The Dixie Merchant*.

While on location for this picture, I received a wire from Sol Wurtzel, second-in-command at Fox studios, saying that if I would lose twelve pounds, they would put me in *Sandy*, a best-selling novel running as a serial in the daily papers. I got down to one hundred pounds in two weeks by eating nothing but canned spinach and canned tomatoes.

*Sandy* was one of the early "flapper"

Madge with Charles Farrell in *Sandy* (1926) (National Film Archive, London).

Madge dancing the Charleston in *Sandy* (1926) (National Film Archive, London).

pictures. In it, I wore a gin flask under my garter, and I danced the Charleston on a table top, much as I was doing in real life. It was a story of the modern girl and her attempt to free herself from traditional restraints.

Louella Parsons, the *Examiner* gossip columnist, always knocked me about the time each of the options on my contract came up. I think that she did this to everybody so that the producers could renew actors' contracts at a lower salary.

At this time, she wrote, "Just as long hair is again the style, Madge has cut hers off."

The famous Polish artist Tada Styka came to Hollywood. With much publicity, he selected the Five Most Beautiful Actresses and painted a portrait of each. They were Marion Davies, Pola Negri, Gloria Swanson, Billie Dove, and me.

The L.A. *Examiner* conducted a poll of Los Angeles photographers as to whom they considered the most beautiful, and I won. My picture, taken by each photographer, was printed in the paper.

One reason that I was chosen was because I had spent a great deal of time and money having my picture taken, although I was not vain and never thought myself to be pretty. I would cry so much seeing my rushes that I had to stop going. I wanted so much to be beautiful—even more than I wanted to be a good actress—that I didn't want to look ugly even if the script called for it.

In 1926, *Photoplay Magazine* conducted a popularity poll. I did not reach the top ten, but I was eleventh. The top five women were Clara Bow, Gloria Swanson, Pola Negri, Colleen Moore, and I was fifth among the women.

It was this same year that I was raped. I went to a party at Ciro's; next to me sat a young, blond, healthy-looking bachelor—a haberdasher. He asked me to marry him. Since I was outrageously attracted to him, I fail to see why I refused him. Instead, I got up on the dance floor and danced a solo. Now this was not an unusual thing to do in those days; many actresses did impromptu Charlestons. However, it was a strange thing for me

Of this photo, Madge says: "Glad the twenties are gone—good riddance! This was a fashionable dress at the time."

to do as I was considered demure and quiet. Mickey Neilan (with whom I was no longer in love) took me home. He thought that I had had too much to drink.

A few days later, I saw this haberdasher again. He was at the next table at a party

Painting of Madge by the Polish artist Tada Styka.

hosted by Joseph Schenck, one of the biggest of the movie moguls. My escort was Nick Schenck, his brother. They were all astonished when I spent most of the evening dancing with the tailor.

The next day, he phoned, and I let him come to see me. He raped me right in my sitting room.

There had been a story in Hollywood—started (I think) by Lilyan Tashman, a great and cruel wit—that "Madge's mother always holds her douche bag." That night, the story came true.

Strangely enough, I saw this man again. I should have hated and avoided forever a man who gave me such a horribly violent introduction to sex. I have never gone to a psychiatrist, but I wish that I had gone to one then, and I wish I could go to one now. Perhaps they could tell me why I behaved this way. After all these years, I still cannot understand my behavior.

I visited him at his Art-Deco penthouse. This man was not handsome; he had a sleepy, bland face and so far as I know, he had no interest in anything but business and golf. I didn't love him. I didn't even like him. I never became a real friend to him either.

A few years later when his business was in trouble, he asked to borrow $50,000 from me, but I refused. I would not have dreamed of lending him the money, although I could have afforded to do so.

The kindest interpretation that I can put on this association was that this was my first man, so I felt a sexual bond. I was cold sexually and remained so.

I hesitate to say that I knew Howard Hughes because I did not have an affair with him. I first met him when a young man named John Considine, who had inherited a theater-chain fortune, phoned me. He said that Mr. Hughes wanted me as the leading lady in a film that he intended making which was to be called *Two Arabian Knights*. I told him that I was under contract to the Fox Company, and he would have to contract them.

"Well, Mr. Hughes would like to come over to your house and discuss it, anyway,"

Considine explained. Then he added, "What you need, young lady, is a good agent!"

"Why don't you volunteer?" I quipped.

"I'm no agent; I'm a rich young man," he replied.

Hughes called on me the next evening. As my butler showed him into the drawing room, he looked suspiciously from side to side and behind as if he feared that he was being followed. At this time, he must have been about twenty-three years old, very tall and thin, with a small head, and a pleasing face. He was hard of hearing, as were his two uncles—Rupert Hughes, the novelist and director, and my singing teacher, Felix Hughes.

I noticed that Howard sat on the very edge of his chair and looked as if he might take flight any moment. Later, I learned that this was his natural manner. After the second lull in our conversation, he asked me if I had a deck of cards.

"I do tricks," he said.

I got the cards, a special engraved set, and he tore them in two with one hand. The surprise that I showed was genuine, and he liked my reaction.

Later, when I moved to my big house on Los Feliz Boulevard, he came by often—sometimes with a group, sometimes alone.

At this time, my boss, Winnie Sheehan, began to take a personal interest in me. Mr. Sheehan was rather stout with broad shoulders, and large, light blue eyes. He had been a policeman and knew gangsters like Dutch Schultz very well. He loved to tell ribald jokes and loved my being offended by them. We attended parties and social events together, and one night, he took me to see the mansion that he was building on a wooded hill in Beverly Hills. It was still mostly scaffolding. We climbed to the second floor and looked over the tree tops toward the city.

"I'm building this home for you," he said.

I answered, "I'm in love with someone else," referring to the mean and married Mr. Herbert Brenon. Strangely enough, I went to bed with Mr. Sheehan that night.

# Chapter Four

**T**hen came the most joyous time of my life. I had always wanted to go abroad. Mr. Sheehan said that the Fox company would pay most of our expenses because the trip could be used as publicity for my next picture, *Seventh Heaven*. It was to be a war picture. I would be met in Paris by the chief photographer of Fox newsreels, "Brick,"* and his camera crew, who would photograph me at the battlefields in France of The Great War. I can only compare this trip to the rapturous times of my early days in New York City.

At the dock, I got the send-off of all send-offs: magnums of champagne tied in ribbons, the press and cameramen scurrying around me. I can still hear the ship's horns as the *Olympic* moved slowly from our shore.

In the togetherness of a ship's crew and its passengers, there is a mysterious tie and an exultation born, perhaps, of the fear men of the land feel for the mighty deep. The ship's orchestra began, and we wondered if we would ever come home again.

It is said that the twenties were a blasé time. I disagree. It was a time certain "Pandora's boxes" were opened by the economic facts of big business. We were living in a bubble that we knew would burst. This secret knowledge must have influenced us and permeated, at least subconsciously, the lives of even the most ignorant and thoughtless. I wanted to see everything, to do everything. I was certainly not blasé, and no one could have been more receptive to every new sight and sound.

We had hardly entered our stateroom and closed the door when we heard a knock. It was Sir Thomas Lipton, the English tea magnate.

*Al Brick

"I just read the passenger list and saw your name," he said. "I thought that I had better hurry, before somebody else gets here. Will you and your mother have dinner with me?"

They say that if a girl catches one millionaire, it is easy for her to catch more. When one falls, they all fall—like dominoes.

We had dinner with Sir Thomas, and I still have the pictures taken of us. Besides Sir Thomas, I discovered a short, stout, elderly man and a long, tall, lean one who were always together, and whom I kept coming upon unexpectedly in corridors, around corners, and down hatches. The short one— grey-haired, dark-eyebrowed—began to smile at me from behind pillars and posts, finally introducing himself.

"I'm Adolph Ochs," he said, "owner of the *New York Times*, and this," he indicated the tall, lean man, "is Mr. Pulitzer."

Mother and I had dinner with them at the Captain's table every night of the six-day voyage to Cherbourg.

Next to our table sat the great Russian singer Chaliapin. One of the diversions of the voyage was watching him eat cheese. He would order dinner, then fruit, and then a whole Camembert cheese pie. His capacity for cheese was almost as great as his repertoire.

I became tremulous with excitement by the presence of Lucrecia Bori, the great Metropolitan Opera star. My admiration for her was almost masculine. I did some "around the corner" peeping and "accidental" bump-into's on my own. Bori wore mostly black or red lace gowns, and she was vivacious and svelte. She resembled my mother.

Other sources of excitement were the food and service. It was like being in heaven for the gourmet aboard a big ship with stewards hovering about like angels, offering to wrap one in a blanket, pushing forward trays of tasty tidbits, their winged white jackets flapping in the soft salt breeze.

I was a would-be gourmet, but I have never been much of a public eater. Ever since the days when I first ate stale bread behind the barn, I have picked at my food in front of people and eaten slowly, If I don't, I choke, and I regret not having enjoyed all the medallions of beef, artichokes, pressed duck-under-glass, smoked sturgeon, and Yorkshire pudding that have been whisked away from under my nose before I have taken more than a bite or two. Since everybody eats so fast, I became a secret eater, sometimes having a bite of something before I went to a dinner or luncheon and nearly always eating something after I got home. I like to eat, especially, while reading a book. Then my animal nature comes out. At the picture studios, I rarely ate in their commissaries but always in my dressing room. Many a young man has been deprived of my association without ever guessing that the reason was that he was a "sandwich man" or a "let's-get-a-bite-in-a-hurry-somewhere-before-the-game" sort of fellow.

When the barmen on board came for orders, Sir Thomas always asked for gin and bitters. We walked the deck in long strides, and he wore a captain's cap, white trousers with a blue coat, a watch chain across his waist, and a small white goatee with a drooping mustache. His manner was jaunty, and his constant smile squinted up his eyes.

The tall tea merchant told me, "Come to England's shores, my dear, and I promise that I'll marry you off to a lord in three months."

The passenger list included Thomas Beer, the author of *The Mauve Decade*, and the young Bennett Cerf, who wrote many years later about meeting me on the trip.

Mama was seasick, and she insisted that our cabin must be right over the ship's rudder. She actually said those immortal words of the seasick: "I wish this boat would sink!"

The chief scandal on the voyage concerned a prominent actor's wife who told all of the gentlemen aboard that she was broke. They all gave, but they also told. However, this lady left the boat at Cherbourg with no fewer than three of the most distinguished young gentlemen on board.

At Cherbourg, Sir Thomas stayed aboard and went on to Southampton. Mama and I left also with three men in tow. One was a handsome young Hollander in the cloth business who had the bad habit of examining the cloth of everyone's lapel. Upon meeting a man, he would grab his collar, look at it closely, and announce the name of the country from which he concluded the suit originated. Unfortunately, he had the same impulse with the ladies and to their intense surprise, would examine the hem of their garments.

Our second acquisition was a young man, Jerry Foreman, who was small in size, but large in Chicago banking circles. He almost ruined the whole trip to Europe for me. He had just been divorced by his wife, whom he loved very much, and he would tell me about it over and over again and weep. I heard the story at Rheims, Biarritz, and under the Arc de Triomphe. He wanted so badly to be on the "rebound" that I could have had him for my own, tears and all, but I cried with him a little and read the tourist guide through my tears. This young man jumped out of a window, killing himself, in the crash of 1929.

The third member of our party was an elderly, retired lumber man from Pasadena. He almost ruined Mama's trip. We didn't expect him to be there, but he usually showed up wherever we went: at the Tour D'Argent and the Russian café—the most popular places in Paris, the Maria Christina in San Sebastian, and the Hotel du Palais in Biarritz. We never found out which of us he was after. I don't think it was either of us. He was just lonesome for Americans and probably read the same tourist guides that we did.

Even today, I can taste the thick asparagus spears and strawberries, large as plums, that were served to us on the train from Cherbourg to Paris. I remember also how thrilled I was at being in the land of Rousseau and Montaigne, of Corot and Millet.

As soon as we arrived at the Hotel Crillon on the Place de la Concorde, I changed clothes and hurried down to the hotel lobby. I wanted to meet the French people at once. The lobby and bar were filled with Americans, most of whom I knew: Hope Hampton, Jules Brulatour, Mr. Ochs, Mr. and Mrs. James, and the *New York Times'* Paris correspondent with his wife.

I wanted to swallow Paris in one gulp, but I was frustrated; the Fox cameraman, Mr. Brick, was ordered to shoot pictures of me wherever I went. I had to stand on the banks of the Seine for three days in a faint mist, waiting for the sun to come out. That's how long it took to get a shot of me looking at the famous river.

At the next place, my photographer almost got me killed. When I went to the Arc de Triomphe to put a great wreath of roses on the grave of France's unknown soldier, where a flame burned day and night, Brick did not get a good picture on the first time. He said that we'd have to do it over again, and I reached to pick up the flowers for another try. A French growl rose to a roar. There were shouts of "canaille" and in English, "pig" as we started to take up the flowers from the grave. As the crowd closed around us, I realized that while Brick was a sweet fellow, he did not understand French, and we retreated in a hurry.

Mama and I wanted to go to the Eiffel Tower and told our taxi driver so. Mama had had three years of conversational French at school; I had studied the language a little, and we had both brushed up before we went.

But we rode around the Eiffel Tower shouting, "Eiffel! Eiffel!" and pointing at the tower for half an hour before the driver consented to understand our French.

Mr. Ochs gave a party at the Café Madrid on the Champs-Elysées at dusk when the tree-lined avenue had the impression of a forest bedded with green lawns. Through the foliage, I could see the former mansions, lighted like lanterns, open to the public as dining places.

The Café Madrid was the loveliest of these, a stately square of ornamented architecture with a mansard roof. Inside, one entire wall was a mirror which reflected the pavilion outside where people danced.

We prepare to live, and we spend time getting over the living we have done, but we really live so little. I think that I was really

alive in Paris. Every morning, we went to the Musée de Louvre when it opened. I could hardly wait to get in. I believe that my first sight of the Winged Victory of Samothrace affected me more than anything else except, perhaps, the enormous paintings by David, who was the Emperor Napoleon's favorite artist. We would remain in the Louvre, unable to believe that we were actually standing before some long-loved friend, some esteemed companion like da Vinci's "Bacchus" or David's "Madame Recamier." When the Musée closed at night, we would go back to the hotel, change into evening clothes, and then go off to Montmartre.

I don't think that we missed a single café; Mama, being very sociable and appreciative of talent, usually invited the entertainers at one café to accompany us to the next one. In this way, we would accumulate quite a large floorshow of our own before the evening was over—when "the dawn crept with silver-sandled feet down the wet and cobbled street." And did our feet hurt! We had blisters on blisters.

When Mr. Ochs invited Mama and me to the races at Auteuil, most of the rest of the party were French people who worked for the *New York Times* in Paris. At the track, men rudely walked around me in circles, commenting and gesticulating about me in a most lively way. Strangely enough, they looked only at my feet, rarely above my knees.

"It's your shoes," one of Mr. Och's Parisian friends explained. "They can tell you are an American by your shoes."

The myth of my knowledge of horseflesh was exploded at the racetrack. Mr. Ochs had graciously bought all of the ladies a ticket on a horse for a large amount. After inspecting the horses for the race, I changed my ticket for one on another horse. Mr. Ochs' won. The ladies confided to me that what they had won would pay the rent on their apartments for the entire year.

At the Palace of Versailles, I asked the guide to show us the servants' quarters.

"Where were the kitchens?" I asked. In all my life, I had never seen them described. Where was the washing done? Where did the

In the trenches of World War I in France; advance publicity shots for *Seventh Heaven*.

seamstresses work who made the embroidered gowns?

"Oh, the kitchens are in the basement about a quarter of a mile from where the court dined," he said. He was sorry, but he had no permission to show them. So we tourists of the world never see where the workers lived. We see only half of the world. Someday, I should like to see the servants' quarters of Versailles.

Of course, we went to the Folies Bérgère. Maurice Chevalier was there. He sang "Petite Peton" and "Valentina." In fact, at that time, all of Paris seemed to be singing "Valentina."

At the finale, each girl, in the almost-nude, sang a song, "My California Rose." To my surprise, I recognized the song as one composed at my piano in Beverly Hills by Tippy Grey, and the lyrics as the words that I had written for the music:

I like the daisies and forget-me-nots
But most of all, I love my California Rose.

Each girl wore a nosegay at three strategic positions as she represented each flower in the song. I did not sue for royalties as I realized that without the girls, the song was nothing.

To illustrate the complete absence of servility in the French, Mama and I went to France's most distinguished hairdresser. After a long consultation with the chief artist there, the verdict was that Mama should have a henna rinse on her midnight hair. This she rejected vehemently, but when we emerged from the beauty parlor, Mama, to her utter consternation, was a redhead.

Orders came from the Fox Company to proceed to the battlefields. I was photographed in my pale green linen Lanvin suit and my new tan cloche walking through the woods of Chateau-Thierry. I jumped over trenches half filled with rust-colored water and saw stretches of tangled barbed wire, foxholes overgrown with verdure, broken trees, and foliage rooting again under the constant rain. And I heard the meadow larks and mocking-birds calling for new life. We walked through Belleau Wood and posed on cannons.

I'm glad that I went. Ever since, I have known that I must work for peace, for life, against the stupidity of men warring against men. They obviously need to join hands in the fight against hunger, ignorance, and disease. I believe that mankind can learn to improve his environment, control his nature, and throw off greed and cruelty like an outmoded garment.

I thought that the French children were the most beautiful children that I had ever seen—so delicate and fragile. But the French people were not very tall, and the men looked as if they were walking in a hole. The French women were not as I had expected. Most of them were so-called "dirty blondes" with light grey eyes, slender, staccato, and brisk. They dressed simply, used little make-up except around the eyes with liner on the inside of the lashes, a thing that I had never seen before. They wore their hair almost straight and glued to the head.

In Spain, the men were beautiful with rolling black eyes that cast sparks as they glanced around. They used impassioned gestures, suave movements, were grace incarnate, and I am describing only the waiters! Sure enough, at the Maria Christina Hotel in San Sebastian, we found our retired lumber man from Pasadena still shouting, "Garkon!" for "garçon," still protesting loudly every "addition," and telling everybody how much better everyone did everything in America.

We intended to go to Germany, Belgium, and the Scandinavian countries (we did not want to go to Italy because of Mussolini), but instead, we returned to France.

France seemed to be an almond green tapestry, threaded with silver streams, ornamented with chateaux, its industrious farmers making it a land of cream and wine. I loved the little village of Barbizon just outside Paris, the home of the painter Millet. Here is where I wanted my home to be. The Barbizon painters caught the heavy shadows and quick sparks of sunlight that filtered through the foliage. They caught the huddled houses of mortar and whitewash, and made them realistic to me.

And then, we spent a week at my home away from home: the Palace of Versailles. Mother and I had lived there in our imaginations since the days when I had played the part of Pollyanna.

We began our residence with the two-volume *Memoirs of the Duke de St. Simon*. We feared, hated, and were awed by Louis Quatorze. His fripperies were absurd, but his

taste was superb. The reckless Duc d'Orleans gave us bad moments with his dissolute ways. We were aghast at the escapades of the Duchesse du Barry and filled with animosity towards the shrewd Madame Maintenon. The king had so many beautiful mistresses that it was hard to keep them sorted. We went hunting and to war with the courtiers, had secret rendezvous, and suffered for the sorrows of our friends, all the while mincing through the tapestried rooms and parquet floors of the Palais de Versailles.

By reading other memoirs, we associated intimately with Louis Quinze. Of course, we knew to what his and Madame de Pompadour's extravagance would lead. But her exquisite taste made her the arbiter of luxurious fashions for a hundred years. We saw her pictures painted by Watteau and Fragonard, and her canopied bed. We stood in Marie Antoinette's unbelievably tiny sitting room, and we saw the first and only bathtub in Versailles. We saw Fontainebleau and the Petit Trianon. Then we left France.

The crossing of the English Channel was very rough, and we bumped into everybody, but no one we knew. In London, I was met by two hundred cheering people, bearing flowers. My ego was not greatly inflated by this, however, because I knew that Fox Film Company's office force had been given the day off and were told to meet me.

We went to the Cecil Hotel, which was patronized mostly by the English. I loved them at once because they were so calm, so kind, so polite—so different from the irritable and argumentative French.

My young Chicago banker, Jerry Foreman, followed us to London and wept on my shoulder at the Changing of the Guard and at the Tower of London. I studied pre-fifteenth century England because my first known ancestor, John Philpott, had taken part in the killing of Wat Tyler, the leader of the Peasants' Revolt. For this, he was made alderman, or Mayor, of London. (I have spent some years writing an historical novel called *Seeds in the Wind* about this period. My hero is John Ball, the de-frocked priest. Alas, it is not yet published.) At the dark walls of the Tower, I

Madge arriving in London.

could imagine the clamour of the peasants begging, threatening, attacking for their freedom.

We drove over the rolling green country, shaded with dignified oaks, to Windsor Castle. It looked huge, but as most castles are, it was a shell like a movie set with houses in a circle around a courtyard.

We also visited the estate that Lord Byron bought, supposedly, from one of my mother's ancestors. It was called "Derden," which was Mama's maiden name.

Sir Thomas Lipton hosted a party for me at the Kit Kat Club. We sat around a table that was fifteen feet across and, sure enough, there was a lord seated next to me. Sir Thomas was being true to his promise. Between the soup and salad, the peer leaned close to me.

"I don't love my wife," he whispered. Between the dessert and nuts, I leaned toward him.

"Where is she?"

"Sitting straight across from us," he replied.

I don't remember any of the other guests at this party except Elinor Glyn and her sister, Lady Duff-Gordon. Elinor Glyn had so dominant a personality that it was difficult to remember the other people present. She was tall and strong with the features of an empress and a manner to match. I remember only one remark that she made to me. Her keen blue eyes, heavily lined in black, observed me as if she were deciding whether to lift or to lower my station in life.

Then she said, "I think you are pretty, even if you do have a big mouth."

# Chapter Five

Back home, I was informed that I was not going to do *Seventh Heaven*. I walked into William Fox's office without waiting to be announced and caught him in his shirt sleeves.

"I want to get out of my contract!"

Mr. Fox looked at me resignedly. "You can't get out of your contract," he said.

"You promised me the part, and I worked during my own vacation on publicity for *Seventh Heaven*. I want to get out because I'm not happy here."

"I'm not in this business to make people happy," he said and sighed. I think that I cried a little.

"I'm sorry," he said kindly. "It's not my choice. I wanted you and I still prefer you. It's Frank Borzage. He wants Janet Gaynor."

How I wished now that I had allowed Borzage to dirty up my nails as much as he had wanted to!

I was so angry with Winnie Sheehan that I sent back the Sealyham Terrier that he had bought and had waiting for me in London.

However, I forgave him (partly) in a few days after it was announced that I would do a picture with Edmund Lowe that was called *Black Paradise*. Roy William Neill was to direct.

I went with Winnie to the party given by Lilyan Tashman, Eddie Lowe's spiteful wife, which celebrated the start of the picture.

As Winnie and I walked through the door, Tashman said in a voice loud enough for all to hear, "Well, just back from Paris, and you're wearing a dress like I had three years ago." Lilyan was famous for remarks just like this one. It made Winnie Sheehan's day. He couldn't stop laughing.

I must tell about my last meeting with Lilyan Tashman. I was parked outside of the Beverly Hills Hotel, waiting for someone.

Lilyan stepped out of a car and walked by, looking as slim and as elegantly dressed as ever. When she saw me, she stopped and I expected the usual insult.

But to my surprise, she called over to the car, "How are you? You know, I've always liked you. Have you heard? I've got cancer," and she waved good-bye rather gaily. She died soon after this.

After *Black Paradise*, I was cast in *Summer Bachelors*, Allan Dwan to direct.

A few years ago during a talk to the cinema students at UCLA, I described how different directors would direct a scene. Dwan used sarcasm. He would say, for instance, "To the left, you see your love approaching. You fear that he doesn't love you any more. He comes up and kisses you tenderly. You burst into tears of happiness and relief—if you can manage it."

Ince would have yelled, "You see him coming. You love him. God, how you love him! What pain you feel—you are in an agony of suspense! He kisses you! What happiness! Cut! Let's do it again!"

Borzage was just as emotional, but quieter. He would weep as he directed. He would sob, "You see him. He means everything to you. He may not love you any more! He is your whole life!—Doesn't he care for you now?" By this time, Borzage would be in tears. "He kisses you! Oh, what joy!" Frank would be too choked up to go on.

When Lewis Milestone was King Vidor's assistant on *Love Never Dies*, he directed some of my scenes. I think that King Vidor was helping Milestone start his own directing career. Their method was my favorite. They would take me aside and explain exactly what they wanted, then keep on talking the scene until they got it. This is the method that Vidor

With May Allison (right) in *The Telephone Girl* (1927) (National Film Archive).

used in the silent days, and it is still done now.

I obeyed the cameraman's directions rather than the director's. My favorite cameramen—Hal Rosson, Ernie Palmer, or Henry Sharp—would take me aside before each scene and say, for instance, "Don't turn your head too far to the left. If you do, your nose gets a streak of light that I don't want," or "Try to keep your chin up! With your face down, you lose my effect."

My next assignment was *Bertha the Sewing Machine Girl*. This was about the last straw! I again went on no-speaking terms with Winnie Sheehan. I liked Irving Cummings, the direc-

tor, but there was no way the film could be good.

When the picture was completed, I received a letter from Herbert Brenon, my unlit flame, offering me the starring role in *The Telephone Girl* at Paramount Studios. At the same time, Daniel Frohman (with whom I carried on a weekly letter-writing project for fifteen years) wrote that he had urged Paramount to sign me for *The Telephone Girl*. I never knew which one really set up the role for me. My option with Fox did not come up for a few months, but I packed up anyway and went to New York. Some sort of settlement must have been made with Fox because Paramount paid my salary—

eight weeks at $25,000. Because of the two weeks lost between pictures, I would have made more under contract to Fox.

Mother and I engaged a lovely, five-room, two-story apartment at the Beaux Arts, then a fashionable hostelry.

As soon as I could get Mama out of the apartment, I invited Brenon to see me. I had known physical, brutal sex, the sex I had fantasized as an adolescent. I knew friendly, unemotional sex with Winnie. Now I hoped to discover what sex was like with a man whom I loved tenderly and who loved me emotionally. I was filled with extravagant expectations, though my love was now older, greyer, and plumper. I remember as if it were yesterday the bed on a dais in the small upstairs bedroom. No word was spoken, and at one point, I crawled under the bed. The encounter engendered no great emotion; but only tenderness, friendliness, and kindness. It was impersonal, no great event. Oh, where was my dream, my vision of joy?

I said only three words to him: "I felt nothing." I was as unloving as he. I never went to bed with him again.

The next morning, we had a quarrel. I was to wear my curly hair straight, he said, "like a typical telephone girl." So for three mornings and after only a few minutes of instruction, I worked in the Paramount telephone exchange as a telephone operator (with straight hair). Never before or again were so many lines crossed in a studio's offices. And I hated Brenon with a heart full of rage. I couldn't learn to operate the exchange, couldn't learn sex, didn't know anything about love. We battled through the eight weeks of the picture.

May Allison was in it. She was one of the beauties in the old scrapbook that I kept in San Antonio, Texas. She was still very beautiful.

Warner Baxter was the leading man with Holbrook Blinn and Lawrence Gray in other roles.

My disappointment in love and my troubles with *The Telephone Girl* did not dampen my social life. Adolph Ochs, owner of the *Times*, invited me to his home to meet Mrs. Ochs and

his family. Mrs. Ochs showed me her jewel collection. I was surprised that she preferred her gorgeous collection of aquamarines to diamonds. In the Ochs sitting room was a large painting by Bougereau of a girl holding a child. Mr. Ochs said that when he looked at it, he thought of me, but I did not see a resemblance.

Because he was fond of me, my picture appeared quite often in the *Times*. However, when I complained that one of his critics was rough on me, he told me bluntly, "I never interfere with critics on the paper."

It was near the end of 1926, and the night life of the speak-easy era was in full swing. We were all enjoying prohibition by drinking or looking for drinks. Neither Mama nor I missed much. Our group usually included several comedians known for their off-stage, off-screen humor; among them were Walter Catlett and Bert Wheeler. Dressed up in clothes by Bendel, Bergdorf-Goodman, or Lanvin and wearing diamonds, pearls, chinchilla, and ermine, we sneaked down dirty alleys looking for secret doors. When we found one, we knocked the secret knock, and an eye appeared at a peep-hole.

"It's Bob or Chuck or Jack," someone would say. Sometimes a bill or two passed through the aperture, and we entered a dingy joint rowdy with half-drunk patrons—noisy, smelly, and heavy with tobacco smoke. The banging of music mingled with a myriad of voices, chairs scraping, yells, and the breaking of glass.

I remember Jimmy Durante's place where he sang at the piano, and Texas Guinan's, and the place that was raided on the night that we were there. The police were bashing in the door, and Mama was running back and forth in front of it with a martini glass in her hand. Doubled up with laughter, we hid behind tables while the bootleggers and the waiters swarmed in frantic activity. Tables were cleared, bottles were tossed into trap doors—everything had been prepared in advance for a shakedown, for that is what it was. There would be a pay-off, and the next night, business would carry on as usual. When the

A still of Madge in *Ankles Preferred* (1927) (National Film Archive, London).

cops entered, hot and mad, there was nothing to be hot and mad about. We all sat quietly drinking our water.

Before *The Telephone Girl* was finished, I had a call from Winnie to come back to Fox. When I returned, I signed a new contract for over $100,000 a year.

On my visits to Winnie Sheehan's beautiful house, we were almost always joined by his favorite priest. I think that he was trying to convert me. He thought it a happy miracle that the priest laughed at his smutty jokes and did not scold him. He did so want me to become Catholic. When the Father drank a little wine with us, it put him in an ecstasy of charmed disbelief and pleasure. They smoked cigars together, and Winnie acted as if he was experiencing the companionship of God.

"Look at Father," he would say. "He enjoys good wine and a good story as much as anyone else!" Sheehan was of the same mold as a typical Irish cop.*

He loved to play jokes, especially on me. One day, returning to the pretty white bungalow that the Fox Company had given me, I found most of the studio executives gathered near my door. They nodded to me and seemed preoccupied as I passed by, so I concluded that the gathering had nothing to do with me. I went on into the bungalow and a few minutes later, went into the bathroom and sat down. Bang! The loudest rendition of "The Star-Spangled Banner" blared forth from a loud speaker on the roof, triggered by the

*He had been prominent in the New York police department.

toilet seat. As soon as I could, I went outside. The crowd around my dressing room was roaring with laughter, and Winnie Sheehan's face was red with mirth.

The parties that I went to with Sheehan were not wild. They were usually games of one-upmanship. Each hostess tried to have the most unusual decor or cuisine, the latest gown or hair-do from Paris in order to establish her status. Quite a bit of pushing and shoving was used to gain advancement or aggrandizement.

One wild party that I did attend took place in a hotel where we threw popcorn at each other until the floor was carpeted with it. I once attended a party at Catalina where Errol Flynn threw a young boy who had been annoying him out of a high window down into the sea. It was lucky that the boy missed the rocks below and was able to swim.

I was not a participant in the wildest party that I ever saw, which was held at my own home. I watched the proceedings from an upstairs landing. The doorbell rang at midnight. A group of fifteen people, most of whom I knew and who frequently visited my home, were at the door. They pushed past my butler, who had been asked to tell whomever was at the door that I was not at home.

"Not at home!" I heard a voice above the noisy chatter as they traipsed into my living room. "Who cares if she's home or not?"

This group went to the kitchen and the butler's pantry and drank up everything that they could find. The butler asked me what he should do.

"I've asked them over and over again to leave," he told me. To the sound of music, the party then spread onto the lawn where they played ring-around-the-rosy, and screamed and hollered till dawn. That was the end of my allowing my house to be used as a wayside inn. No more of that, I decided.

These progressive parties that went from house to house in Beverly Hills were very odd. The party began at one home; moved to another when the liquor and food were gone; and then, augmented by a few strangers, continued so that, with the "jump-ons" and

*Ankles Preferred* (1927), a film about a working girl, starring Madge and Lawrence Grey. It made more money for Fox, says Madge, than any other picture of the time.

the "drop-offs," the parties rarely ended with the same people who began them. One found oneself in a strange house with strange people at what was, technically, the same party.

It was a wild time in Hollywood. The writers wrote wild parts for us to play, and we played these parts off-screen as well. Hollywooders lived unreal lives, believing that activity was life, and that things brought happiness. We were tired and sleepless and weary of all the nothingness, but we ran faster and faster to catch each gold ring on the merry-go-round that grew louder and more raucous, drowning out thought. After it was over, we saw that we hadn't gone anywhere at all. We looked, but we had not seen. We ate, but we were still hungry. Better to have eaten stale bread with the rest of the world than to have been a flame so easily extinguished.

With James Hall in *Silk Legs* (1927) (National Film Archive, London).

Once, a well-known director appeared at my door, breathing heavily.

"Let me in!" he cried, never stopping, and he ran through the house shouting, "I just want to be happy!"—echoing the words of a popular song. Out of the back door he went and across the yard.

Then his wife rang the doorbell, ran through the house, saw her husband's figure going over the fence, and followed him out and over. Why they ran through my house, I never knew and I wonder if she ever caught up with him.

Being a friend of the head of the Fox company didn't help me get better parts and pictures because Fox made few good pictures at this time. I had fought for *Seventh Heaven* and lost.

For *Silk Legs*, in which I appeared, Arthur Rosson was the director. Then came *Ankles Preferred*. This picture made more money for Fox than Tom Mix's picture released at the same time, and he made $10,000 a week.

There were charming people at The Fox Studios such as Hugo Ballin and his wife, Mabel. He was both a famous painter and director, as was Harry Lachman. The director F. W. Murnau came from Germany. We all visited his strange sets* for *Sunrise* that had a built-in, exaggerated perspective, growing quickly smaller and slanted. These artists often used my house and my ear because they needed a sounding board that was honest enough not to steal their ideas. I was the ideal listener as the writer walked up and down the room talking to himself. Others who came

*designed by Rochus Gliese

With James Hall and Joseph Cawthorn in *Silk Legs* (1927) (Wisconsin Center for Film and Theater Research).

were Paul Bern, Joseph Hergesheimer, Carey Wilson, Benjamin Glazer, and Sadakichi Hartmann.

Hartmann was about sixty-five years old, part Japanese and part German, and he was so cadaverously thin and shabby that it was difficult to tell his age. Mama knew that he needed food and drink; and she plied him with these necessities as he stuffed our ears with tales of Whitman, Emerson, Verlaine, and Mallarmé, all of whom he had known personally. On every visit, he left me some of his poems and took away some little gift from Mama that was not quite so ethereal.

At this period, I passed through my Mae Murray, or moue-ing period, and the Pola Negri lowering phase seen in my portraits of this period. I even attempted the cold, quizzical leer of Swanson but only with fair success.

I had many beauty tricks, some rather dubious. For instance, I thought that my lower lip was too full and used to suck it in. Many a scene, I fear, would have been better without my disappearing lip. I never wore a brassiere or girdle, and I started the halter neckline to hide the bone at the back of my neck. I think I started the ankle-strap style in order to hide a fullness above my ankle.

My Scots-Irish grandmother came up from Texas to visit us. Her name was Texanna White because she was born on the Texas-Louisiana line. My grandfather had come to Texas from Kentucky. They were both school teachers. Later, he became a lawyer and a judge, and then a justice of the peace for twenty years in Amarillo, Texas. He was beautiful with heavy, silky, white hair; a long white beard; and merry blue, blue eyes. When he was fourteen, he had joined the Confederate Army and fought for four years. Northerners were always "damn Yankees" and aliens to him. Although he and Grandmother had raised two black children who turned out well, they both hated black people for no longer being slaves. In 1921, they belonged to the KKK.

Grandmother was tall, strong, and the most energetic and industrious person I ever knew. I never saw her without work in her hands. When she walked, she carried a bowl of batter, or cream, and beat it. Sitting down, she churned, made sausage sacks, or sewed dresses and hats of buckram. She was a devout Baptist and Prohibitionist. She talked like Don Quixote and always had a bottle of Peruna by her side. Peruna was later found to be 99% alcohol.

She remembered hiding from Indians with other women and children in the cellar. The white men were away, and the Negro men would fight the Indians off. She didn't care much for Indians—or grandchildren, either. She called them both Comanches.

She thought that dancing was instantaneous damnation. When I was ten years old, she told me not to swing too high, to remember that I was a girl, and to keep my dresses down. She thought a girl should have a beau and get married early, and from the moment that she arrived at our house, she worried about me.

One night, she came up to my bedroom and cried, "Muggie, you must get married." ("Muggie" is what I called myself when I was a small child.)

"But Grandmother, I can't. There's nobody who wants to marry me." She wiped her tear-filled eyes and put an arm around me.

"Listen to your old Grandmother. You must get married or you will get tuberculosis."

"Well, I'll try," I promised her, wondering if she thought I was living an immoral life. Grandmother put her head down on my bed and wept. All of the regrets of a lifetime gather around me as I remember the scene. I do not recall putting my arms around the poor, dying, old woman. Many a dress had she made for me, and many a chicken had she plucked and fried. Many a caress and many a merry joke had passed between us. But I was not impressed with her ideas, which were alien to me. Perhaps my youthful heart was a little hard.

Mama said that Grandmother used to come to her bedroom at night and cry.

She told Mama, "Annie, you should have had more children."

"But, Mama, why bring that up now? It is too late for me to have any more children." Grandmother wasn't just trying to give advice; she was seeking tenderness and affection, and I wish I had given it to her.

She didn't stay long; she said she couldn't stand our climate. She went back to Amarillo, Texas, where the temperature drops below zero and strong winds blow. Perhaps the climate of our love upset her.

About this time, I received several proposals of marriage, all of which had good possibilities. Unfortunately, I did not speak up with sufficient alacrity. Number One was the handsome scion of a Los Angeles philanthropist named Clark.

At a party, he took me aside and said urgently, "Come on, let's get out of here and get married."

He must have noticed a certain indecision.

"Come on," he pulled me toward the door. "My plane's at the airport. We'll fly to Las Vegas." The party was very crowded, and we were separated while I hesitated. In the meantime, he proposed to a well-known actress who moved more quickly. They left the party and were married. Very happily, I heard.

Number Two was a director who proposed to me on bended knee before everyone. While I was cogitating, he not only bent his elbow, but he bent his knees again to another.

Number Three was a handsome leading man who had a habit that made me stall: he would stare straight ahead of him as if he were in a trance. I learned later that he was thinking

In a racing car with Marjorie Beebe for *Very Confidential* (1927) (National Film Archive).

ot oil because he did not remain an actor for very long, but he became the head of his family's Texaco oil interests instead.

Of course, I was pursued by the usual deranged individuals who bother anyone who receives publicity. Mama, who answered some of my fan mail, was impressed by one letter. The man said that he wished to see me as he had written a play for me, and we allowed him to visit us. He was a dignified, middle-aged man. Soon after, he began writing letters threatening to kill Daddy, Mama, and me. When he hid in the shrubbery in front of our home, we called the police to have him taken away.

About this time, I found that a dram of gin helped steady my nerves. My excuse was that I had a phobia about posing for still pictures that made me rigid and jump as the shutter clicked. I suffered from this aberration from the time when I saw Maurice Tourneur humil-

iate a poor extra woman who inevitably moved when stills were taken. I wish that I had gone to a psychiatrist, but I never did; eventually, I got over this embarrassing problem.

It was prohibition, the time of the bootlegger, and no one, not even Mama, thought it odd that I kept a twenty-gallon bottle of gin in my bedroom closet. I took some to the studio with me each morning in a glass Collarium bottle. Collarium was an eye-wash. It had an eye-cup stopper that was loose and leaked fumes. Before going on the set, I would drink an eye-cup full of gin. Although the blue glass Collarium bottle held only ten ounces, the liquid gave off terrific juniper odors that overpowered the scents of my favorite perfumes: "Christmas Night" and Coty's "Jasmine." I attempted to disguise these odors with cloves that I kept in my gold-finished dressing case.

*Very Confidential* (1927) (National Film Archive).

I regret this use of liquor, but I regret as much my use of that Collarium bottle. In my defense, I must say that nearly everybody in those days carried a flask of some prohibited refreshment. I carried one under the garter of my rolled stockings.

One reason that I did not become an alcoholic was because I reversed the old saying, "I never drink when I'm working." I seldom drank when I wasn't working. I tell with shame the fact that I needed the gin because it was at such variance with the image of serenity and self-confidence that I wished to project.

Although I was becoming very angry at being cast in lightweight and silly comedies, I wrote one of them myself. It was called *Soft Living*.* I had been "Pickfordish," "Gishish," "Mabel Normandish," even a half-hearted "Swanson;" but in these comedies, I used Harry Langdon as my model. I thought that

he was a wonderful comedian, and besides, I thought that I looked like him.

In the picture that I wrote, I escaped down a fire escape wearing a fat man's trousers, which I lost in the lobby of a fashionable hotel. That was the day that Mr. and Mrs. Adolph Ochs, owners of the *New York Times*, chose to visit me at the Fox Studio. Later, Mr. Ochs wrote saying that he thought it was a shame that I was not cast in parts more suitable to my ability.

I wrote another story for myself. I called it *The Red Dancer* and took it to my immediate boss, Sol Wurtzel. It was about a girl dancer who accidentally turned the tide of battle during a revolution. Sol told me that the story would not work as it was too serious a subject for comedy. Fox did the story a few months later as a melodrama with Dolores Del Rio. I got no credit for the picture and still don't understand why I didn't demand it.**

*story credited to "Grace Mack."

**story credited to "Eleanor Brown;" adapted from an original by Henry Leyford Oates, said Fox.

(Courtesy of Robert S. Birchard)

(Courtesy of Robert S. Birchard)

Madge in *Soft Living* (1928) (National Film Archive).

*The Play Girl* (1928).

*The Play Girl* (1928), which a poster describes as "A Diamond Miner who works the Canyons of Broadway, with Madge Bellamy and Johnny Mack Brown, Walter McGrail, Lionel Belmore."

## Chapter Six

A few men friends would drop by our house: Richard Dix, Howard Hughes, Leslie Fenton, Lawrence Gray, Tippy Grey, and Bill Parnell, who wrote the music for my pictures. I had no women friends. I liked Sue Carol, Olive Borden, and Janet Gaynor, all of whom worked at the Fox Studio, but I never saw them socially. One girl whom I liked a lot came by my bungalow at the studio just to talk with me; her name was Jane Peters. She was later known as Carole Lombard. She was working in westerns. A handsome, healthy-looking girl, very frank and forthright, she quizzed me about different directors and their methods, and about pictures soon to be made. I saw that she was ambitious and determined to learn.

There now appeared a new girl on the lot, and I felt very threatened. Everybody seemed to expect great things from her. She was straight from the New York and London stages. I'll just call her "G." There was a rumor going around the lot that Winnie Sheehan, the big boss, was seeing her. Since I had not been going with Winnie for some time, it was strange that I felt so overwhelmingly jealous. Even my maid of five years, Adele, sensed my misery. She attempted to assuage my anguish by sharply criticising the newcomer.

"Miss Bellamy," she consoled me, "that girl may act good, but she's got a real ugly shaped head." Dear Adele, I rewarded your faithful service and soothing companionship with nothing!

I had never before in all my life been jealous of anybody, so I convinced myself that I must love Mr. Sheehan.

Oddly enough, at the same time, I liked Miss G. She was so friendly and confiding, so real. I particularly admired her habit of carrying with her a French lesson book, which she studied even on the set.

Although Winnie and I were not now bedfellows, he still escorted me to parties and to afternoons at Malibu with the Raoul Walshes. Now he ceased to phone his little "Black Widow" (a name he called me because I often wore black), and Miss G. received his attentions.

All of this sent me back to the tailor, who, when I refused to lend him $50,000, got it from someone else. He now had the big building that he wished to buy and a sumptuous penthouse atop the building. There was a garden, a massage and steam room, a tiled atrium with therapeutic sprays, and a couch with a long mirror beside it where, nude, we embraced without affection or passion in encounters like impersonal athletic workouts, admiring ourselves in the long mirror. It makes me sick to think of it after all these years. Perhaps I had nothing better to do, or perhaps I was rubbing my nose in sex to cure myself of it.

We did not talk much. We didn't have anything to say to each other. I once gave him a copy of Joyce's *Ulysses*, which was banned in America at that time. Contemptuously, he threw it in a drawer.

At the time, I was reading D. H. Lawrence.

"That mystical sex stuff is detrimental to you," my mother said. "I wish that you wouldn't read it."

I don't think it was what I read that made me so frantic. I was twenty-eight years old and had never experienced sexual pleasure or satisfaction, or love of any kind. Nearly thirty years old, I felt like a woman of fifty who sees life passing her by. I had no close companionship with anyone except my mother. The parent-child relationship was one of criticism and great expectations.

My tailor told me that he, as well as Sheehan, was having an affair with Miss G. He said that she had an anatomical characteristic that made her almost irresistible. Naturally, I began seeing someone else.

The "else" was a thirty-eight-year-old stockbroker. I doubt that he ever sold any stock, but so he called himself. I did not sleep with him and had no intention of doing so; we just went to parties or the Coconut Grove to dance.

The strange fact is that while I was earning over $100,000 a year and was called the prettiest girl in Hollywood by many people, I had no one to take me places.

I would like to write that I fell in love or at least felt some affection for someone, but it would not be true.

In those days, actors and actresses were not accepted in the old clubs like the Jonathan Club and the California Club. My tailor friend could not take me with him to the Bachelor Club dances. The picture people attended only the Mayfair dances and the Little Club.

Logan Metcalf, my stockbroker, who claimed to be the stepson of a former senator, urged me to marry him many times, but I had no intention of doing so. His mother, a lovely, gracious lady who resided at the Ambassador Hotel, hoped that I would become serious about her son.

We had been out dancing nearly every night for several months. I had made two pictures which, though silent, still employed orchestras in them—Woody Herman's and Stan Kenton's. The pictures were *Very Confidential* and *Soft Living*. Although they had been made some time earlier, the bands still played "Why" or "Very Confidentially—Ain't She Sweet?" when I entered a night club. I loved this and felt like royalty.

One night, Logan Metcalf and I came home as usual at about three o'clock in the morning. We were met at the door by both Mama and Papa.

"You're not going to marry him?" Mama cried almost hysterically.

"Of course she's not," shouted Papa. Turning to my escort, he continued, "Now you get out of here and don't you come back!"

I don't know why, but I turned to this stranger and said, "Come on; let's get married."

I was twenty-nine years old and felt I should be married and have a home of my own. If I was tired of being bossed by my parents, why did I choose a domineering person like him who was eleven years older than I?

We drove to Tijuana, Mexico, but I insisted that we spend the night first in San Diego at the Ulysses S. Grant Hotel. I always said that I would never marry a man without first having slept with him. Well, we spent the night together, and he was impotent. I thought it was because he was scared. Strange to say, this pleased me mightily. I felt that this showed great respect for me, so we went across the border and were married.

When we returned to the Ambassador Hotel to see his mother, she gave me some of her jewels. Then we went out to my home, and Adele met us at the door with a panic-stricken face.

"They're gone! They said they're not coming back. Your Mama and Papa are gone! They aren't coming back!"

They were, indeed, gone and had left no forwarding address.

My new husband consoled me by saying, "It's a good thing they're gone! I don't want you ever to see them again." Of course, I contacted a detective agency at once.

My husband had another idea. He insisted that I leave pictures. I must call the studio and ask that my contract be abrogated at once. This may sound as if he were bossing me, but it is what I wanted to hear. I had been complaining bitterly, both to him and to my parents, about the hard, unproductive work that I did in an endless string of inconsequential pictures at Fox. Although these pictures, about five in a year, made a great deal of money for the Fox company and were very popular, for a very ambitious actress, they were not enough. I felt that I was capable of much more.

Perhaps my consort was just humoring me when he urged me to quit work because he knew it was what I wanted. I phoned Sol Wurtzel who promised to see us on the next day. When we went into his office, Logan explained my wish to retire. I remember how hard Sol looked at me. Some years later, he told me that I was white as a sheet. He said that he would have to speak with others in the company and would let us know if my contract could be terminated.

Then he took us to my bungalow on the lot. It had been decorated with white roses and the whole front of the little house was wired to hold the flowers. A large bell hung over the entrance, which was also covered with roses.

The next day, I told Logan that I had to go to the studio for fittings for my next picture, which was true. I told him that I would be home about six o'clock. I arrived at six-thirty and was hit by, of all things, a box of orchids.

We were going to a premiere that night. The next morning, he told me that he wanted $14,000 to buy a Deusenberg automobile. I was stunned by this demand, but I wrote the check and gave it to him. He immediately tore it in two. He had changed his mind.

"We will go to your bank and have the account turned into a joint account!" he said. That did it.

"This marriage is a terrible mistake!" I told him. I tried to leave the house, but he locked me in my bedroom. Later, he went into my bathroom and cut, or rather nicked, his wrists. They didn't bleed very much, but I agreed not to leave him. In the meantime, Adele was running around looking wild-eyed. She didn't know what was happening.

The next morning, I convinced Logan that I had to go to the studio, and he let me go. I drove away in my town car with Jess, Adele's husband, who was my chauffeur. I didn't go back, at least not as long as he was there.

The detectives found Mama and Papa in Long Beach. I went there to get them, and they came home with me, although they would not talk to me. So ended what the newspaper called my six-day marriage. What did the man expect?

We went to Jerry Giesler, a prestigious divorce lawyer, who advised me to let Metcalf get the divorce because, otherwise, it would be an ugly affair; my spouse had threatened to fight the divorce. Logan insisted on fifteen minutes alone with me in the lawyer's office. He made a good pitch, but I refused to speak or look at him.

After the divorce, my ex-husband wrote me a few times, but I tore up the letters unread. About five years later, I saw him again. He told me a sad story about his financial difficulties, and I gave him back the rings that he had given me.

Then Mama began a new campaign. My parents had my power-of-attorney from my first days under contract in Hollywood. They did all the buying and, later on, the selling. I did not like to shop, so Mama selected and bought all of my clothes, cars, dogs, jewelry, house, and everything else. Now Mama bought me a $25,000 sable coat, diamond bracelets and rings—she also bought me a new home—without consulting me, or even showing it to me or my father before the purchase.

One day, Mama said, "Come, I want to show you something." We drove over to Los Feliz Boulevard and around a magnificent villa. I was too awed to speak. It was three stories tall and a quarter-of-a-block long. It was beige stucco with a red tiled roof. The driveway circled the house. At the front were formal gardens like those at Versailles with steps at various levels where waterfalls and fountains spilled over stones to the street, thirty feet below. At the back of the house was a huge half-moon solarium and terrace that overlooked lawns and trees around a small, artificial lake.

The house was a copy of the Duke of Alba's villa in Spain. It was built by Maurice Tourneur, my French director of *Lorna Doone*, when he thought that he was going to live in America (he had returned to France). His artistry showed in this lovely place. He had

# "THE CEDARS"

THE NEW ITALIAN MANSION recently completed by Mr. Phil Hunt (owner)
IS OFFERED FOR SALE BY
MR. AND MRS. CARR, Agents - 6331 Hollywood Boulevard - Hollywood, California
TELEPHONE HEmpstead 9806 - Residence GLadstone 5340
Courtesy is extended to any "Realtor"

Madge's home on Los Feliz Boulevard—built by Maurice Tourneur and modelled after the Duke of Alba's castle in Spain.

# "The Cedars"

—

The location of this palatial residence cannot be surpassed by any other home in California. It stands on its own knoll in a park of three acres formerly known as Tourneur Park, situated one block south of Los Feliz Boulevard, with a private driveway off of Commonwealth Avenue. The property *faces* the mountains and commands a permanently unobstructed view from Mount Baldy to the Pacific Ocean, while on the south a gorgeous panorama of the entire city is presented. The design is Italian inside and out, a duplicate of the Duke of Alba's palace. It is constructed of hollow tile, concrete and structural steel. In its surrounding landscaped gardens are magnificent fountains and ponds.

The multiplicity of detail and colossal magnificence of the interior precludes any attempt at individual description. Suffice it to say: The entrance hall, with its vaulted dome nearly fifty feet in height in black and white marble, has cathedral art glass windows and a balustrated marble stairway leading up to an upper hall with vaulted ceiling and art glass windows. From this hall a number of Italian arches divide the marble stairways leading to the magnificent dining room (with its double iron grilled plate glass doors and enormous cut crystal chandelier) and the upper living quarters. The decorations are mostly in old ivory and art stone. The hall terminates at the entrance to the Grand Reception Room with a huge adjoining solarium, and the mahogany library on its left. The sleeping room suites are so situated as to provide a view of the surrounding mountainous landscape in every direction.

(South View and Gardens)

(A Northern View of the Mountains)

The interior of this palatial residence is divided into the following number of rooms: Grand Reception Room, 46x23; Solarium or Music Room, 42x22; Library, 28x13; Dining Room, 27x17; Billiard or Card Room, 21x17; Kitchen, 20x15; Breakfast Room, 13x12; Maid's Suite (east wing), 26x12; Laundry (east wing), 28x15.

There are four suites of bedrooms—two on the main floor in the west wing and two on the second floor. These suites comprise bedroom, sitting room, dressing room and bath, with the bedrooms alone approximating 22x17.

There are a number of extra or store rooms, pantry, cedar-room, lavatories, etc., and two large rooms with bath and closet space for servants over the four-car garage.

The bath rooms have all glass inclosed showers, Belgian marble washstands, Venitian mirrors, medicine cases and are finished in either orchid, light blue or black and white marble with a Roman bath in the main suite.

The dressing rooms have an unusual amount of closet space, mirrored top wardrobes and linen closets.

Madge Bellamy riding in style.

sold it to the Hellman banking family, but they never moved in. The house was still without flooring.

As Mama and I entered the black-and-white marble vestibule with its stairway winding up two stories and its huge crystal chandelier, we looked into the great drawing room; my legs actually shook.

I made one remark: "I'll never be able to furnish it." I felt like a little dog that had just been handed a gold-plated bone.

From the baronial hall, we walked to the solarium, which occupied one-half of the circular terrace. Each bedroom included a suite with its own marble fireplace, sitting room, bath, and dressing rooms walled on all four sides with mirrors. The large bath had a marble sunken tub and a red Venetian glass window that, at sunset, lit the white marble like a brilliant flame. A large play and gaming room on the first level faced the water.

Upstairs, on a clear day, all of Hollywood and even the ocean could be seen. Mama's room was to be decorated in the Empire style,

I decided. After reading Madame Ramuset's memoirs of the days of Napoleon and seeing a picture of Josephine, I discovered a great likeness between Mama and the Empress.

With my knees quaking, I took what pleasure that I could in decorating and furnishing it. I bought dozens of books on period furniture and rugs. While I began to furnish my big house, I sensed that it was temporary, just as if I were a fortune teller.

This white elephant of a house tied up most of my money. It isolated me, too. My father lived at the farm most of the time, although the top floor of my new house was furnished as his apartment. My mother lived at our beach house, so I was alone with Adele and her husband, Jess, our butler and chauffeur, and a few other servants. I never liked it—it was so big and uncozy. I made my habitat of one small suite, sitting room, bedroom, and bath, where I took all of my meals. I rarely wandered over the immense dwelling.

I suspect that Mother bought the house to keep me working. I had married badly, been divorced quickly, and I think that she and my father feared that I'd give my money to someone or do something foolish. They wanted the cash invested. They thought a beautiful, new home would keep me interested, but it didn't work. I had liked the home on Beverly Drive in Beverly Hills. It was small, but I felt that it was big enough. It was near people whom I knew who would drop in to see me. The Los Feliz house was isolated. The nearest house, half-a-mile away, was Earl C. Anthony's, and he dropped in very rarely.

I am trying to analyze why I did not have close friends. Now, in my old age, I have two or three . . . why didn't I then? My Father had said that I was "dogmatic." Perhaps I was not as tolerant as I believe I am now. Also, I viewed men as adversaries in their role of admirers and sweethearts.

Since childhood, boys and men have been my friends. I felt no hostility towards them as males. But when eroticism showed its (ugly?) head, either in me or my male friend, I felt hostile. In examining this emotional phenomena, I believe that in childhood, I received the message that the sex act involved submission by the female, the granting of a favor to the man for an exchange of goods and services, or a miserable necessity in order to have babies. This script was given to me, I believe, by my mother, who told me about the birds and the bees, progressing to the seed in the mama's stomach put there by the father, causing the poor mother great pain because it hurt very much when the baby was born. Later, my father continued my sexual education by impressing upon me the fact that there were "bad girls" who were impure: girls who had lovers before marriage or women who, when married, were untrue to their husbands.

When I was about twelve years old, I read my first novel, *The Scarlet Letter*, and I saw the injustice of woman's lot. I began to believe in equality for women, and as I read the magazines that my mother received from a radical young cousin—magazines like *The Masses*—this belief was reinforced. Subconsciously, erroneously, I incorporated all of this into an antagonism to my sexual

partners or a feeling of exaggerated subservience to them. This led me from tolerating my rape to avoiding relationships where neither of us felt love, respect, or friendship. Thus, my subconscious produced the horrible results of my coldness and the eccentricity of my sexual encounters. I never had a real love affair.

Joy had left my life, and it is hard to write about it now. When people attain their material goals and do not find satisfaction and pleasure, they receive a deep, and often unrealized, psychological shock. The very rich, who seem secure, develop a psychotic dread of revolution or social change. This insecurity begets greed, cruelty, and war. We know that all things return to dust, all will rust away. What we possess is only lent to us, and we really possess nothing beyond what we use and enjoy each day. My possessions made me feel less secure because I knew that it takes money to keep money, and I was full of fear.

When my house was finished, I gave a party and invited some of my directors and their wives; Sol Wurtzel and his wife; Howard Hughes; and my tailor, whom I had begun seeing again. I invited a new girl in town named Lili Damita, who later married Errol Flynn. The moment that she and the tailor looked at each other, I saw what was happening and lost him for a few weeks.

Howard Hughes dubbed my mansion "Madge's sanitarium." He came to the "sanitarium" many times, always rather ill-at-ease. We played and sang at my Knabe piano in the solarium and then rode around the hills singing.

I resumed going to my tailor's penthouse, where we admired ourselves in the long mirror beside his antiseptic couch. He said that my house looked like Barker's furniture store.

I was too stupid to be happy, to appreciate each day, each moment, each hour. It has taken me many years to develop the serene joy of just living.

My three years in the Italian-Spanish castle were the most unhappy years of my life. I must have had a premonition that I would lose this home, causing great depression. I may have foreseen the upheaveal in the picture business with the coming of sound, the lower salaries, the end of the star system, the changes in management and power. I felt that my perch was tottering.

In addition, my mother and I were estranged. I considered her interest in others to be traitorous. Now in my late, late life, I rarely think of her. In order for me to remain healthy, I have to shut out her memories. But the music of Chopin speaks to me as if it were her voice, and I remember my tenderness for her. I can bear to listen only for a short while. If I feel her presence in the music for too long, the curtain of death between us becomes too monstrous to face.

My father was busy with the farm which he bought at Perris, California, and named "Fairview Farms." It was near Louis B. Mayer's horse farm. It was so large that it was shown on the map of California. Father, who had learned much about farming while he was a teacher of English at Texas A & M, put some of the acreage in wheat for dry farming. He drilled fine wells run by electricity and installed underground concrete pipes to irrigate some of the land for potatoes and watermelons. All of this was accomplished before water from the Colorado River was brought to the valley.

Then my father subdivided part of this land, laid out streets, and began to sell lots. He took a partner, who later gave him much trouble. They built a large pavilion on the property and chartered buses to bring crowds of people out to a free lunch and a lecture by my father on the beauties of California and of Fairview Farms, in particular. Many realtors do this now, but he was the first. He sold many lots. I'm ashamed to say that I went to the farm to hear him only once.

Dozens of prospective buyers were fed free of charge at long, outdoor tables. All that they had to do was listen to Daddy talk. And what talks he gave! Mama kept copies and published them a few years later when she had a small newspaper. They were so compelling that reading them now makes one want to buy a little farm and have one's own vines and

fig trees. I spoke with a man a short time ago who did not know that I was related to W. B. Philpott, the real estate orator. The man said, "You should have heard that man speak! He was a real spellbinder!"

My father was a sentimental "flower of the South" sort of gentleman, but on the lecture platform, his wit made the audience laugh hilariously. His talks were not only sales talks, but covered all subjects. Considering the crowds that came to hear him every Sunday and the great expansion of Fairview Farms, they were not only poetic and dramatic, but highly successful. His lithe figure moved up and down the platform, gesturing, shaking his fist, clapping his hands to his head, and laughing with his audience, but in such a refined and quiet manner that he might have been speaking at Oxford. When I heard him lecture, I was so impressed that I wanted all sales of the land stopped at once. I wanted to keep it all for ourselves.

Until this time, moving pictures were black and white. Daddy was interested in a color camera, and with another man, he invented a camera that took pictures in color. The process used a crystal prism and was completely unlike other processes that were being developed. I know Daddy's camera worked because he took some beautiful pictures of me in a green and orange batik dress playing around our big house with my Pomeranian, Peggy.

Besides the interest in color, there were rumors that "sound" was coming to Hollywood. The whole studio buzzed with the talk of "talkies." There was panic, bedlam, and enthusiasm. I obtained a libretto of *The Dollar Princess*, a musical by Leo Fall, and carried it around under my arm, perhaps because the part called for a great deal of singing by the princess.

The press built the coming of talking pictures into a crescendo of speculation. Would they succeed or fail? Who would rise with their advent? Who would fall? How long would they last? And why should we change, anyway?

At last, the great day came at the Fox Company when all of us made tests before the sound camera. Strange to say, no dialogue

Madge (right) with Janet Gaynor and two Fox Company writers.

was given to us to memorize or suggestions on what to say. Afterwards in the projection room, we had a difficult time concealing our mirth at the grammatical errors made by some of our actors.

I was not pleased with my test. I thought that I sounded like a twelve-year-old boy. However, my test was considered a success, and I was chosen to be in the Fox Company's first talking picture. My voice was considered distinctive.

This announcement evoked the following from New York movie critic Richard Watts, Jr.:

Recently, the Fox people offered a private showing of some Movietone tests that had been made by the Fox stars. One who attended them tells me that the voice of Miss Madge Bellamy proved much more suited to the purposes of the talking films than did that of Miss Janet Gaynor. Somehow, I cannot see how any trend in the cinema that would hail Miss Bellamy as a more valuable performer than Miss Gaynor comes under the head of progress.

The talking picture that I was to do was *Mother Knows Best* by Edna Ferber. It was based on the life of Elsie Janis, a great vaudevillian, famous for her impersonations of the great actors and singers of her day. I wanted to impersonate Galli-Curci, who was a friend of mine, and Raquel Meller singing "Who Will Buy My Violets?" Raquel was a wildly popular Spanish concert and nightclub singer, but Mr. Sheehan insisted that I do Anna Held, Al Jolson, and Harry Lauder. We were in accord on Harry Lauder. I think that my singing and

Madge in William Fox's picture *Mother Knows Best* (1928) with Louise Dresser.

dancing in his *For She's My Daisy* were the best things that I did. However, singing "Mammy" like Jolson and "For I Just Can't Make My Eyes Behave" in the raucous manner my coaches insisted was Anna Held's style required me to use a new blatant, lower voice. What success that I achieved was accomplished with hard work. By forcing my lower register up into my throat, I was able to sing in a loud voice around middle C. It was dear Bill Kernell who helped me learn these songs. Bill wrote the theme song, "Sally of My Dreams," and dedicated it to me.

In this first talkie, the microphones were placed about the set. and it was necessary to face the mike into which you were to speak. The actor might say, "Do not leave me, darling!" while facing away from his darling because the microphone was hidden in the folds of the tablecloth behind him.

In reply, she would walk a couple of feet away from him to murmur, "But, darling, I shan't leave you" into a mike that was hidden in the draperies.

While making *Mother Knows Best*, I was surprised to find that I had a mike in bed while I lay near death.

Working in this picture was a happy experience, for my director was the talented and kindly John Blystone. The part of my mother was played by wonderful and beautiful Louise Dresser. I was with her again shortly before her death at age 86.

In this first Movietone picture, only half was done with sound.

Some critic said, "The sound does not come

The theme song by William Kernell for *Mother Knows Best* (1928).

Madge as Harry Lauder, a Scottish singer, in *Mother Knows Best* (1928).

on until after the audience has become absorbed in the story, but so tellingly dramatic is its injection as to make the brief scenes unforgettable."

The critics were unanimous in effusive praise for the picture, and for Louise and me. The premiere at the Carthay Circle was attended by such celebrities as Janet Gaynor; Norma Shearer; Doug Fairbanks, Jr; and Joan Crawford.

The next morning, one of the papers said, "A really big picture has been brought to the screen. *Mother Knows Best* scored a brilliant triumph at its Hollywood Premiere. . . . If this first Fox picture production with Movietone is a forerunner of what will be developed in movies with a voice, the screen is in for a greater revolution than prophesied."

Louella Parsons wrote, "Madge Bellamy is Hollywood's most recent sensation."

Another critic said, "Madge Bellamy evidences a maturity and expression undreamed of. . . ."

Harrison Carroll, in the *Herald*, wrote, "I shan't forget for a long time Madge Bellamy's scene with the baby of her girlhood chum, the chum who married the neighbor boy and who knew nothing of fame. It becomes to me one of the most touching scenes ever filmed."

Edwin Schallert said, "Miss Bellamy's work is bound to be sensationally rated. Her performance as a whole will raise her to the estate of one of the most successful screen stars. Both Miss Dresser and Miss Bellamy register splendidly. The words spoken by her would indicate that Miss Bellamy's voice will prove exceptional."

# Chapter Seven

Since my impersonations of Harry Lauder, Al Jolson, and Anna Held in *Mother Knows Best* were so highly praised, I felt that I would succeed in a musical picture. A singing teacher and an accompanist came to the big house several times a week, and I studied everything from Mozart's "My Mother Bids Me Bind My Hair" and Bellini's "Costa Diva" to Victor Herbert's "Kiss Me Again" and "Sweethearts."

With the libretto of *The Dollar Princess* under my arm, I went to the studio and urged them to produce it with me in the lead. I felt more ambitious and joyful than I had since my first New York days when I was so sure of success.

My father was expecting great things for himself with his color-picture camera. He took the camera to the Fox studio where they considered it for a while, keeping us in breathless suspense.

Sol Wurtzel called me into his office to tell me that I was to do another silent picture called *Fugitives*. Kenneth Hawks, Mary Astor's husband and Howard Hawks's brother, was to direct. I was overwhelmed with anguish, but no talking picture was scheduled on the lot at that time, so I could not object.

When the picture began, I discovered that there had been an upheaval in the hierarchy of the studio. The first morning on the set, there were, as usual, the director, cameraman, crew, actors, Adele, and my dresser (a lovely young woman paid by the studio to assist me). There were also four young men in business suits, strangers on the set, who were bank employees. They watched and reported on time lost, money spent, progress made, or the lack of it. They sat unsmiling on the set, consulting with each other in whispers or taking the director aside to deliver instructions.

One was assigned to me and repeatedly sent me back to the hairdresser or to the wardrobe department. He kept my dresser busy re-adjusting my attire. They were like locusts on the set.

I did not realize that the entire industry was undergoing a big upheaval; positions of power at the top and on down the line were shaking. In a short time, Winnie Sheehan at Fox would be replaced by Darryl F. Zanuck.

While I was making this picture, Adolph Ochs and his wife came from New York and stayed at the Ambassador Hotel. When I went to see them at their bungalow, he took me inside and spoke seriously.

"Get your money out of the country," he warned. "Put your money in banks in Canada or Switzerland."

How I wish that I had understood! He was alerting me to the big stock market crash that came in October and the horrible depression that followed.

When this picture was completed, the front office called and told me that I was to appear in a picture called *The Lady from Hell*, another silent picture. I was distraught, for the director was to be an actor named Robert Armstrong, directing for the first time.

Bargaining with Sol, I said, "I'll do it if you let me select my own director."

Sol said, "You can select your leading men, but not the director or the picture."

"Then I quit," I replied. "Please tear up my contract!"

I remember how sad Sol looked.

"Go away, wait for awhile, and think about it," he told me in a very gentle manner.

Madge in *Fugitives* (1929) (National Film Archives, London).

I did go away, but I came back to his office later that afternoon. Evidently, he had talked with the powers-that-be, for he spread out a new contract for three years with yearly options. I was to receive $25,000 more a year than I did on my present contract.

Then I said the words that I have regretted all of the rest of my life. They were disastrous words, considering the state of the economy and the picture industry.

I said, "I don't want it. I want to get out!"

Sol Wurtzel remained a good friend of mine for many years, and he was certainly a good friend at this time, for he sadly and kindly urged me to change my mind and be sensible. I said no and left his office and the Fox Company.

Within two days, the local Los Angeles gossip columnists had me leaving Fox because I was ill, had become grossly fat, had become temperamental, or had broken morality clauses. Not one assumed or believed that I had left of my own accord. Whenever anyone left any studio, Louella Parsons and the others printed horrible or pathetic tall tales, and when a new contract was signed, they changed their stories.

Universal Studios engaged me for the leading role in *Tonight at Twelve*, a successful stage mystery thriller directed by Harry Pollard. The leading man would be Norman Trevor. It was one of the first talking pictures to be made at Universal.

I was paid $16,000 for this picture, one-half

In *Tonight at Twelve* (1929). (National Film Archive, London).

of what Fox paid me per picture. A phone call from Winfield Sheehan at Fox to come in and see him should have made me overjoyed. Instead, I went there in a sulky mood. Winnie greeted me in a tentative manner, not sure what to expect. We shook hands gravely, I sat down, and he sat down behind his big desk.

"We are going to produce the well-known stage play *The Trial of Mary Dugan* by Bayard Veiller. We think you would be fine as Mary. I have been authorized to offer you the part."

"I'm not interested in doing it," I answered without hesitation and got up to go.

He looked puzzled and astounded, and I, too, am still astounded at myself. Why did I do this? A thousand sleepless nights haven't solved the puzzle for me. Evidently, I felt resentment towards Sheehan, but why? For

not loving me, in spite of contrariness? Is that why I refused this offer of a big dramatic part, a role that I wanted to play? Writing this now, I remember that I reacted similarly to other opportunities at this time.

Edgar Selwyn called me to the MGM studio to talk with him and his brother Archie. The "Wyn" in their name was joined to the "Gold" of Sam Goldfish to create "Goldwyn"—which Sam took as his own name.

I told them that I didn't want supervisors on the set when I worked. I expect this finished any chance of my signing on at that studio.

Perhaps I chose not to work, not to succeed, because I was ill with unhappiness.

At Columbia Studios, Harry Cohn, the famous insulting Cohn, insulted me once more.

He called in Frank Capra to meet me, then

said, "You used to be the most beautiful girl in pictures, but you aren't now." I should have known that he always deprecated anyone with whom he wished to do business. He had beaten me down before signing a contract with me at previous times, but this time, I got up and left.

Then I did a talking picture with Kenneth Harlan called *Riot Squad*.

In October, 1929, the stock market crashed, and the disaster spread over the world. Half of the mansions in Beverly Hills and Hollywood were put up for sale, including mine. The few buyers offered a tenth of the previous value. Ruth Chatterton, Claudette Colbert, Ina Claire, Tallulah Bankhead, Helen Hayes, and other stage actors, young and old, were brought to Hollywood at one-eighth of the salaries that we movie actors had been receiving.

I had no offers, and in six months, I began to feel the pinch. Mother insisted that I was blacklisted. The studios were ruled by about five men who played gin rummy and golf at the same club every day. They drew up the blacklists.

*The Trial of Mary Dugan* eventually went to MGM and Norma Shearer. I never dared to tell my mother of this offer. She would have thought me demented.

For awhile, I thought that if I had had enough business sense to get backing and had produced my own pictures, I might have survived. However, Winnie Sheehan lost his post at Fox a short while after I left. He produced his own picture with his own money, but hardly anyone saw it because his rivals had ganged up on him and obstructed release of the picture. He lost most of his money fighting to get it shown, and he never made another picture. With monopolies controlling picture houses, it was almost impossible to produce an independent picture. I felt defeated and suffered great embarrassment.

My parents advertised that I was selling my home because I was leaving the country, but everyone knew that it was a forced sale because of bankruptcy. Then I found out that I still owed $150,000 on the home, and no

buyers would pay more than that sum for it. So, after a year of unemployment, I lost the house.

An auctioneer brought truckloads of furniture into the house, sold his furniture at high prices, and let my furniture go at absurdly low prices. I listened to his monotonous voice until I heard him auction off my rare art books for $1 an armload. I called to Jess, my butler, and had him relay to Mama and the auctioneer that the auction was off.

As the crowds drifted away, I lay on the stairs, sobbing. If I really wanted failure, I had it. I had not lost a loved one—a child or parent—or had an illness; I just lost a lot of "things." It was the most awful, the most tragic, the most pitiful time of my life.

Mama ran a shop on Hollywood Boulevard called "Hollywood Couturier." It had been partly my idea to sell beautiful, handmade clothes at reasonable prices. Mama engaged a Frenchman to make the dresses and help to run the shop. I don't know that he ever sold a dress before I fired him and closed the place. He had run up bills all over town for ads in theater programs, for hundreds of fancy boxes, for silks and woolens, laces and seamstresses. After he was gone, I was left with dozens of dresses of lamé, fine silk, and Chantilly lace—all made for models six feet tall and weighing no more than ninety pounds.

We moved into the back room of my vacant building in Santa Monica with the leftover furniture that included two Renaissance straight-back chairs, a very large dining set, a Venetian bedroom set, and numerous prayer rugs.

Has anyone moved so quickly from a palace to a hovel? I lay in the Venetian bed crying most of the time. Mama, passing by, gave me angry and disgusted looks, and I felt like a baby.

Scenes like this were enacted all over the United States in 1930. Although financiers were jumping out of windows, I felt as if I were the only one with the bottom fallen out from my world.

I had lived the story of Cinderella; now it was the Cinderella story in reverse, a story common to American society—the success who becomes a failure. I tasted the bitterness of this experience. As the climb upward has its excitement, the climb down has its drama.

Had Mama planned this move to a vacant building as a punishment? Had our money disappeared completely? We received $20,000 from the auction, and still had the beach house and the farm. If my father had ever made any money from the farm, he had put it back into it. His big barn was full of water-logged potatoes that were unsaleable.

In a few weeks, we moved into the beach house. Or, rather, I holed up in it. Looking back, it seems incredible that I did not employ an agent to try to obtain work. I received one offer for twenty-four weeks at $3,000 a week, doing the three singing impersonations from *Mother Knows Best*: Al Jolson in black-face; Harry Lauder, the Scotsman; and Anna Held.

It was a godsend; I should have leaped at it, but I refused the offer. I knew that I couldn't do those impersonations four times a day, changing orchestras and theaters, hotels and trains, make-up, and costumes. So I stayed at the beach. However, five years later, I did attempt it; those five performances a day, three songs, each with skits and blackouts, required leather lungs and an athlete's health. At this time, however, I knew it was too much for me, so I stayed at home at the beach.

The Depression was worsening. Our property was on the ocean front in Venice with large celery fields behind us where the workers were striking for a living wage. People all around us were being evicted for non-payment of rent. The strikers and their families were starving.

Mother and I took care of three of the strikers' children, each from a different family. All of these children had rickets.

Community committees were formed in Venice to force the authorities to help these people humanely. Such a committee was formed at my house. We went to the strikers' homes and organized them into groups to meet in front of the city hall, demanding milk and food for the children. Of course, there were no government bureaus then to care for the poor and hungry. Groups went to homes where people were evicted onto the street, carried the furniture and personal belongings back into the house, and helped the tenants resist evictions.

Seeing all of this poverty around me and fearing poverty myself, my compassion was further aroused for the poor and downtrodden. I felt a passionate pity for them, and a burning indignation at those who caused this deprivation and would not help alleviate it.

I was drawn to those who felt as I did, the twenty or thirty people—men and women—who were actively trying to help. We tried to make the unemployed, penniless people understand their rights and tried to show them what to do to help themselves. My store buildings were vacant, so I turned them over to these committees. Mother Bloor, the famous octogenarian, spoke there.

Of all of the people who met at our house, I remember only one vividly. He was a pale, blond, young man named Morris. I felt that he was ill and wouldn't live long. He wore an old black overcoat, indoors and out, and he sweated as furiously as if he had been running to accomplish what he had to do. He was the driving force of this socially conscious group of people. His energy pushed us on; his straight, fair hair flopped over his wet forehead, and his coat-tails stood out behind him in the rush of his movements.

I read *Das Kapital* (as did many others) and envisioned a society where all would be equal, have enough for their needs, and all would be friends . . ."Equality, Liberty, and Fraternity," "Do unto others as you would be done by," or as Jesus said, "Love one another." We were wildly hopeful for what Franklin Roosevelt would do.

In all of my years in Hollywood, I met no socially conscious people. The most friendly people whom I met were the reactionaries like the Hugheses, Howard and his two uncles. Rupert Hughes, the novelist, was especially fond of me. He supported every elitest cause for the rights of the well-born and rich. It was strange that the people most opposed to my philosophy were attracted to me. The only cause that I espoused concerned cruelty to animals in pictures. Once at Universal

Studios, I left a picture for two days because they had purposely tripped a horse, breaking its leg. The only philanthropic gesture that I can remember making was a hefty yearly contribution to the Childrens' Orthopedic Hospital.

I stayed at the beach house for three years without working or even getting an agent. In fact, I never had an agent during my entire career.

In 1932, the zoning was changed around my buildings. I was taxed to enlarge and broaden a nearby street, leaving my buildings in a cul-de-sac. The earthquake of 1932 cracked these buildings beyond repair, and I had them torn down. This cost me $5,000.

When I received a wire from a representative of Preston Sturges, the famous playwright, asking me to come to New York to audition for the leading role in his new play, Mama and I left at once.

We checked in at the Ambassador Hotel. New York City looked different. The Great Depression had produced bread lines, or soup lines as they were called, on the dirty streets, and people sold apples on the corners.

When I went by myself to see Preston Sturges at his apartment, he answered the door. We were alone. Sturges was as handsome as a movie star, reminding me of Ronald Colman, especially in manner. He wore his hair brushed up. The small room was filled with exotic furniture, Rococco sculpture, and many ornamental objects. Parted curtains revealed another room of Oriental splendor with canopied sofas, pillows, lamps, and burning incense—like an Arab sheik's tent. Sturges, himself, wore a magnificent maroon brocade dressing gown.

He led me to a small table, and to my surprise and relief, he had a butler serve me tea and cake. I sat uncertainly on the edge of my chair, balancing my cup, while he told me the story of his new play.

The part that I was to play was somewhat like that of the girl's role in his famous play Strictly Dishonourable. A young and innocent girl was determined to tempt an older man into seducing, or "ruining" her as they say. Sadly enough, it was a part that I had played

in real life some ten years earlier. Evidently, I still looked suitable, for Sturges asked me to try out in his Strictly Dishonourable, which was playing in Philadelphia, to see if I would be right for the new play.

Mother and I went to Philadelphia, and I played there for three weeks. This part was one of the most charming modern roles written for a girl. In a shocking and risqué scene, the young virgin disrobes before the audience down to her "teddy bears" and climbs into the leading man's bed to await his arrival.

While we were in Philadelphia, I got a call from Bernie Gimbel asking me to come to see him. He was a good-looking young man who told me that he admired my speaking voice and wished to employ me to advertise Gimbel's Philadelphia store on the radio. I'm afraid that I refused this offer rather arrogantly, considering advertising beneath me. Later, this scion of the Gimbels married pretty Sally Phipps, who had appeared in several movies with me.

Mama discovered that Robert McCormick, owner of the Chicago Tribune, was stopping at our hotel. She called him and said that she would like him to meet her daughter, Madge Bellamy. He invited us to his suite at once. For the visit, I wore ruffled pink taffeta pajamas, highly unsuitable for the occasion. It embarrasses me now to think of it, and I am glad that Mama accompanied me. Nevertheless, in a few days, I received an offer from the Chicago Tribune to star in their new radio serial.

As for Preston Sturges, the playwright, he never showed up in Philadelphia. I read in the papers that his new comedy production in which I was to appear had been called off, that he had accepted an offer to direct pictures and had gone to Hollywood. There, almost at once, he became well-known and honored as the director of some really fine pictures.

Back in New York, I tested for some radio parts at the William Morris Agency and then signed the contract to appear in the Chicago Tribune radio serial. I went alone because Mama had to stay in New York for repairs on our car. I found out how much I needed her.

## Chapter Eight

From the time that I read Rousseau's *Confessions* and Isadora Duncan's *My Life*, I hoped that when I came to write about my past, the perspective of time would help me to comprehend why I had done or refrained from doing certain things. Now, so many years later, I don't understand those strange and baffling days any more than I did then.

I checked into the Congress Hotel and went to the studio for rehearsal. It was all very smooth and underplayed as we stood in front of microphones with our scripts. The only suggestions that the director made concerned our distance from the microphone and the speaking volume.

I went back to the hotel and found that $500 which I had hidden in the lining of my sable coat had been stolen. This added to the deep depression that had come upon me, although I should have been grateful that the thief left my coat. I felt that my life was in ebb, going nowhere; I had no love, no companionship, little money. Youth was slipping away, as was fame.

But with a radio contract for $2500 a week for twenty-five weeks, I shouldn't have felt depressed and humiliated. What a fine new opportunity in 1933 to start a great new career in radio! Many other stars were doing the same.

The program was to go on live at nine o'clock. I had dinner in my room and got dressed to go. I felt very nervous, but since it was still the time of prohibition, I could not order a drink. Instead, I took a swig of perfume. I had never done such a thing before—or since. It was Guerlain's "L'Heure Bleue," and it tasted awful! I have hated the odor ever since.

After this dreadful drink, I lay down on the bed with my hat on—a small turban—and fell sound asleep. When I awoke and looked at the clock, it was past nine. I had slept for over an hour and missed the broadcast. Why couldn't I have gone to the station and explained this lapse by saying that I had overslept because I was very tired? My absence would probably have been excused, and I could have continued in the program the next week.

It isn't what happens to you, I now know, but how you take it that makes the difference. I considered this a catastrophe and felt a ton of guilt. That night, I walked out to the well of the hotel, stood on the fire escape, and looked down four stories to the pavement below, wishing for the courage to jump. I stood there for a long time, crying.

The next morning, a phone call asked me to come to Colonel McCormick's office at the newspaper. I was ushered into a magnificent room by two very polite gentlemen and was seated in a large chair opposite a large desk behind which sat a very large gentleman. If I had entered with insouciance and laughingly explained how I had, unfortunately, overslept, I may have been forgiven. Instead, I was as grim as a prisoner about to be sentenced for the crime of murder or, at least, grand theft. I don't think that I said a word.

After a pause, the very large man behind the very large desk asked, "Do you know Robert McCormick?"

I said, "No."

Why I lied, I don't know. I was scared. Visions of breach-of-contract suits were dancing in my head. When a release from the contract was put before me, I signed it with relief. So great was my fear of a lawsuit that I just signed away $25,000.

When I left the newspaper office, I found myself surrounded by newsmen. I told them

Madge, Bela Lugosi (center left), and Robert Frazer (right) in *White Zombie* (1932).

nothing except that the contract was terminated, but one newsman was so ingratiating that I accepted his offer to take me back to the hotel. Instead of the hotel, he took me for a long ride. I told him everything, including drinking the perfume that evidently made me oversleep.

He said, "I wish that I had known; I'd have brought a high-ball myself."

He must have been really sympathetic, for he wrote nothing about it. The newspapers said the contract was cancelled by mutual consent.

The next morning, I had an early guest: Jay Hormel, head of the meat company. I could hear that he was in a state of agitation, so I let him come up. We had met on the ship going over the Paris in 1927 when he was on his way to meet his wife.

Jay was a dark, wiry, little man with a strange blue complexion; no doubt his blue-blood was showing through. His black hair

was slicked down, and he had a permanent five o'clock shadow. In the seven years since we had met, I had not seen nor heard from him or his wife.

When he came nervously into my hotel suite, his hands shaking and his eyes red, I was surprised to hear him say, "Let's go away together! South America! Anywhere! What do you say? Will you? I must know at once!"

I thought that he must have taken some drug.

"But you are married," I reminded him. "I couldn't possibly run anywhere with you."

He took this refusal surprisingly well, even though he remained distraught. Then he said good-bye and almost leaped out of the room.

I heard later that he had been in a traffic accident that morning. When I met him with his wife years later in Palm Springs, neither of us ever mentioned this strange episode.

Later the same day, I received an enormous bouquet of red roses. The card said, "From your admirer Sidney Spiegel. I am downstairs. Will you meet me?"

I went down. The scion of the Spiegel mail-order house was an exuberantly active and enthusiastic young man—plump and of medium height. He had light brown hair; large, Germanic grey eyes; and a lovely fair complexion. He was not exactly handsome or charming, but he told me most convincingly that I was his favorite actress, that he adored me, and loved me madly. So I went to bed with him that night.

The next morning, Mama arrived in the motorcar. I told Sidney good-bye, and we left for Hollywood. Mama never asked me what happened to my radio contract, and I never told anyone else about it excepting, of course, the sympathetic, young newspaper man, who, as far as I know, told no one.

I marvel while writing these lines at how close Mama and I were, yet how uncommunicative. We avoided touchy subjects, and although we questioned and judged each other's actions, we were silent and non-committal as strangers to each other.

Hardly had we unpacked in Hollywood when I got a telegram from Phil Goldstone, an

# PUBLICITY SECTION "WHITE ZOMBIE"

## "White Zombie" One of the Eeriest Pictures Ever Brought to Screen

### Story Describes How Black Sorcery Is Employed in Haiti to Exhume Dead Bodies and Make Them Work

"White Zombie," one of the eeriest and most fantastic stories ever pictured for the screen, will have its premiere at the .............. theatre on .................., and American movie fans will thus learn, thousands of them for the first time, of the occult practices in Haiti in which by processes of sorcery dead bodies are dug from their graves and put to work as slaves.

Rumors have been reaching the United States for years of these sinister practices, and now, for the first time, light is thrown upon them by a screen presentation. The story of "White Zombie" is based upon personal observation in Haiti by American writers and research workers, and, fantastic as it sounds, its entire substance is based upon fact.

**Lugosi Starred**

"White Zombie" was produced in Hollywood by Edward and Victor Hugo Halperin, independent producers who have made countless successful pictures in the past decade, the story being an original by Garnett Weston.

Bela Lugosi, who came into prominence in this country with his stage and screen creation of Count Dracula in "Dracula," has the principal role in this newcomer, and his portrayal even surpasses that former work of artistry. He plays the role of a sinister fiend who traffics in the exhumation of dead bodies in order to man his sugar cane mills and his fields. He also has nine of the Zombies as a personal bodyguard, a bodyguard which perpetrates heinous crimes at the behest of their hypnotic alter ego.

Madge Bellamy, who retired from the screen two years ago in order to devote her time to stage work, makes her screen comeback in the principal feminine role. Joseph Cawthorn also plays one of the principal roles, as do Johnny Harron, Robert Frazer, Clarence Muse and Brandon Hurst.

**Photography Beautiful**

The settings and photography of "White Zombie" are among the best ever done for the screen. They include, for example, a castle in the Haitian mountains which is one of the largest of its kind in the history of motion pictures. This, with the tropical scenery of Haiti, makes an unusually striking background for this weird story.

The story tells of a young American couple who become entangled with the leader of the Zombies in Haiti, the result of which the young bride is placed under the influence of a powerful drug which relegates her to the mental plane of a sleep-walker. She remains in this state for several weeks, and it is only after all but superhuman efforts on the part of her husband and an American missionary that happiness is wrested from tragedy.

Bela Lugosi *in a scene from* "White Zombie"

*3—Two Col. Scene (Mat .10; Cut .50)*

## "White Zombie"

### With Bela Lugosi

Directed by Victor Halperin

Produced by Edward Halperin

| | |
|---|---|
| Photography | Arthur Martinelli |
| Story and Dialog | Garnett Weston |
| Settings by | Carl Tritschler<br>Ralph Berger<br>Howard Anderson |
| Musical arrangement | Abe Meyer |
| Sound engineer | Pete Clark |
| Editor | Harold McLernon |
| Assistant directors | William Cody and Herbert Glazer |

Running Time: 74 Minutes

CAST

| | |
|---|---|
| Murder | Bela Lugosi |
| Madeline | Madge Bellamy |
| Dr. Bruner | Joseph Cawthorn |
| Beaumont | Robert Frazer |
| Neil | John Harron |
| Driver | Clarence Muse |
| Silver | Brandon Hurst |
| Pierre | Dan Crimmins |
| Chauvin | John Peters |
| Von Gelder | George Burr McAnnan |

## Actress Collapses After Seeing Own Death Role

### Madge Bellamy Scared to Death By Own Portrayal in "White Zombie"

Hollywood has finally produced a character portrayal so infinitely realistic that when it was flashed upon the screen it scared the life out of the actress who portrayed it.

The portrayal is in "White Zombie," the picture which comes to the theatre on , and it was done by Madge Bellamy, who returns to the screen after a two-year retirement.

The story of "White Zombie" concerns itself with that black sorcery practiced in Haiti which has to do with dead bodies being re-animated and put to work in mills and fields. Reports of these eerie practices had been seeping into the more populated sections of Haiti for years, and recently an American author verified them through personal observation.

Miss Bellamy, in the story, is placed under a spell by the leader of the Zombies, a sinister sorcerer who traffics in dead bodies secretly dug from the graveyard, and, after she is pronounced dead by her family physician and interred in a large mausoleum, her body is disinterred that night by the Zombies and taken away to a mountain retreat. There the sorcerer brings her back to life, but only permits her the animation of a sleep-walker.

Miss Bellamy went through these scenes one morning, and late that day she and other members of the company went into the projection room to look at the result. That part of the sequence in which she is seen lying in a coffin was flashed upon the screen, and, after taking one look, Miss Bellamy let out a piercing scream and bolted for the door. And nothing could prevail upon her to return.

Now Miss Bellamy is a convert to cremation.

## Bela Lugosi a Hermit and Mystic; Spends Time in Mountain Retreat

### Star's Private Life Much Like That of the Screen, Except That It's Benevolent Rather Than Sinister

Bela Lugosi, who will be seen at the .................... theatre on ........... when "White Zombie" has its premiere is as much a Hollywood superstition as is Greta Garbo. More, in fact, for even the elusive Garbo may be seen in public once in a while.

Lugosi's very name has become synonymous with strange, secret powers, and this is not altogether due to "Dracula" and his other eerie portrayals. There is something of a mysterious, hypnotic quality about the man himself, particularly about his deep-set eyes, and the reason appears to be that he has probed life too deeply.

**A Decided Mystic**

But probing life is just what he has devoted his thought to. Seldom has he dwelt upon this ambition, for he has few intimates and, with the exception of his studio visits, he is seen in public infrequently. He remains in his inaccessible retreat in the Hollywood mountains, and his constant companion is a half-wild malamute dog which howls at night just as if it were more wolf than domestic pet.

The star unintentionally put all of his philosophy into one paragraph one day recently, when an interviewer managed to corner him at his home. Lugosi had been looking off into space toward the Pacific Ocean, when he suddenly swerved around and said:

"People — thousands of them — chained by monotony, afraid to think, slinging always to certainties and terrified by the unknown. They live like ants. I want to get away from people. I must get away somewhere where I can be free.

"And I can do it soon, too. Not many more years and I will have enough of this world's goods to pursue my own course and to pay for whatever research I desire to make. I'm going into the mountains, completely away from people, to study.

**His Longest Speech**

That is the longest speech anyone ever heard Lugosi make in Hollywood. But it proved what everyone believed—that he is a mystic and that he shall not be happy until he is off by himself in some remote mountain retreat, where he can think out the things which have been on his mind since the war.

"I have lived too completely, I think," he said on a subsequent occasion. "I have known every human emotion. Fear, hate, hope, love, rage, despair, ambition—all are old acquaintances, but they have left nothing to offer me. Only study and reflection remain. I must know what I have learned. I must analyze all my theories and be alone to think."

Bela Lugosi has specialized in eerie portrayals. He has characterized souls in torment—inscrutable and mysterious rolês. And those who know as much of him as it is possible to know are convinced that there is something in his own nature which mirrors these odd roles. They are certain that those inscrutable eyes of his know a lot about hypnotism, for example.

### Short Synopsis "White Zombie"

Madeline Short, a New York girl, arrives at Port au Prince, Haiti, to marry Neil Parker, her fiance, who works in a bank in that city, but on the ship she had met Charles Beaumont, a wealthy plantation owner who prevails upon the young couple to be married in his palatial home. Upon their arrival at the plantation, Madeline and Neil soon learn that there was an ulterior motive in his invitation.

Ignoring the marriage plans, Beaumont tries to win Madeline's love, and when he fails he lays plans to forestall the wedding. He calls upon "Murder" Legendre, a sinister necromancer, and obtains from him a deadly drug, one pin-point of which divests its partaker of all intelligence and the entire five senses.

"Murder" is the leader of the Zombies—that is, dead bodies dug from the graveyard and, through a process of sorcery known to the natives, permeated with suspended animation and put to work in the sugar mills and fields. He has scores of these at work, and he is always accompanied by a bodyguard of nine of them, the most sinister group ever assembled.

Under the guise of friendship, Beaumont gives Madeline a rose as a parting wedding gift, but he places in it a pin-point of the potion. She smells the flower and shortly thereafter falls to the floor and is pronounced dead. She is buried, but "Murder" and Beaumont immediately have the body exhumed by the Zombie bodyguard, who carry it to "Murder's" mountain castle. There Madeline is brought back to life sufficiently to be able to walk, eat and do a few odd domestic jobs. But she has less mental animation than a sleep-walker, and she is continually under the dominance of the necromancer.

Beaumont is happy in having Madeline with him, but a few weeks later her lifeless expression brings home to him the heinousness of the crime he has committed. He pleads with "Murder" to bring her back to life, but, as "Murder" has other plans, he secretly puts some of the potion in Beaumont's wine and then he too goes under the dominance of the sorcerer.

Meanwhile, Neil has discovered the empty grave, and he confides in Dr. Bruner, an American missionary who has been in Haiti for thirty years and who is conversant with the island's black sorcery practices. The two suspect foul play, and, with the aid of an old native witch doctor, they manage to journey to the castle in search of Madeline.

"Murder" discovers their presence and, by hypnotism, tries to get Madeline to murder her young husband. The missionary prevents this, after which the sorcerer directs his Zombie bodyguard to kill Neil. They start after him, but Neil, who had been standing at the brink of a precipice, accidentally stumbles and falls to the ground and the relentless Zombies walk one at a time over the cliff. The missionary then strikes "Murder" over the head with an iron bar, the result being that Madeline comes partly back to life, but as soon as "Murder" recovers consciousness she returns to her former state.

The sorcerer then starts to escape into his castle, but at that moment Beaumont succeeds in throwing off the effects of the drug sufficiently to grapple with him, and the two hurtle over the cliff to their deaths.

Thus released from her bondage, Madeline regains her animation, and she, Neil and the old missionary turn their steps to happiness.

## Lugosi Once Fled Firing Squad in Hungary

### Price Placed on Head When Revolution Swept Native Country

Fugitive from a hanging squad, with a price on his head! This was the rather unwelcome role which a few years ago was forced on Bela Lugosi, the famous Hungarian actor who is now appearing at the .............. Theatre in "White Zombie."

In the revolution in his native Hungary in 1918, Lugosi was one of the principal lieutenants of Count Karolyi, who seized the reins of government, and was given the newly-created post of Minister of the Theatre. This was not only because he had been an enthusiastic adherent to Karolyi's cause, but because he had long been the theatrical idol of the country, appearing as leading man for many years at the National Theatre in Budapest.

"Soon afterward, however," says Lugosi, in recounting his adventures during those hectic days, "the royalists regained control of the government, and whenever they could find a member of the Karolyi party, they proceeded to hang him. And so I decided to go away from that place. I had no desire to attend such a necking party. I escaped into Austria, then went to Germany, and finally proceeded to the United States, where I resumed my theatrical career in a new environment and in a new language."

The story of "White Zombie" treats of the occult practice in Haiti of trafficking in dead bodies, which by sorcery are re-animated and used as slaves.

### He Turns Modiste

A director of a motion picture, if he is a good one, is able at all times to undertake jobs which do not usually come under his attention. Take the instance, for example, of the picturization of "White Zombie" by Victor Halperin.

In the picture, which comes to the .......... theatre .................., Madge Bellamy is supposed to appear in an undressed state in her boudoir, and for the scene she purchased a long slip. But when the director saw the slip he said "No." He thereupon procured a scissors and made the slip into two other garments, a brassiere and a pair of knickerbockers. And a bit of lace from the prop department completed the job.

Bela Lugosi *star of* "White Zombie"

*2—One Col. Star Scene Head (Mat .05; Cut .30)*

**ACCESSORIES**

**8 x 10 stills (25 to set)**
**11 x 14 lithos (6 to set)**
**Trailer** ..........
**Scene Mats** ..........
**Ad Mats** ..........
**Press-books** ..........

**—Order Direct From—**

*Goodwill System Exchanges, Inc*

630 NINTH AVENUE
NEW YORK, N.Y. 10036

Phone: [212] 246–6660–1

Publicity and background material for *White Zombie* (1932) (Courtesy of Stephen Jochsberger).

independent producer, offering me the leading part in a picture called *White Zombie* with Bela Lugosi, to be released by United Artists. It was written by Garnett Weston. This picture was made on the back lot of Universal Studios in eleven days. The great scenes of castles and cliffs were painted. Bela Lugosi, who had just played Dracula, and who, one would expect, made a big salary, did this picture for $500. I got $5000—a sixth of what I had earned per picture at Fox.

*White Zombie* became a classic and made millions for Phil Goldstone. Collectors' magazines still advertise prints of it for $350, and it is in demand for private collections. I have seen it on television many times. Just recently, I answered questions by telephone to an audience in Arkansas after a showing of the picture.

Through the television station there, I heard from Victor Halperin, the wonderful director of *White Zombie*, who phoned me from Sulphur Springs, Arkansas, where he now lives. In those eleven days that we worked together on the picture, I learned to love and respect him very much.

After this picture, he and his brother, the production manager for Goldstone, were engaged by Paramount. Their first picture there was *Supernatural*. They tried to get Paramount to employ me for the lead, but the studio insisted on signing that girl I had known at Fox Studio as Jane Peters—her name now was Carole Lombard.

During the making of *White Zombie*, my father took over the role of my chauffeur and helper. He and Bela Lugosi became friends. They were both rather ceremonial in manner. Perhaps manner states the mode of mind. When I am asked so often what Bela Lugosi was like, I am tempted to say that I almost had my neck bitten.

The picture had a wonderful story based upon the fact that in Haiti, at one time, plantation workers were given a native drug that made them work without rest or food until they died of exhaustion. Then, too, it was also a love story. Robert Frazer, the actor who was supposed to be in love with me, played his part with touching conviction.

Mama, Daddy, and I were excited, happy, and hopeful during Roosevelt's first days as president, but we were disappointed that he did not nationalize the railroads.

I had been home only a few days, already at work on *White Zombie*, when Sidney Spiegel arrived from Chicago. He proposed to me in the garden of the Miramar Hotel at Santa Monica.

"I know that you are sleeping with that black Jew," he said, meaning Phil Goldstone. (How could Speigel, himself a Jew, say such a thing?) "I hurried here as soon as I heard. I can't stand the thought. I want us to be married at once."

Since I had concluded that nothing mattered but money, I should have said yes, but all I thought was, "How odd to want to marry me when he has heard and believed such a thing about me." How strange men are, I thought; how competitive, how indifferent to fidelity. I felt no love for him, for I was repelled by his appearance. Since I had last seen him, his front teeth had been removed.

I answered him by saying, "Oh, I can't marry you. I would probably be untrue to you." This silly remark did not faze him.

"You'll have children, and you'll have to be true," he said.

I dated Sidney off and on for five years. I don't think he really loved me, but was just movie-struck. As my career continued going down, he cared less and less for me, and I became more and more fond of him, a pattern of emotional behavior that I've always followed. Instead of "love 'em and leave 'em," I leave 'em and then love 'em.

The fact was, I turned down Sidney, one of the most eligible young men in America, because I thought that my career was in the groove again, and I didn't think that I needed love, a man, or money. I never wanted a man when I had a job. And no man wanted me when I lacked a job.

Next, I did an independent picture called *Gigolettes of Paris*, directed by a Frenchman, Alphonse Mostel. The leading man was Gilbert Roland, whom I expected to be cynical and worldly. To my surprise, he was a very gentle person, not at all the sophisticate.

Madge with Buck Jones in *Gordon of Ghost City* (1933).

I sang a little song in this picture, but it didn't seem to set the world on fire. I have seen *Gigolette* several times on television. It's a pretty, very slight picture.

Suddenly, I had a plethora of beaux, and good Sidney Spiegel phoned me nearly every night to sing "Good Night, Sweetheart" to me. Oil was discovered at the beach, and Union Oil paid a monthly sum to hold my land for drilling.

I went into a picture called *Riot Squad* with Pat O'Malley. This picture did not amount to much, and I was frantic because wonderful pictures were being made at this time.

Some of my good friends were song writers: Bill Kernell, who composed "Sally of My Dreams" for *Mother Knows Best*; Tippy Grey Johnson, who wrote "Pennies from Heaven;" and the very handsome Sam Coslow, who wrote "Thanks for the Memory" and "Cocktails for Two."

Sam arranged for me to sing in a coast-to-coast radio broadcast with Paul Whiteman. After the broadcast, I knew I had been awful when Paul Whiteman saw me to the elevator and, in saying good-bye, patted me kindly and sympathetically on my shoulder. In confirmation, my widowed aunt and her three children, who had come from Texas to stay with us, greeted me with lugubrious looks and my mother was crying. No one commented on my performance, and fearing the worst, I asked no one about it. I went to bed at once.

Then, the only thing that I was offered was the lead in a serial with Buck Jones at good old Universal Studio. Normally, stars were too grand for serials, but my misfortunes were continuing.

The Union Oil Company cancelled the lease on my property because the city council had re-zoned my beach property as undrillable. The oil company drilled behind my property and immediately to the left. (You can be sure that they slanted their pipes onto and underneath my house.) This made my land unsaleable; who wants to build a beach house where globs of oil are deposited on its sands? Janet Gaynor and Mae Murray's houses nearby were nearly ruined. It was so unjust. What's more, the government demanded $14,000 for back taxes from me.

So I accepted the serial. It was called *Gordon of Ghost City*. I am proud of it now because I am included in lists of western stars. Also, I read recently that *Gordon of Ghost City* has been selected as one of two old westerns to be shown on a regular basis to school children. In the thirties, for a feature actress to appear in a serial was considered worse than death, but I needed the money.

People asked me about Buck Jones. He seemed a sweet, kind person, but I thought that he was mean to his horse, the famous "Silver." When the horse was fractious, he would exercise his control over the spirited animal by riding him repeatedly towards a wall. This may not have been cruel but necessary. However, I was proud that I could

Portrait of Madge; reverse side is stamped, "Studio G.–L. Manuel Freres, 47, Rue Dumont–D'urville, Paris."

and did ride him without using such measures.

Sidney Spiegel came to Hollywood to see me, and I went to Chicago to meet his family. We had a very quiet dinner with them. During the conversation, Sidney's father discussed Peggy Hopkins Joyce, a much talked-of beauty.

"She's no beauty," the senior Spiegel said. "She has freckles all over her."

Sidney was distressed that I had condescended to be in a serial. He had seen some of it.

"Your hair looked terrible," he mourned. He was disappointed that my career was not going better. I realized again that it was the picture actress, rather than me, about whom he cared.

Daniel Frohman, with whom I still corresponded regularly, asked me to come to New York to appear at the annual "Actors' Fun Benefit" in one act from a restoration comedy with the British actor Philip Merivale. I took the train at once for Manhattan.

I hadn't been on the train long before two young men approached me who said that they were Nat Perrin and Arthur Sheekman, writers for the Marx brothers. They invited me to dinner and asked me where I was staying in New York. I planned to stay at the Barbizon-Plaza, the cheapest, most respectable hotel for women in the city. But, ashamed to admit my economy, I gave them the name of a more glamorous hotel.

I hadn't been in the Barbizon-Plaza's lobby for more than a few moments when I heard myself being paged. It was my two young writers, who asked me to dinner at the Pierre Hotel and to the theater afterward with their employers, the four Marx brothers.

I laughed so much at the dinner table that my cheeks ached. The brothers flew around the table changing places, vying for the seats next to me. They swapped plates in sleight-of-hand exhibitions and juggled food.

During a pause in the mirth, I turned to conversation to my favorite topic by saying, "The middle class is disappearing."

"I know," answered Groucho as Chico left the room. "He just left!"

Years before, Mother and I were seated in the front row of a theater during a play in which Groucho played a hotelman turned real estate salesman. Mama was a good audience, and we laughed so hard that Harpo played the show towards us, squatting in front of us every other gag to blow bubble gum at me.

Now, at this evening at the theater, I seemed to have difficulty keeping my purse on my lap. Every few minutes, someone would reach over me or change seats, and the purse would fall to the floor where there would be a scramble to pick it up. For a long time afterwards, I didn't know the reason for all the commotion. Some years later, Arthur Sheekman told me that Groucho and his brothers were trying to get hold of my purse long enough to put some money in it. Staying at the Barbizon-Plaza made them realize that I was short of funds.

The benefit in which I was to appear was at the Amsterdam Theater. After the performance, Dan Frohman said, "You and the other woman were good, but the men were awful."

The other actress, who was leaving a Broadway play, suggested that I try out for her part—but the play closed.

Then someone suggested that I meet George Gershwin as he was looking for a girl for the lead in his new musical *Of Thee I Sing*. I met him and producer Sam Harris in their office and an audition was arranged. There was just the piano player, myself, Gershwin, and Harris in a small room. I have no idea what I sang, but I *can* imagine how! Gershwin sat stonily, his baleful eyes upon me, his long narrow chin thrust so high that he had to gaze through half-closed eyes.

When I finished, there was a long silence; then I heard Sam Harris whisper to Gershwin, "George, she'll be all right. She's just like Molly King."

Evidently, Harris' opinion did not count, for another refugee from talkies, Lois Moran, got the part.

I next appeared at another big benefit (not given for me, alas). As I stood in the wings waiting my turn, I suddenly realized each performer was doing his thing—singing, dancing, or reciting. They hadn't told me that this was expected, and I had prepared nothing. When I walked out on the stage and faced that great audience, I hadn't the slightest idea what I was going to do, but I had an inspiration.

I remembered Peter Pan, who walked down to the footlights and, spreading his arms, inquired plaintively, "Don't you believe in fairies? Please say that you do." Of course, the audience always responded vociferously. I, too, had said similar lines in the play *Dear Brutus*, also written by James Barrie. At the end of the second act, I would run to the footlights holding out my arms, crying, "Oh, I don't want to be a Might Have Been," and the audience always responded wildly.

So now, I ran to the edge of the stage, and extending my arms, I cried, "Oh! Aren't we all having a wonderful time for this wonderful cause!" Of course, the house came down with applause, and I ran off the stage as fast as I could.

Since I received no job offer, I decided to prepare my own act. I marvel at what I attempted, all alone and very scared in the caverns of that great city. First of all, I went on a search for song writers in all those entwined cubby holes, noisy with practicing and production efforts, where nameless musicians, singers, and dancers sweated and swore in concentrated creation.

It was at night that I was most frightened by echoes of the past day, and the stirring of a new day's eerie sounds reverberated against the empty cement and stone streets. Anyone who hastens alone through the early morning streets of the city feels its nightmarish aura: the sudden flashes of light or sound, the ominous holes of darkness, the screeching brakes of cruising taxis and unmarked cars, the banging of ashcans, the chatter of riveting in boarded excavations, the clang of manholes dropped in place, the early arrivals appearing out of the subways, the hawking cries of newsboys' "Extra! Extra! Getcha Extra!," the climb to one's own cubby hole to find exhaustion more often than sleep as the frazzled mind dreads the breaking day.

I found two song writers who wrote three

songs for me, and I composed the lyrics. They rehearsed me in them for about a week. One song was to be sung in the style of Greta Garbo, one as Lupe Velez, and one as Anna Held. I reneged on the Al Jolson in black-face and the Harry Lauder.

After running around to several agencies, I got a contract to make personal appearances in upstate New York towns on what was called the "straw hat" circuit. I found a shabby, time-worn agent to travel with me in his car from place to place with my suitcase in the back seat. Having even less hope than I, he seemed the very picture of dogged, mechanically plodding determination. I am grateful for his kindness and respect. As for myself, I felt like a disembodied spirit, hating the smelly dressing rooms, the packing and unpacking, the dressing and undressing. My act could not have been too bad, for I was booked into the big houses.

Then I discovered phenobarbitol. It could be obtained in any drug store without a prescription, and I bought it by the quart. The pink, syrupy liquid tasted like a sweet liqueur that I liked very much. It made me sleep well at night and kept me from feeling anxious about anything.

The first performance at Fox's enormous Brooklyn Theatre began at eleven o'clock in the morning. The second show was at two, the third at five, the fourth at eight, the fifth at ten o'clock. I went on stage with a rousing rendition of "You Ought To Be In Pictures." Whenever I hear this old tune, I see myself walking into the bright lights and hear the applause of the the big old movie houses.

I sang my songs and did two or three black-outs with the master of ceremonies. Black-outs were quick sketches like the ones on *Laugh-In*, always ending with a suddenly darkened stage. All this was done without a microphone.

On what proved to be my last performance, the stage manager met me in the wings.

He said, "They couldn't hear you."

I answered, "Well, the applause was just as strong as ever."

"They felt sorry for you," he answered.

I quit.

The phenobarbitol may have affected my throat. It also could affect the vascular system. The fact was, the tour was too much for me—as I suspected that it would be.

During this period, I met a dark, intense, young, Jewish man in an agent's office. The last week of my engagement, we looked at apartments together, and I signed a lease for one. We spent one night together there. In the middle of the night, he went back to the other twin bed.

"You don't like me very much, do you?" he said.

"Oh, yes, I do," I countered weakly. But I left him and New York on the next day.

I read that Sol Wurtzel, my production head at the Fox Studios, was in town at the Carlton. I phoned him and he invited me to dinner with him at Billy La Hiff's Cafe. As we were having our coffee, Billy sat down at our table. He was a popular New York figure known for his geniality and kindness. He knew most of the Broadway characters by their first names and could tell an anecdote about each one.

How he knew that I needed a job, I don't know; but he turned to Sol and asked, "Why don't you sign her up?"

I saw why he was such a beloved person. Wurtzel looked over at me.

"All right, I will," he answered.

# *Chapter Nine*

*I*n a grim mood, I left for Hollywood and the Fox Studio the next morning. When I arrived at the studio, instead of being called to the front office to sign a contract, I was sent to the photographers.

They gave me many of the pictures made that day, and I still puzzle over them. Why, in the sophisticated era of Greta Garbo and Joan Crawford, were my poses sweet and childish? I look like an unsophisticated girl of sixteen, my hair in careless curls and my face wearing little make-up. It was the time of the woman, not the girl. I had always used make-up artistically in making my mouth more shapely, my eyes softer and larger; why keep reverting to my teens? Did I believe that I could still be the naive ingénue?

A few days later, they made a new set of pictures of me. A marvelous hairdresser cut my hair in a short shingle, pulled it back from my forehead in a style that I had avoided because I thought my hairline was far too high. I used to glue my curls to my forehead to hide its height. A make-up man did my face in the new style with a wide mouth, penciled brows, heavy upper lashes, and nothing on the lower lid. This style did not last long, and only Marlene Dietrich continued using it. I wore a long, tight, drop-shouldered dress. In those pictures, I look ten years older than I did in the pictures made the week before.

At home, there was turmoil. My New York friend wrote asking what to do about the apartment lease that I had signed. Mama saw the letter before I did, and she was enraged. Not only had I been living with a man, but paying half of the rent!

Fortunately, the barbiturates that I had used in New York were suddenly unobtainable without a prescription, and this ended my last encounter with drugs. They had calmed my nerves during my six-week-long stage career. I don't think that I could have survived that strenuous experience without them, but they weakened me and gave me a sore throat.

Back at the studio for a test, I was on the witness stand, undergoing a cross-examination. A scene in another test with a new girl called Andrea Leeds took place in a dive where I sang "Frankie and Johnny." It later turned out that Andrea was dying of consumption.

When I saw the tests, I was not impressed with myself. Someone, perhaps her agent, loudly praised Andrea, but no one mentioned me. So I was surprised to get a small part in a Lawrence Tibbett picture. He was the famous Metropolitan Opera tenor.

Before it started, I was invited to a party given by the studio for A. H. Giannini, the president and founder of the Bank of Italy; Nelson Rockefeller; and the head of the Chase First National Bank of New York. I learned that these people had been former investors, but now were the new owners of the Fox Company. They were taking over direct, day-to-day control. William Fox was out of the company, and Winnie Sheehan was almost out. The studio had provided me with an escort for the party, a writer whom I had not met before.

The large party, held in the Commissary, was attended by Fox stars and people from other studios. At the next table sat D. W. Griffith, whom I watched with interest as I had never met him before. I also jealously watched Winnie Sheehan with a new starlet.

When dinner was over, a studio employee

said that Mr. Giannini had asked us to come to the reception line to meet him. He then introduced my escort and me to the chairman of Chase First National Bank, and to another man whose name I did not hear.

"What was the name?" I asked.

As he answered "Rockefeller," my escort announced in a loud voice, "What we need around here are more Communists!" The men froze and raised their hands to the ceiling as if it were a hold-up. I don't remember how we got out of there.

Later, I realized that my partner had been quite drunk. I often wonder what effect this incident had on his career, and did he ever work for Fox again?

And what effect did it have on my career? In the Tibbett picture, I worked for the first time in a picture in which I did not have the lead, excepting my first two roles. Mother thought that Winnie Sheehan had had me black-listed when I left Fox and that he was still being vindictive.

There were a number of reasons for the ruin of my career. I was intransigent when I should have been cooperative; I fell out with Sheehan over his religion; stage stars were preferred over silent stars; and, what is more, I believe that I was literally going out of style. There are styles in women and styles in men, just as there are styles in acting. My mother complained that she had always been out of style. As a girl, she was a mere slip, but the great beauties Lillian Russell and Anna Held displayed hour-glass figures. I began as a petite, dainty Pickford type and managed to make only one transition to a wild and naughty flapper like our leader, Clara Bow. In a poll taken in 1926, I was the fifth most popular woman star after Gloria Swanson, Mary Pickford, Clara Bow, and Colleen Moore.

In the Tibbett picture, Wendy Barrie, an English actress, had the feminine lead, which was really a very small part. I was left with only one scene in the finished picture.

However, Norbert Lusk, a New York critic and personal friend, wrote in his review: "All this dreadful picture proves is that Madge Bellamy is as beautiful as ever."

Just the same, the sweet, coy, cute, naive type of women were being superceded by the wisecrackers like Carole Lombard and Jean Harlow or the sophisticated women like Joan Crawford and Claudette Colbert. In this transition, I never got a change to change my style. Neither did Gloria Swanson, Colleen Moore, or Clara Bow.

During my first day on the picture, I was sitting behind the cameras and the hairdresser was using a pencil to darken the hair around my forehead. Two women extras sauntered by, rolled their eyes as they looked at me, and broke into laughter. Of course, I knew that I was being made fun of, as did my hairdresser, who looked up quickly and said reprovingly, "I do this for all of the stars." I realized then that this little incident reflected my fall in status.

Nowadays, stars do "cameos" in pictures, and no one thinks the less of them, especially if they are paid well for their small stint. In my day, anything less than the leading role was, for a star, the end.

There was a class system on the set. Stars did not speak to extras, and dress extras did not associate with lesser extras. Stars received exaggerated deference, and extras watched the stars with admiration and awe. Now I thought that I felt derision.

My exaggerated sensitivity was responsible for most of the mistakes of my life. However, my evident fall to a lowly estate didn't depress me too much. Back in my dressing room, I began to sing "Mighty Lak' A Rose." I had resumed my music lessons with Felix, the uncle of Howard Hughes.

My dressing room door was open, and a voice called from below, "Is that a record playing?" I went out to the railing of the balcony. There was Lawrence Tibbett wearing the scarlet doublet and white ruff of Faust.

When I told him who I was, he said, "Let me introduce you to our musical director. You have a lovely voice."

This he did and I was thrilled, encouraged enough to have a record made. On one side was "Mighty Lak' A Rose," and on the other side was "Only A Rose." I escaped from my troubles by imagining myself in love with Mr.

Madge in the 1930's (National Film Archive, London).

Tibbett and imagining myself as a successful singer. But I did nothing to further either cause.

During the few days that I worked in this picture, I watched Tibbett with love and admiration, and forgot my horror at playing such a small part. There was some excuse for my admiration for Tibbett. The screen did not project the magnetic personality that was so evident on the stage and in person.

Vigorously, I renewed my singing lessons. Like his nephew, Howard Hughes, my teacher was very deaf and not a very good teacher. I went to him, primarily, because I was so fond of his wife, Ruth Stonehouse, a silent screen actress who had begun in films in 1911 at the Essanay Company and must have made dozens of films.

She and her husband were eccentrics, but of the two, she was the more odd—different in every way from everybody else. They lived in a beautiful house with gardens near the Los Angeles Country Club where they played golf every morning. She had an unusual taste in clothes, such as wearing white tennis shoes with black socks; a long, wrinkled coat over a short, plaid, irregularly hemmed skirt; and a demure, flowered hat. She never came downstairs from their bedroom until noon, and I never saw her eat anything but crackers and buttered radishes. I also never saw her take a drink, but she was often high or suffering from a hangover.

Ruth, thin to the point of emaciation, had magnificent breasts, large and high. She claimed to have had so many lovers that she couldn't remember their names. She may have been bragging; she loved being outrageous.

One night that I spent in their home, Felix came to my bed. I pretended that he was walking in his sleep and took him back to Ruth. She said that she appreciated this as she hardly had enough of him to spare.

At one of their many parties, I met Howard Hughes with Jean Harlow, who was making *Hell's Angels* for him. She did not impress me in her grey, light crepe dress cut to "there." She was my father's partner at bridge that evening, and afterward, I asked him why he had played so poorly.

"It was Miss Harlow's neckline," he said. "I couldn't keep my mind on the cards."

Ruth thought herself to be quite an authority on the bust and told me that Jean had what she called "ribbon" breasts, which were bound with tape to make the admired "pointiers."

Jean's heavy, dark eyebrows gave her a sinister look, but her face changed when her eyebrows were thinned to a high arch. A fragile and frail little girl, she photographed almost buxom and coarse. She worked as an extra in several of my pictures and married two friends of mine—men who seemed unlikely to attract a glamorous movie star.

Her first husband, Paul Bern, was a brilliant man-about-town, producer, and writer. He was short, plump, and far from good-looking. He killed himself shortly after they were married. Many times, he was my escort to parties and premières, but I did not think of him as a beau. He just like being seen with motion picture actresses.

The other man whom she married was the dear and wonderful cameraman Hal Rosson. He photographed me in seven or eight pictures. A quiet, shy, little man with a diminutive face, he may have been shelter from the storm for Jean.

When I received my record, I took it with me to a luncheon at a restaurant in Beverly Hills. The proprietor discovered that I had it with me and insisted on playing it then and there at the restaurant. As the notes of "Only A Rose" wafted through the large cafe, I noticed several notes slightly off-key. People were laughing and voices were merry before the record was put on, but now it seemed to me that they were laughing at my singing. I crouched lower in my seat and never made another record or tried to promote my singing again.

Some people think that to be unhappy is to be intellectually mature, but now I think otherwise. Anyone wise enough about himself and the world can be happy—all by himself, all within himself—in spite of catastrophe and sorrow. The being, existing, experiencing, is wondrous. This is being alive! At this period, I was far too stupid to be happy.

To be cast in a "Charlie Chan" picture was

the pits, and the woman in these pictures was a zero. On my first day's work with Charlie Chan, several chairs on the set were marked with names of the cast, but no chair bore my name. One day, the assistant director asked me to get up because I was in the chair with the character actor's name on it. There it was! I realized that I was a nobody, "declassé," ruined.

When someone introduced Myrna Loy, she tactlessly remarked to me, "My, you can certainly fall fast in this business." Now, in my wisdom, I would laugh at such a remark and agree with her. But at that time, it was deeply wounding.

I continued with the picture, which took all of ten days to shoot. Both the leading lady and I were seen only briefly in the finished picture.

During this shoot, I reached the lowest point of my life. Being suddenly relegated to the lower class affected me strangely; I made a pass at Ray Milland, the leading man in the picture. The others had gone to lunch, and Ray and I were alone on the drawing room set of Charlie Chan.

I said, "Kiss me."

"Here?" he exclaimed in surprise.

We parted with the suddenness of a fade-out. I didn't look him in the eye for the rest of the picture.

A week after the picture was finished, I was called to the studio again to meet the ferocious foreign director of a forthcoming picture. The studio lackey introduced me to him on the busy set. Was his name Propatkin? I have forgotten. I doubt if he finished the picture and it was his last one. Though I had not seen the script, I knew that I wouldn't like the part.

"I do not want to do this part," I said firmly. "I want something better."

Only the old phrase "a towering rage" could describe the director's reaction.

"Take Miss Bellamy away!" he shouted. My escort and I swiftly made our exit and marched in silence to the office of the new head of the studio, Darryl Zanuck. His assistant, Otto Schreiber, greeted me from behind his large desk.

"What happened, Miss Bellamy?" he asked.

I answered, "I asked for a better part."

"Well," he said, "that seems a reasonable request. We'll see what we can do."

I left his presence and the studio, did not respond to calls from the studio, and decided that my career in pictures was over. I wasn't going to be embarrassed any more. All the kings' horses could not have pulled my career together again.

These new men in charge of the picture business did not know me. The fact that Jim Grainger, the publicity head of Fox, said, "Madge never made a picture for us that did not make money" evidently meant nothing.

But I had not given up work. A young writer came to me with his new play called *Intermission*. I agreed to do it, and we rehearsed for ten days at the Geary Theater in San Francisco. It was a light farcical comedy with all of the action taking place in the foyer of the theater. In the first act, everyone is seen entering the theater, the second act is the intermission, and the last act has everyone leaving the theater. We had an unusually strong cast with the great Blanche Bates playing one of the roles.

Our troubles began at once. The nervous playwright rewrote and changed lines and scenes until we were all half crazy. By the time that we opened, the play was so ragged and disjointed that it was hard to tell what it was about or what the author had originally intended. Everyone felt spattered with the frantic writer's bloody sweat.

On opening night after the performance, Mama came backstage to tell me that the man seated next to her had said of me, "She can't act herself out of a paper bag." Mama never failed to rush and tell me anything bad she had heard about me.

*Intermission* lasted for one week. The plot was about a woman with a gun in her hand who pursues her unfaithful lover to the theater—a situation remarkably like one in my own life that took place a few years later.

Even though I refused to work, the Fox Company did not stop my weekly paychecks. Had their bookkeeper not been told to stop? Did some secret friend keep me on the payroll? Or did the corporation incongruously have a conscience and was repaying me for the fact that I had been with them eight years and had never made a picture that did not make money?

It is said that after Greta Garbo made her last picture at MGM, *The Two-Faced Woman*, in 1941, she was called into Louis B. Mayer's office and received $250,000 for the cancellation of her contract. I repeat this to help people understand these strange times. The flaws in the first awkward, squeaking, talking pictures were eliminated as the technology of sound improved. We silent picture actors were left behind when the new microphones, sound cameras, and voice mixers appeared. Anyway, the checks gave me security, although I didn't know when they would end.

I began a three-year course of bed hopping, or one-night-stands, in search of—what? I am now in my eighties, and think I know the answer. I never have gone to a psychologist, but if I had, he may have said that I did it to spite my mother and to win my father. My father adored my mother and told me that I wasn't as pretty as she was except when I wore make-up. He always called her "Sweetheart" and was extremely jealous of her (with good cause). Was I jealous, too?

After I moved away from Beverly Hills, my current intellectuals no longer dropped in to see me. My few friends came from Santa Barbara and Palm Springs, and belonged to a group that hated themselves and others. No one whom I knew had any interest in public affairs. They were concerned with who slept with whom, who said what about whom, who wore what, who had what, and who had lost what.

I was aware of the rising youth gangs of Hitler, the changes in Russia, and the millions of unemployed in the USA; but I was uninvolved in any of it.

I was on a man binge, and most of these men were millionaires. Perhaps I was trying to find a rich husband. Perhaps I was like the girl who went out only with millionaires because she didn't know anyone who wasn't a millionaire.

## Chapter Ten

My father told me one day that he was in serious trouble at the farm. His partner was selling the lots before they completely owned them. Even I knew that this was fraudulent, and I told Father to go at once to the Farm Commission and explain to them that this illegal behavior was taking place despite his protests. This was sensible advice, but it proved disastrous.

Father, as president of the company, was indicted with the culprit and brought to trial with him. He had never discussed the purchase of this enormous farm with me, the building of the largest steel corrugated barn in the state, or what crops to plant. Nor did he consult with me when he drilled five wells run by electricity, divided the land into lots, took on a partner, or anything else. My mother treated me the same way.

They had my power-of-attorney and signed all checks. I criticize myself now for my moronic behavior. My interest lay in other fields, and I made no protest. Now that they are long gone, I am glad that I never reproached them. They had no intention of hurting me, and I was foolish not to control my own assets. I could hardly have done worse with our money.

When at last they asked my advice, what happened? My father was indicted for fraud. He pleaded "nolo contendere"—neither guilty nor not guilty. My heart was wrenched to see my father brought into the courtroom, the very picture of humiliation and shorn dignity.

He was found not guilty, but his partner was given eight years in prison. This affair broke my father and he took to his bed. He was an invalid until his death four years later. My mother found a letter from the judge in his wallet saying how sorry he was that a "man like you should have been put to such a trial." Beside the crumpled, much folded letter was a poem that I had written and sent to Father years before:

> Through grief unchartered, gallant and free,
> You guide your ship of life upon a storm-tossed sea;
> No wreck upon your heart has left a scar.
> Your cargo is of dreams, your eyes are on a star;
> No work or deed is lost, no love is gone,
> And all will moor at last so tenderly
> In promised lands of your soul's destiny.

The trial was not the last of our Fairview Farm troubles. People who bought lots sued Father, and one lawsuit included me.

When I was called to the stand, our lawyer whispered to me, "If they ask where you bank, say that you don't know." That was the first question asked of me.

The next morning's headline was, "Madge doesn't know where she banks, she says."

I was so embarrassed that I was sick. As my Father had my power-of-attorney and I signed few checks, I may not have perjured myself, although it certainly made me out to be a fool. We won the case, and I was not held liable.

I didn't join the "American Brigade" to fight against Franco in Spain. I retreated instead to the race tracks at Santa Anita, Hollywood, and Del Mar; and the social clap-trap of Palm Springs. The Springs was only a village, but it was a very busy one with visitors and tourists moving in and out—just as it is today.

The social queen was Ona Brown, the 45-year-old ex-wife of director Clarence Brown. She claimed to have engineered his career, and I believed it because she was a

Left to right, top: Madge, Jane Merrick, Ona Brown (director Clarence Brown's wife), and Adrienne Ames. Left to right, bottom: Captain "Babe" Dawley and Roy Randolf.

marvelous people manipulator. She planned parties for people and invited guests whom the host or hostess often did not know. She was rewarded with a few gifts and the sheer fun this activity afforded her. A typical chorus girl—gay without wit, busy without productivity. She had a nice, full figure; natural reddish hair; lots of freckles; a merry smile showing crooked teeth; and dancing, grey eyes smudged with carelessly applied mascara. This was Ona, who often invited me to spend weekends at her cottage. It was fun being there, and she asked me because I attracted people. Ona promoted many a bachelor party in my honor.

On Easter Sunday, 1937, she told me that among the people coming from San Francisco were Stan Stanford and his patient and tolerant wife, Camilla.

"He's the funniest, wildest, most perpetually hung-over drunk in the whole world," Ona continued. "She's a former stage actress, but plain." I had never heard of her.

"She evidently knows when she's well-off . . . she puts up with everything. Gordie, an old beau of mine who used to be very rich, is coming with them. I dropped him years ago when he lost his money, long before I married Clarence, but we're friends. They are bringing with them a man named Murphy who's getting a divorce. Gordie says he owns half of Humboldt County."

When I came into the living room to meet the guests, Stan Stanford was standing, apparently about to speak.

"Ah-ha!" he said. "Here is another student. Please be seated." His manner was professional.

"Now," the speaker continued, "I cannot proceed with my lecture without my customary instruments."

He turned to his practical-looking wife. She and Ona rose and went into the kitchen, returning with a colander, steak knife, and egg beater. Taking this paraphernalia, the "doctor" called for his patient—his wife—to lie down on the sofa. This she did while the "physician" performed an operation, explaining his procedure as he worked.

"I am opening the epiglottis," he said, making quick strokes in the air with the butcher knife over her abdomen.

"Ah-ha!" he exclaimed, waving the egg beater. "Just as I thought—a duodenal ulcer. Nurse!" he called to Ona, "the colander, please." He removed a hunk of something from the imaginary wound and placed it in the colander.

"I leave you, my students, to dress the wound. The operation was a success." We all laughed hilariously.

Ona took the "doctor" to the bathroom to wash up. In a few seconds, he returned, followed by a flustered Ona. This time, he was armed with a pair of scissors, and it turned out that I was to be the patient this time.

"I'll shorten her dress," he declared as he stooped to my hem. I rose and he pursued me around the room.

"I want to get a better view of those legs," he shouted as I ducked behind Gordie, Ona's old boyfriend, who rose to protect me. The chase ended when Ona thrust a highball into Stan's hand, and he fell back exhausted onto the sofa beside his wife. I ended up with Gordie's arms around me. His round belly pressed against me.

"I feel like a knight in shining armor who has rescued the lovely princess. Don't I deserve a kiss?" So I responded with a kiss and a hug.

Gordie was the short, round, graying type of person who often seem to think that I was made for them. The "man named Murphy" was a raw-boned, long-jawed, long-legged lumberman named Stanwood Murphy. His teeth were yellow and his red-brown hair was thin. It was later that I noticed his beautiful, flat, broad shoulders and soft hazel eyes.

Ona took us to see the guest house that she had rented for the group, and then we all went to the Palm Springs Tennis Club for dinner. The merry Stan acted as a surrogate waiter, insulting us and people at nearby tables as he passed plates, snatched napkins, and poured wine.

Afterward, we returned to the rented house, and Stan, his wife, and Gordie began a bridge game. The solemn Stan and I begged off, got into the car, and made a tour of the surrounding dunes and ravines.

I found that my friend was short on chit-chat, but long on narrative. Once started on a tale of a hunting or fishing trip, he never stopped. Near the end of the drive, we parked on a hill at sunset to enjoy the glorious panorama.

Not greatly attracted to him, but feeling mischievous and bored, I put my arm around him and said, "I really like you." He retreated like a startled elk.

"You work fast!" he said, blushing furiously.

My old hatred of men welled up inside me, and I thought, "He's going to find me the slowest worker he ever saw."

We were together for the rest of our stay. Every evening, the others played bridge, and Murphy and I drove around while he talked. Details about hunting trips, guns that he'd owned, dogs and horses that he'd had, fish that he'd caught. All he did was talk and I listened. When he left, I promised to visit his lodge near Scotia, a lumber town, where he was the head of the lumber company. He wrote me long letters about fishing and hunting, and I went up to Scotia with the group a month later.

At first sight, I fell in love with his lodge. It was on a bend of the Eel River where a creek that ran under the house turned a mill wheel and continued with a gush into the main stream. Giant trees sheltered the glorified log cabin that was built high and square with a gallery all around. On the road that wound by the Eel on the way to the house were fences enclosing thoroughbred horses, kennels with howling hunting dogs, and aviaries filled with quail.

Inside the big cabin were Stan Stanford and his wife, the bland Camilla; and Murphy's older brother and his wife, who was a former stage actress named Marion Cockley. She was a blonde beauty with a very subdued personality. In the scrapbook that I began in early childhood and which I still have, were pictures of dancers, opera singers, stage actresses, and movie actresses. I found Marion Cockley's picture in my scrapbook. When younger, she was almost a double for Marion Davies. I felt friendly towards her, and I think that she liked me; but she seemed suppressed by her cold, censorious husband.

That evening, Townsend Netcher, a famous playboy and Chicago department store heir; and Faith, the tall, lanky, former wife of actor Doug MacLean, joined us as well as Gordie, who later proved to be a good friend to me. Drinking began at four o'clock and continued through the evening. We played bridge uneventfully until Netcher and his girlfriend had a furious fight. She climbed the stairs to her room and slammed the door, the usual termination of their evenings, I found out later.

From my window when I retired, I enjoyed the full moon reflected on the river below, the tall trees on each bank, the low flying bats sailing back and forth, the delicious, pine-scented air, and the rhythmic sound of the millwheel close to my room.

I was almost asleep when a knock came on my door. I opened it. It was Mr. Murphy in his pajamas. He said nothing and I didn't say anything either. I just shut the door in his face.

In the morning at the breakfast table, I said that I must go home immediately. A few eyebrows were raised, several knowing eye contacts were exchanged, but no one urged me to stay or asked for an explanation, including Murphy.

I joined Mama at the beach house, and in a few days, I received a long letter from Murphy, telling in detail of his activities— fishing, boating, hunting.

We exchanged a few friendly letters, and he came to Los Angeles to visit me at my beach house. Mama didn't like him because she found his talk about boating, riding, and hunting boring. She cared not at all for those things. Mama, of course, did not approve of anybody with whom I went out.

He asked me to marry him, I consented, and we left the next day for Las Vegas. When we reached Yuma, it was late, and we spent the night there—our first time in bed together. As usual, my response to him was fresh from the freezer. He was excited and I thought that this showed a great passion for me. I found later that he had been impotent for some time and was greatly agitated about how this attempt would turn out.

When we got to Las Vegas, we went to bed again. Then he got up and began to pace the floor of the motel room wearing only his striped shirt. He explained to me how dangerous it could be for us to be married publicly. The year before, he was divorced from a crazy alchoholic wife who tended to take off her clothes and run down the street, screaming. At the divorce trial, she seemed completely sane and was awarded his beautiful house. He had two teenage sons, he said, and if it were known that he had married again, his ex-wife would make a big scandal. In other words, he did not want to go through the marriage ceremony.

"We'll be the same as married," he said.

I must have been love-struck, for I said, "That's all right with me."

We went to the World's Fair in San Francisco and laughed a lot, perhaps because I was so exhilaratingly happy with this homely, hopelessly inarticulate man. Perhaps he laughed a lot because it was weird for him to have fun.

We returned to Los Angeles for the racing season. I was, and still am, clever (or lucky) at the race track. My constant wins were noted by the *Herald-Examiner's* sports writer, and my selections for the day were printed on the sports page. Strangely enough, when they were printed, my selections rarely won.

At the ranch, I rode the ungaited colts, and using my father's lore, I found that I could gait them to single foot and pace. At night, we went canoeing in a nearby pond with a headlight on the bow. We shot frogs on the lily ponds and fished on the Eel for steelheads. We enjoyed planning our meals, although we both were always dieting. We rode about the countryside looking for leeks, truffles, or other ingredients for a sauce.

At this time, my father was bedridden at the farm and when he grew worse, I went home to see him. He suffered from prostate blockage and refused to have an operation.

My mother said, "If we insist and he dies, we will blame ourselves."

Back with Stan at the ranch, he declared, "I want you to go back to work."

"What for?" I inquired.

"Think what you could do for me," he said. "You could buy me a yacht."

I was astounded because instead of planning to buy him a yacht, I was looking forward to getting the mink coat that he had promised me for some time.

Later, back at the farm to visit my sick father, I received a call from the Selznick studio. They were thinking of me for *Gone With The Wind*. When I went in, I met several men in the casting office. The part was the one eventually played by Ona Munson as the madame who ran the local "bad" house and who was the mistress of Rhett Butler before he met Scarlett. In the book, she was a fairly well-developed character. In the finished picture, she had only a few scenes. They said that I looked too young for the part. Clara Bow was also considered.

Stan and I had been together for a year when we took a trip to Mexico. It was the happiest time of my life. We hunted, carrying our rifles to one picnic after another, but never shooting anything. Once, in an old hotel, the antique bed fell in on us. It left us bruised but laughing. This happy time was really the last for me, for Stan began to change.

He said that his brother had told him not to marry me when we stopped at his brother's place in Pasadena on our way to Las Vegas to get married. I remember how joyfully we entered the large, beautiful house. I wore orchids, and Stan was flushed and beaming. I thought it was odd that his brother asked to speak with him privately. They were absent for some time while I got better acquainted with his wife, Marion.

About a year later, Stan decided to make me over. First, I had to throw away all of my makeup. When I visited the guest house to see Marion, I would borrow a quick smear of her lipstick.

Upon my return to the big house, Stan would stare and say, "I see you have been visiting again." This was said with the usual stiffening of his neck and the elaborate jerking away that was his physical expression of extreme displeasure.

Among Stan's guests were an old windbag of a retired banker and his equally old and fat inamorata, who always agreed with whatever the banker said. We played bridge with these people every night, and I often won.

Then they could criticize my playing with, "If I had led with a heart, my partner would have known that I had the queen." It was unheard of to lead with an ace when I had only a ten, etc.

Once when I was visiting my father at the farm, Stan sent me a picture of a clown that his friend, the banker, had given to him because "It looked so much like you!" I know now that I should have stayed on the farm.

I blame the old banker and his girlfriend for the loss of my lipstick and, eventually, all makeup. Soon after, my long curls had to go in exchange for a small knot of hair. Meals became meager—toast and stewed fruit for breakfast, salad for lunch, cheese fondue for supper. Every morning, Stan and I lay on our backs, side by side, our feet pointing toward the far end of a long room. We would wiggle our bottoms across the hardwood floor in order to reduce our waists and derrières. Stan decided that I should lose eighteen pounds. I would then be 100 pounds, which was what I weighed when I first arrived in Hollywood, and my boss, Thomas H. Ince, said that he would star me if I gained ten pounds. I never weighed more than 115 pounds when I was in pictures. No doubt Stan was preparing me to star anew.

I visited Stan's office several times and toured the lumber mill at Scotia, near Eureka, California. It was a noisy, scary place, and the danger was real. In those days, there were few safety precautions. The narrow cat-walks had slender boards for railings, and circular saws swirled down below. The cities of Eureka and Scotia were noted for the large number of one-armed, one-handed, and fingerless men on the streets.

I never talked abut politics with Stan Murphy. Evidently, he had little interest in the subject. I can't imagine now what we did talk about—not movies because we saw only two together: *Penny Serenade* with Irene Dunne and Walt Disney's *Pinocchio*. He had a book at the lodge on the ancient history of Mexico which I read and found extremely interesting. He had never read it. He did read *Captain Horatio Hornblower* and, to my surprise, *Bambi*. His favorite record was "Old Man Mose," which he played at dinner most nights.

Once politics was discussed at the lodge with the old banker, who was the most reactionary old cuss I ever knew. At the time, the ship full of Jewish refugees from Hitler's Germany was on the high seas. No country, Roosevelt's America included, would let them in.

The old banker remarked, "It ought to be blown up at sea!" I should have left such company at once.

The fun had gone out of my relationship with Murphy, and the masochism had not yet begun.

Although I received letters and phone calls from Murphy, I spent less and less time with him. I always returned to Mama and Papa after a week or ten days with him. In Los Angeles, I saw him most often at Townsend Netcher's beach house.

Weekends there were attended by a variety of men, pretty young models, and other hopefuls. Many cameras were always snapping.

Stan, looking over these snapshots, remarked to me, "You don't photograph very well, do you?" Without makeup, he was right.

However, Stan and I had some wonderful times when we were alone together. He had a way of kissing my arms that turned me on.

He would say, "Oh, how I love these little arms," and I would melt. Sometimes, I would kiss him under his chin where I could just barely reach. This brought him great sexual excitement, often twice at night and two or three times in the morning, every day and night—this from a man who had been almost impotent when we met! It was my only success with him, although I was still completely frigid. I faked it sometimes, but I must not have fooled him for he told me that he would like me to have an operation. It wasn't necessary because I could have an orgasm alone.

My frigidity, I believe, was caused by a deep fear of men. If I had known a little tenderness or even a little common humanity in my first sexual experiences, things might have been different. Perhaps not. I had not felt any sexual stirring until I was twenty-five years old, and then I ventured into a physical relationship out of curiosity and the fear of becoming an old maid.

As a child, I believed that sex hurt. I used to throw rocks at the rooster when he mounted the hen, which I considered a brutal act.

Two friends of Stan often joined us: a pedantic, little man and his long, lean, tousle-headed wife. I doubted either one of them really liked Murphy, but they liked life at the lodge. The man was one of those people who don't excel at anything but feel they were born into the world to criticize others.

We visited this obnoxious couple in their home against my objections and their obvious rejection of me. I noticed that Stan and this tousle-headed woman locked eyes. The husband may have noted their attraction to each other, for he began to corner me and became more friendly. He may have had a little wife-swapping in mind.

# Chapter Eleven

*U*nlike most liberals, I was against the war, but Mama and I helped pack bundles for the troops, some of whom we knew from March Field.

My checks from the Fox Company stopped as mysteriously as they began and in my diary, I wrote, "Oh, my God! What shall I do now?"

I received a telegram asking me to come to town to see about doing a new stage play in Hollywood financed by Shirley Temple's father. We opened to good notices at the Libra Theater in Santa Barbara, then moved to a theater across from the Pantages Theater. The play closed there after the first night, knocked into a cocked hat by the critics. I didn't blame them because I couldn't figure out what the play was about either.

One critic said that my acting was "like a clock that did fine at first, but gradually ran down."

As I came out of the Knickerbocker Hotel, a man I knew spoke to me, and we left the building together. Just then, Stan appeared, saw us together, and became very indignant. For some reason, I chose this moment to tell Stan that I loved him, something that had never been easy for me to do.

However, this seemed to be the wrong time to say it and the wrong man to say it to, for he answered very skeptically, "You love me? Ha!"

I received a telegram and a letter from the author of a new Broadway play to be directed by Otto Preminger. The play had been written with me in mind, and I wanted desperately to go to New York. But I did not have the money. I didn't even think of turning to Stan because when one of his sons shopped for school clothes and brought them to his father for approval, Stan objected strongly to the cost of the clothes.

I wrote to Joe Schenck, head of the Fox Studios after Winnie Sheehan left, telling him that I did not want to lose this chance to start up my career again in a profession I loved very much. It must have been an appealing letter because he sent me $1000, and I set out.

In New York, the two young writers of the play had rented a lovely little apartment for me, and they took me at once to see Otto Preminger, of whom I had never heard. I always considered the director to be someone unimportant who just annoyed actors.

When I worked with Barrie's great English director, Iden Payne, in *Dear Brutus*, I agreed with his words, "I tell the actors what has to be done and then let them do it their own way." I resented a director who acted out the part exactly as he wanted it and had the actor imitate him. However, at my audition on the stage at the Belasco Theater, Mr. Preminger did not try to direct me. I held the script in my hand and read from it for the first time.

I was surprised to see several other well-known actresses there in the darkened theater, waiting to read for the part. None of us got it. The part was given to the much older, but lovely actress Violet Heming. She was at least sixty years old.

When the young playwrights introduced me to Preminger, he said, "It seems both of these young men are in love with you." I took this to mean, "Why else would they consider you for this play?"

The writers wanted me for the play even after it was cast and took me with them to the out-of-town opening. I thought that Violet Heming was more suited to the part than I. It was about a former movie star who becomes the social leader of New York high society. However, the authors wanted the part to be incongruous—as it would have been had I played it. They may have been right, for the play did not last more than a week on Broadway.

I was desperate and went to an agent who found a part for me almost at once as the ingénue in a farce called *See My Lawyer* that had been a hit in New York some years previously. This was the road company. For the two weeks that we reheased, I moved to the less impressive Barbizon hotel.

On Sunday at an actors' meeting, I saw the newly famous Armenian novelist William Saroyan.

He saw me, too, and although we had not met, he called after me, "I'm at the Great Western Hotel!"

When I got home, I wrote a letter telling him how much I admired him, having just read "The Man on the Flying Trapeze" and thought it wonderful. He came to see me right away. (People tell me that my letters are really great.)

I talked with him about Hemingway's *Across the River and Into the Trees*; evidently, this was the wrong thing to do, for I never saw Saroyan again.

I also met Herbert Yates, the corpulent president of Republic Pictures, who took me to dinner at a restaurant where rodeos were held—a rather strange place to eat. Gene Autry was there, too, but he did not have dinner with us. He sat at a nearby table and played his guitar throughout the meal. He was a star even at that time.

The company left for the road. A critic commenting on my playing an ingénue wrote, "Madge Bellamy, who refuses to grow old." I took the critic to dinner and scolded him for not saying, "who refuses to get *older*."

I was having difficulty sleeping. The cheap hotel where the company stayed was very noisy, and I complained to the management. It turned out that the noisy ones were members of our own company who, evidently, were told of my complaint. They *all* stopped speaking to me.

A few days later, I received a beautiful letter from my father and answered it at once. As I walked to the theater that freezing cold night, I fell down on the icy sidewalk and was blown by angry winds straight across the frozen street on my bottom. Then when I was sitting before my dressing table mirror making up for the evening performance, a knock came on the door—a telegram.

It said, "Your father died this evening. Mother." My mirror reflected my mouth opening wide as if I were screaming, but no sound came out.

A second knock came on the door—"Fifteen minutes."

Into my mind came a thousand memories of my father's face. Then came another knock.

"On stage, please!" I got up and went to the wings. The eyes of the other players were on me, coldly watching; the curtain went up, I went on, and continued through the whole performance with no mistakes; my usual performance in that raucous comedy. The laughs came, the curtain fell, and I went back to my hotel room. No one had spoken to me or looked at me. How could I have continued in the play as if nothing had happened? But I did.

I must have spoken to the management, for notices of the play's closing were posted on the wall of the theatre the next day.

For two more days, I continued in the part, and as the curtain fell that closing night, another actress in the play said to me contemptuously, "Well, I never could have done it." Evidently, she was referring to my continuing with the play for two days after my father's death.

The next morning at the railroad station on my way back to California, the other actors showed me no kindness or sympathy. Actors are convivial, sympathetic people; but I was disliked by this company from the first. Perhaps they felt that I considered a road company beneath my talents. Their attitude reminded me of animals in the wild who turn on a wounded or aging leader.

Mama met me at the station without an embrace or even a word. She was too infuriated with me to speak because I had not come home immediately. The funeral had been held on the second day after my father's death, and I missed it. Why was the funeral so soon? Perhaps in order to punish me.

A large flower arrangement had arrived at the funeral inscribed "To Dad." We found this embarrassing because I had never called my father "Dad." Someone else sent it, probably the dreadful Herbert Yates, who had followed me to Detroit and whom I had, evidently, told of my father's death.

One night in New York, I slept with Yates and told him that I was broke, begging him to put me in a picture. Never before had I given myself in exchange for work. I should have known that it wouldn't succeed because respect is lost and the puffed-up ego of the producer cannot accept paying you or helping you in gratitude.

My mother said, "Your father's last words were, 'Where's my baby? I want my baby.'"

My mother had an autopsy performed on my father. There was no cancer, but his kidneys were so dessicated that they fell in ashes at the autopsy, no doubt because of his prostate trouble.

During those four years of my father's illness, my mother nursed him with infinite care. From the time that I was a small girl, she told me that she didn't love my father, but her care for him was without flaw.

Once I made up his bed. When she felt the sheets, she almost screamed, "They are damp! How could you?" She remade the bed at once.

For a time, we three were alienated from each other. My mother reproached me for having mishandled my career. My father's puritanical standards made him reproach me for the men in my life. He reproached my mother, too, for the same reason. Mother reproached my father for being what she called a "visionary": too many dirigibles, magazines, steambath tubs, real estate projects. I blamed them both for the loss of my money, poor investments, and strange deals. Yet, we clung firmly together, and they refused to divorce each other no matter how violently they quarreled.

Then we reached the nadir of our finances. What to do? We thought of the big trunk in the barn that had not been opened for years. It contained unanswered fan mail. When the studio stopped mailing out pictures of me upon request as they had done for years, I stored the letters in this trunk. These letters usually contained a quarter or half dollar asking for a picture. We went to the barn, opened these letters, and found enough money to sustain us for awhile.

Papa's papers were in his lawyer's possession, and he told us there was nothing of value among them—no deeds, no stock. I was so desperate that I phoned Stan asking him what to do.

He said, "Deed the farm to me and send the papers to me. I will see what I can do." Since I didn't trust him, I sent nothing.

Mother and I decided to sue the lawyer. We lost the first suit, brought a second, and lost it also. I was a poor witness on the stand because I was ill-informed and vague. Mama blamed me for our lack of success.

I still had my diamond rings and decided to pawn or sell them. Herbert Yates had a side business, Yates Industries, and I went to see him. When I was ushered into his office, I explained my plight. I hoped that he'd have pity and do something for me, but he sent me to his Yates Industries. I turned over my rings to them on loan for $5000—about half of their value, I thought.

It was daring of me, but I accepted a part in another stage play, the starring role in *Holiday Lady*. After three weeks of rehearsal, it opened at the Belasco Theater in Hollywood.

To open a new play without a previous try-out was a nerve-wracking experience; before the Hollywood crowd and critics, it was awesome. They didn't like it. The main reason? It was too risqué. Yet, there was not a dirty word in it, and today, it would seem as mild as milquetoast. They could not forgive the fact that the third act took place in a house of prostitution.

In the story, a woman married a man who

MADGE BELLAMY starring
in "HOLIDAY LADY"

*Belasco Theatre*

In the play *Holiday Lady* (1946).

does not know her past. When he finds out and denounces her, she returns to a brothel. At the end, her husband finds her and forgives her.

Everyone concerned had great hopes for this play. *Life* magazine sent a camera crew to photograph the dress rehearsal in case we were successful here and later, in New York.

My dressing room was filled with flowers.

Grace Kingsley, a Hollywood critic and a friend of mine, came backstage and cried, "Oh, Madge; how could you do it?" She was really shocked. How times change!

I went home to Mama and told her, "That's the last time I'm going to try to do anything."

# Chapter Twelve

When Stan did not hear from me, he wired me to come to Hollywood to see him. I met him in a bungalow of a well-known hotel. I bitterly recalled that the last time I was at this hotel, I had not sneaked in. Then, I had registered and the management had sent roses to my suite.

Stan told me that while I was away, he had visited the farm.

"It's not much of a place, is it? The house, I mean." Of course—the house was an old five-room frame building, but why had he gone to see it?

He said, "I don't want to get married." He repeated to me how dangerous his ex-wife was with her drunken sprees and running down the streets naked, and that she now had their beautiful fourteen-room mansion. He paced the floor.

"I don't want to marry! I don't want to marry!"

I said over and over, "You don't have to marry. I'm not pressing you to say that we are married. I'm not urging you to do anything." He doesn't want me because I'm poor, I thought. He went to see the farm to estimate what I was worth, and I was ashamed that he had seen the shabby, old farmhouse.

Later, I understood why he was protesting that he did not want to marry. He was trying to tell me that someone else was pressing him; and in a kind of confession, he was trying to send a message to me that I did not receive.

Another thing that he said haunted me.

"I'm lost," he confided. "I feel like I'm lost." For the first time, he was discussing his feelings with me, and I was touched and confused. He did not ask me to go back to San Francisco with him as he had done so many other times. Besides, I couldn't have gone because something had to be done with the farm.

I could not pay the enormous taxes on the farm now that we could not plant potatoes or watermelons because we could not use the electric wells for water; the attorney had control of the water rights.

As someone said, "Madge, your water-right story is dry."

I really did not want to go back with Stan. I had been hurt too many times by those friends of his. He always wanted groups of people around him, even though they were not congenial to either of us.

It was a strange time to send Stan a gift, especially since my mother and I were so short of cash. But I went to Riverside, about fifteen minutes from the farm, and spent the afternoon listening to records, indulging in an orgy of memories. I chose "These Foolish Things (remind me of you)." Stan had said that this song reminded him of me. Then I chose "Very Confidential" and "Who? (stole my heart away—you, no one but you!)." Woody Herman played this song for me in a silent picture called *Ankles Preferred*. I mouthed the song, of course.

I also selected "Don't Sit Under the Apple Tree (with anyone else but me)" and the overture to *Romeo and Juliet* by Tschaikowsky, my very favorite tear-inducer. I enclosed a poem that I had written a few years before about my love for him, but I had never shown it to him. My mother had once come upon the poem accidentally, and she said that it made her ill.

I began to fantasize, and romantic love took over my every thought and energy. I turned

146

the whole experience into an agony of longing, a frenzy of indecision. I was in a state of paranoia that made reality insubstantial, and my own imagination was the world in which I lived.

> When in your arms the world is far,
> Timeless in space we seem.
> Distant from earth as a star,
> The memory of grief vague as a dream.
> Stilled is fear of the future
> Gone is regret for the past.
> One with you the spell is broken,
> Life eternal ours at last.
> Then part of the dead and unborn we are;
> Distant from earth as a star,
> Free from yesterday and tomorrow.

A few days after sending off my poem and records to Stan, I received a telegram asking me to phone him. We did not have a phone, so I went to the nearby town of Perris.

He said, "I've fallen in love. I'm going to be married."

I dropped to the floor of the telephone booth. It seemed as if I were experiencing the culmination of all of the grief in my life and the loss of all of my dreams. For how long I lay on the floor in that little bus station booth, I don't know. There was no one around when I recovered my senses. Or did I recover my senses?

I went home, packed a small suitcase, and went to San Francisco. When I arrived, I went to Stan's office, but he wasn't in. I found out where he was staying and engaged a room in the neighborhood. It was a few days before Christmas, and I sent a potted plant to his apartment.

In a day or so, I followed the plant and knocked at Stan's apartment door quite early in the morning. He answered, sleepy-eyed in his shirt-tails and looking quite gaunt and raw-boned. Strange to say, I said nothing and he, too, was silent. Then he noticed the morning paper on the floor between us. He stooped down, picked up his paper, and shut the door in my face.

I stood there staring at the door. In those moments, I lost my own identity and became some fictional character, some tragic heroine

of history . . . some Andromeda, Phedre, Niobe weeping for her children. The human ego can take only so much humiliation. It responds by making one's grief larger than life, more important than fact, saving the ego by giving grandeur to grief.

I left that place, that closed door, lifted into the stratosphere of high tragedy. In the following days, I was sustained by the heroic part in which I cast myself. Joan of Arc feels no self-pity! My immolation has made glorious my defeat! I exalt in misery that no one has ever suffered before. I felt majestic, knowing that no one else could ever understand such depths of agony.

Strange to say, my social life became quite active and successful. I had one friend in San Francisco, Mary Howard, the accomplished and, yes, beautiful head of the Association for the Blind in the city. She had an office in a basement room at the Fairmont Hotel on Nob Hill. There she had her typewriter and her piano, and many prominent and influential guests came to donate to the charity and hear her play and sing, which she did beautifully in spite of the fact that she was born blind. She was well-educated and had exquisite manners. She said that she loved being with me because I didn't seem able to remember that she could not see.

There, I met a charming man, a member of the steamship "Dollar" family, who began to take me around a bit. Also, I met a prominent social figure, a member of the Stokes family, who seemed to take a fancy to me. I often wondered what they thought of my living in such a run-down part of the city.

On a pleasant evening, I would bundle up and walk the few blocks to Stan's apartment where, it seemed, he no longer lived. The vacant lot across the street was piled high with dirt and boulders. I climbed on the rocks and sat there looking at Stan's bay window, subconsciously emulating the scene in Goethe's autobiography, *Storm and Stress (Sturm und Drang)* in which he describes waiting and watching at Charlotte's window after he has lost her forever. There, like him, I watched and wept.

Needing a job, I answered an ad for women checking advisers at the Bank of America. I took the name of "Jean" because it is a favorite of mine, applied for the job, and got it—even though I was in no way qualified.

In the basement of the bank, I sat with twenty-five other girls around a big table. Each morning, each of us received a stack of checks and accounts for the same. These were to be compared and any discrepancy noted and turned in. We knew that if we did not turn in the average number of misstatements, we would be fired. Happily, I kept to the average, counting mostly on my fingers. In school, I had not been very good at math.

I was unpopular with the girls because I showed no interest in them. At a party they gave, everyone brought a little gift for some other girl, and I received a yo-yo. They laughed when I walked up to receive it, but I was in another world and didn't mind. I was as unreachable as if on another planet, and they recognized me as an alien.

During my nightly vigil in the vacant lot, I noticed a change in Stan's bay window. It now held a bowl of white lilies decorating the wide expanse. In a few days as I was watching, a truck drove up with a load of white trunks and white luggage. The next morning, the newspaper, *The Chronicle*, announced in the society column that Mr. S. Stanwood Murphy had returned from New York with his new bride, the New York florist June Dibble Almy.

I went berserk and stormed to his office to demand the mink coat that he had promised me for so long. I don't know why I made this fur coat such an issue because I already had a mink coat: Russian wild mink, the best there was, and full-length.

I was told again that Stan was not in, but they invited me to see his large, beautifully appointed office. The smiling executive suggested that we go around the corner to a nearby bar and have a drink. It was all too pat and arranged. I was not fooled and refused the insulting invitation. That night, I left for the farm at Perris to get my little gun.

My mother and I were no longer speaking because we were both so full of pent-up recrimination—she considered me heartless for continuing in the play after my father's death and was disgusted with me for throwing away my career. (I really don't feel that I did.) I was angry with her for holding the funeral without me and mismanaging my affairs—buying the great Los Feliz mansion without consulting me, auctioning if off, and selling my books and furniture at a loss.

She once wanted to turn the basement of my Beverly Hills home into a secret gambling place at a time when I was trying to become one of the industry's respected members of the Beverly Hills elite. She said she was like an Indian who never forgets an unkind word, and I had said some extremely ugly words to her. We came together later, but we remained mentally estranged forever after.

I did not know if the small gun was loaded or not, but I carried it back to San Francisco with me and to my secret nightly "watches." I imagined how I would frighten him in retribution for all of the pain which he had caused me. Seeing the abject fear in his face, I saw him pleading with me, looking ridiculous and scared; but I imagined nothing as wild, unbelievable, and ridiculous as what actually happened.

I saw him leave the apartment only once. That day, I had tied a string across his garage to find out if he was using it. I watched as he angrily jerked the twine loose. It was plain that he knew who had done it.

I hoped that I might see him entering or leaving the Commonwealth Club on Nob Hill across from the Fairmont Hotel, and once I thought that I saw him and his tall bride (wearing a mink coat) entering the door to the Fairmont.

Not having seen him at the club, I decided to go by railroad to Scotia, the location of the head office of the Pacific Lumber Company of which he was the chief executive. When I got there, I went to the spacious bungalow where he had his office, but he was not there. I checked into the hotel in town and phoned.

Stan answered, but what he said was garbled. I understood that I was to stay at the hotel and that someone would come for me.

The person who arrived was Stan's former brother-in-law, whom I had never met. I got in the car with him, but instead of taking me to the lodge, he took me back to San Francisco, talking quickly, expertly, and profusely all of the way.

I told him, "If he doesn't see me, I will climb the tallest building in San Francisco and jump off." This was a new idea to me at the time, and I don't know if I really meant it.

The man talked constantly on the trip back to town and included the terrible troubles of his sister, Stan's alcoholic ex-wife.

When I arrived back in San Francisco, I decided to go to see her. I was under a weird momentum, a mental pressure for action that I couldn't stop. I found the "ex" in her dark bedroom at her gloomy, three-story home. She lay red-nosed and red-eyed under coverlets pulled up to her chin; she was as confused as I about why I was there.

She had not heard of the new marriage, and we both cried about it. I thought that she resembled me with her brown eyes and auburn hair. The new Mrs. Murphy also had brown eyes and auburn hair, and she resembled both of us. Neither of us held any animosity towards the new wife. We cried over Murphy's duplicity and cruelty.

On my next walk to Nob Hill and the Commonwealth Club, I carried my little pistol wrapped in the latest *Harper's Bazaar* magazine, which I intended to read if I could find a seat. Walking by the club, I recognized Stan's car and verified it by its license number.

I stood there no more than a few seconds when Stan appeared. He walked to his car and began unlocking the door. I jumped over the foot-and-a-half ornamental stone fence and fired at his windshield. The shot and the shattered windshield made a terrific noise. That gun was really loaded.

Stan ducked to the ground. At that instant, I was caught in a bear-hug by a man who appeared out of nowhere. He held my hand with the gun straight up toward the sky. I said, "Look out; I'll kill you!" He gave me a push as he took the gun, and I fell in a sitting position with my back toward the fence. Stan

was crawling on all fours towards the club entrance.

Almost like magic, two very tall policemen showed up. They looked at me sitting there with the *Harper's Bazaar* magazine at my feet.

"Is this your gun?" one of them asked.

I said, "Yes, it's just a toy."

"It doesn't seem like a toy," he said, looking at the broken windshield.

"I was just trying to scare him," I explained.

He replied, "Well, I'm afraid you will have to come with us."

As I walked between the two officers, I felt like a tiny bungalow between two skyscrapers. I also felt quite cheerful. I distinctly recall thinking, "Well, I guess I'll go to jail for a long time. I don't care. I'll write a book like *Pilgrim's Progress* as John Bunyan did, or as Cervantes did with *Don Quixote*."

At the jail, they identified me by showing me pictures of myself taken the previous Sunday at a race track in my mink coat presenting the winner's cup. They asked me if I wished to make a phone call.

I said, "No, I have no one to call."

The news photographers appeared. They lit a cigarette and put it in my hand, and I docilely took it. They reported that I wore a tight green sweater and a pleated tan and green plaid skirt, and that I appeared calm.

I was first taken to a jail matron who searched me and took a coin purse containing a few dollars and a key from a pocket in my shirt.

"What's your name?" she asked.

I said, "I'm Madge Bellamy, the actress."

She replied, stony-faced, "That's what they all say."

I was then taken to an office where my thumb was pressed into a box of black ink and onto a white paper. They placed me in a small cell made entirely of bars so that there was no privacy. It had two bunks, one above the other. An open privy was in a corner.

After I had been in the cell for awhile, the matron came to see me.

"Why don't you tell them that you were drunk? It will go easier for you," she said.

"I can't," I told her, "because I wasn't."

# Miss Bellamy Sues to 'Divorce' Murphy

**A. STANWOOD MURPHY**

**MRS. AMY DIBBLE MURPHY**

On grounds—legal in Nevada, too—that they once consented to become married but never went through an actual ceremony, Madge Bellamy, who popped into the headlines here Jan. 21 with a three-shot attack on A. Stanwood Murphy, San Francisco lumber magnate, brought suit in Las Vegas, Nev., today against Mr. Murphy—for divorce.

Mr. Murphy, insofar as California laws are concerned, is married to the former June Dibble Almy, daughter of a British general.

**It was because he had married Miss Almy that Miss Bellamy fired three wild shots from a .32 caliber revolver as Mr. Murphy emerged from the Pacific Union Club, the big-eyed actress said shortly after her arrest.**

She was given a six months suspended sentence for violation of the State Gun Law for that display.

That, presumably, ended the feudin', for Municipal Judge Morris extracted from Miss Bellamy at the trial her promise that she would not again try to get into touch with Mr. Murphy.

Late this afternoon, the United Press teletypes began clicking out a story from Las Vegas . . .

**"The actress, once one of the highest paid stars in Hollywood, based her surprise suit today on a decision handed down by the Nevada Supreme Court in the case of 'The State vs. Zichfeld'," the story said.**

"In the case the state court convicted Zichfeld of bigamy on grounds he had entered into a non-ceremonial 'consent' or common-law marriage with one woman and later married some one else with a regular ceremony. The court ruled the first marriage was as legally valid as the second. Nevada is one of the few states to retain a statute recognizing the validity of common-law marriages."

Mr. Murphy was not available for comment when the story came in, but his personal secretary at the Pacific Lumber Co. of which Mr. Murphy is president, said:

"Pardon me for laughing, but how can it be?"

The attorney who represented Mr. Murphy in the Bellamy affair, Harold Faulkner, said he hadn't seen months," and Miss Bellamy's counsel in that trial, J. W. Ehrlich, remarked when apprised of the news today:

"She discussed that idea with me shortly after the trial, and I advised against it."

The actress charged in her complaint she and Mr. Murphy consented to become married at Las Vegas on April 26, 1941, but never went through an actual ceremony.

Officials of the Clark County clerk's office in Las Vegas told United Press that they had no record of a marriage license obtained by the couple but explained the Nevada statute ruled a marriage is valid without a ceremony if both parties "capable in law of contracting" agree to become married.

Miss Bellamy filed the action under the name of "Margaret Philpott Murphy, otherwise known as Madge Bellamy."

She asked equitable distribution of three million dollars community property, alimony, court costs and attorney fees.

Her complaint also charged Murphy with "having relations" with June Dibble Almy. (Mr. Murphy and Miss Almy are married in California anyhow.)

"Miss Bellamy Sues . . . Murphy" from the *San Francisco News*, Monday, July 12, 1943, page 1.

Later, the jailor appeared, bringing with him two young women.

"Here's some company for you," he explained jovially as he locked them up, too. These two persons showed absolutely no interest in me and whispered between themselves.

After awhile, the jailer came for me and took me to a small cubbyhole office. A man with dark, patent-leather looking hair awaited me.

He said, "I'm Jake Ehrlich, lawyer. Several people have phoned me asking me to represent you. They heard of what happened on the radio."

I answered without enthusiasm, "You can if you want to. I can't pay you anything." I did not ask who had phoned him.

Mr. Ehrlich showed me pictures of the new Mrs. Murphy in a bathing suit, and I recall showing a keen interest in them. Then he took me to a large cell and a man in dark clothes arrived. He was a judge.

"Are you sorry for what you did?" the judge asked me in a very gentle voice.

I began to tremble all over in a completely uncontrollable manner and answered, speaking to the wall before me, "I'm sorry. I won't ever do it again."

"Do you promise you will never try to harm Mr. Murphy again?" he asked.

I nodded. "I promise. I'm so sorry."

They both left, but Ehrlich soon returned. He had procured my release. It must have been on my own recognizance. I have forgotten if there was any bail required.

Ehrlich took me to the place where I had been living and made me use the pay phone. He said that I must thank some of the people who had called him to look after me. First, we called Ed Thompson, a hotel man who was known for being a friend to his friends in need. Then we called Mickey Neilan. I had not expected him to come to my rescue. Neither was at home nor in his office, so we gave up on the calls.

Later, I learned that the reason Ehrlich, this famous trouble-shooter lawyer, took my case was because L.B. Mayer, the MGM tycoon, had called and asked him to do so—not because he was fond of me, but he was acting as a protector of the motion picture moral code. I heard later that Claire Windsor, the silent picture actress who lived in Hollywood with a prominent and wealthy social figure, had phoned Ehrlich and offered to pay the fees.

Ehrlich looked over the room that I had been living in, which was a total mess, like all of the places in which I've lived unless I have someone to pick up after me. The only incriminating evidence was a bottle of brandy, and I was glad to see it was unopened. Of course, the police had been there.

Then Ehrlich and I went to a men's haberdashery where he tried on hats and finally bought one. This was supposed to be a gift for him from me in gratitude for his help, but at the time, I did not realize this. It was just as well because I had only a few dollars in my purse.

Then he took me to his home, and his wife served us a lovely three-inch souffle that was just like eating whipped air. They were very kind and had me lie down on a sofa, covered me with a blanket, and I went to sleep as quickly as if I had done a hard day's work.

# Chapter Thirteen

The radio carried my exploit all over the country. The *San Francisco News* early morning paper had two big headlines that said, "Allies in Tripoli!" "Madge Bellamy in Court Over S.F. Love Shooting." It was January 20, 1943.

In smaller letters, it said, "Only wanted to scare him, she claims." A big picture showed me smoking the cigarette that the reporters had given me. Smaller headlines read, "Three bullets are fired at Bay Area Lumber Executive." Then it said:

Madge Bellamy, whose big eyes, and curvaceous figure thrilled movie fans when some of today's stars still were wearing three-cornered pants, was booked for a personal appearance here today in Municipal Court on a charge of assault with a deadly weapon.

Miss Bellamy came out of semi-retirement last night in a blaze of gunfire. She popped three bullets in the general direction of A. Stanwood Murphy, 53, socially prominent president of the Pacific Lumber Company, as he left the Commonwealth Club on Nob Hill. "I only wanted to scare him," she told police. "I fired the shots on an impulse." Miss Bellamy told the *News* this morning before going to court, "I had been walking along, kind of dreaming of things I would like to do to get even with him, when he happened along. I was carrying a revolver because it sort of comforted me. When I saw him, I whipped it out. But I was as surprised as he was when I heard the shot."

Whether she succeeded in scaring Mr. Murphy was something only he could say, and he wasn't talking. In fact, Mr. Murphy was nowhere to be found. "They left in the car early this morning, and I wouldn't be surprised if they'd gone to the country."

As the first bullet zinged from the thirty-two caliber revolver toted by Miss Bellamy, Mr. Murphy, alerted, identified the approaching object as unfriendly, and took the necessary precautions. Miss Bellamy said, "He ducked," while other reports to police were that Mr. Murphy had violated all traditions of the stately old club by dropping to his hands and knees and crawling around its parking area with the agility of a lumberjack at the cry of "Timber" in one of his redwood forests around Scotia. However he managed it, Mr. Murphy got back into his club without having been contacted by any of the bullets.

"He was the first man I ever loved, and he married another woman," Miss Bellamy, thirty-nine, told police. She made it clear he had not promised to marry her during their several years of friendship, "but he promised not to marry anyone else when he got his divorce."

While she was being questioned at headquarters, Mr. Murphy went to his apartment at 2299 Pacific Avenue, and joined his bride, the former June Dibble Almy, English-born Jean Palou mannequin, and more recently the wife of a wealthy Arizona cowboy and rancher. Mr. Murphy and Mrs. Almy were married on New Year's Eve. Police quoted him as saying he had known Miss Bellamy for four or five years, but there was no reason she should have opened fire on him.

When I was arrested and walked towards the jail between the two tall policemen, my thought was, "Oh, my! I'll never have another date with a man. They will all be afraid of me!" But in jail, I didn't care.

I said to myself, "I hope I am sent to prison. It will be better in than out—better than just more of the same kind of life I have been living."

My arraignment on a charge of assault with a deadly weapon was continued until January 27th. My shoot-out took place on the evening of January 19th. I must have lapsed into a kind of amnesia because I can't recall what I did or where I went after Mr. Erhlich took me to his home. Everything in my mind is mixed up.

However, between January 20th and the 21st, I became completely anesthetized. I felt nothing. I existed in a hazy dream, and I remember little. I know that I appeared in court wearing a broad-brimmed hat, for that is how the pictures in the papers show me.

That is when Mama suddenly appeared in the courtroom wearing my big red fox cape. It was the first that I knew she had arrived in town.

The night of January 20th, Mama and I registered at one of the town's best hotels, and a few minutes later, we were asked to leave. This was the nadir of my life, I suppose, but I was so insensible to everything going on around me that I was not bothered by this insult. But my mother was stony-faced and silent with rage. It was as if some merciful hormone had filled my brain and body. I was passive, not really displeased with anything, a disinterested observer, noting everything, but not reacting normally, as if I were a disembodied spirit aloof from human cares and strife. I really didn't care what happened to me—or anyone else. I was alone—and as self-sufficient as an atom or an oyster.

The next clipping that I have saved from those weird times is dated January 27th and is the same large picture of me smoking the cigarette that the reporters gave me the night of my capture. The headline reads, "Madge Bellamy Faces Gunplay Charge Today."

The other headlines in the paper that morning read, "Allies Thwart Nazi Plan to Lure Spain Into War"; "Britain Hangs 13th Nazi Spy"; "United Nations Get Tough with Franco, Prevent Him Making Deal with Hitler."

The article about me says:

> Miss Margaret Philpott, better known as Madge Bellamy, stage and screen actress, will appear before Municipal Judge Clarence Morris today for preliminary hearing on charges of assault with a deadly weapon. The charges followed an exhibition of gunplay by Miss Bellamy on the night of January nineteenth, when she sent three bullets ploughing into the automobile of A. Stanwood Murphy, lumberman and socialite, just as he was about to enter it in the parking lot of the Commonwealth Club on Nob Hill.
>
> "I didn't try to hit him," Miss Bellamy insists. "I'm an expert shot and I just wanted to scare him. I think I did it."
>
> She told police that Murphy had "led her on" for four years and then jilted her to marry Mrs. June Dibble Almy, divorced wife of a one-time millionaire cowboy. The shooting occurred a few days after Murphy and his new wife returned to San Francisco. Murphy and his wife left their apartment at 2299 Pacific Avenue, shortly after the shooting, and he has not yet come forward with charges against Miss Bellamy.
>
> Through her attorney, J.W. Ehrlich, she obtained liberty on $500 bail on the promise to avoid Murphy and not molest him further.

I remember thinking, as I read these lines, "Oh, God! I'm glad my father didn't live to know about all this!" It was reading the name "Philpott" written in such a context that hit me. My father was so proud of his ugly name. His father had tried to obtain the Philpott estate in England by hiring lawyers for the great sum, in those days, of $3000, but the land reverted to the Crown.

The Philpott escutcheon is the same as that of the City of London: a white sheath with a red cross. It was given to John Philpott for killing Wat Tyler, the leader of the Peasants' Revolt, when the serfs marched on London with their rakes and tools on their shoulders.

A Philpott is in *Fox's Book of Martyrs*; he was burned at the stake by the Catholics for not renouncing his wife and children because his marriage had not been sanctified by the then-dominant Church. A Philpott is noted in books on heraldry as a pursuivant at Court.

In the book *Historians' History of the World*, a Philpott was a great merchant who donated the use of his ships to save the British Navy.

Thinking these thoughts made me ashamed of my deed for the first time since I had done it.

# Chapter Fourteen

*I* did have friends among Murphy's friends. Between court appearances, I literally ran into one of them in the foyer of my hotel: Stan Stanford, who had been with Murphy on the day when I first met him and had kept us amused in Palm Springs five years before. He rushed into me with such force that we were thrown into a bear-hug to keep our equilibrium. He held me a moment and when he let go, I saw tears rushing down his cheeks.

"Madge! Madge! Darling little Madge," he whispered and quickly kissing me on both cheeks, he ran away from me.

This gesture, this sudden, fleeting embrace said a thousand words of understanding and comfort to me. In his heart, he must have been suffering, too, for only a few months later, the headlines read, "Stanford Jumps to Death From the Roof of His Five-Storied Home." How close we were for a few moments, both of us with sorrows and humiliations too great to bear.

Although I should have been wretched, I was not. I did not dread the thought that I would be sent to prison as much as I dreaded having to go on living as I had been living.

The hearing was held on January 27th. On January 28, 1943, the *San Francisco Examiner* ran a picture of the sleekly handsome lawyer, Jake Ehrlich, and me. The caption read:

Must face trial—Starry-eyed Madge Bellamy stands beside attorney J.W. Ehrlich at preliminary hearing yesterday over Nob Hill gunning involving socialite A. Stanwood Murphy. "Target" was absent, but police filed charges.

The headlines said, "Film Beauty Must Face S.F. Gunplay Trial." The article said, "Bellamy affair almost ends with absence of socialite from court. Police file complaint."

On the rest of the page, part of Madge Bellamy's diary was printed, and it ran in the paper like a serial for several days. It was reckless of me to give it to a very likeable reporter, but I did not care what was said about me.

On Friday, January 29, 1943, the papers were full of the account of my appearance at the trial with Murphy present.

Louella Parsons came to San Francisco to see me. She came with her priest. At her hotel, she introduced me to the priest and left us alone. He was sweet and kindly.

Smiling and lowering his eyes, he said, "I did something like you have just done when I was young."

"I wish that what I did had been done for a better cause," I replied. "I deserve whatever punishment I receive."

For those few moments, I felt sweet communion between us. What powers the church attains when it enlists such gentle, forgiving priests! What healing power resides in kindness!

A few moments later, Louella took me aside. "I don't see why you were so in love with Murphy," she said. "I've known him for years and never thought him attractive."

I did not answer her. It was smart of me to be silent because to have expressed my thoughts at that moment would have been a disaster.

I felt like saying, "I agree with you. I don't think him attractive. In fact, I don't love him. I don't love him at all. I'm just mad as hell. My act was one of vengeance, not of desperate love."

# Madge, Rich Target Meet Again—In Court

# 'If Looks Could ---'

Madge Bellamy (right) had her first look—and what a look—at her former sweetheart, A. Stanwood Murphy, smiling (left), as they appeared in court today. Attorney J. W. Ehrlich is in center. —Call-Bulletin Photograph.

News article on Madge and A. Stanwood Murphy; the date of this clipping is probably January 29, 1943.

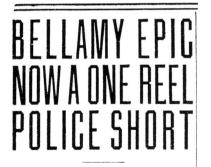

# BELLAMY EPIC NOW A ONE REEL POLICE SHORT

### S.F. Lumber Tycoon Drops From Cast; Felony Charge Reduced to Carrying Concealed Gun

"Ambush at the P. U. Club," highly press-agented courtroom drama of sweet memories, good shootin' and fast footwork, underwent drastic revision in production yesterday.

Originally billed as a feature-length, super-smash, it was whittled down to a one reeler through an abrupt change in schedule which left Miss Madge Bellamy in the starring role but dropped A. Stanwood Murphy, socialite lumber tycoon and presumption leading man, clear out of the cast.

The change was announced in the municipal court of Judge Clarence Morris as Miss Bellamy appeared for a rsumption of her preliminary hearing on felony charges of assault with a deadly weapon—charges resulting from what Murphy described, in his single, fleeting court appearance last week, as "an unusual occurrence," on the evening of January 19.

**(He said he came out of the Pacific Union Club, noticed .32 caliber bullets pinging around him, and went back into the club.)**

### BACKS LEADING MAN.

Before Miss Bellamy could speak a line yesterday, she found herself in a "B" picture with no leading man. Judge Morris dismissed the felony charge against her and police re-arrested her on a simple misdemeanor charge of toting a gun.

The effect was to take the entire matter out of the realm of high crime and put it into the police courts. Because the charge is now that of carrying a concealed weapon, without a license, the fact that the bullets spattered close to Murphy becomes irrelevant and Murphy's further appearance as a witness becomes unnecessary.

Because Miss Bellamy's motives for exercising her roscoe are without bearing on the reduced charge, all the lovely lines she had concerning her four years of association with Murphy will be left on the cutting room floor.

### NOT GUILTY PLEA.

Miss Bellamy entered a plea of not guilty to the new charge and waived jury trial. Judge Morris set next Wednesday for hearing, and released her on bail of $100. If found guilty, she faces a maximum penalty of six months in jail and a fine of $500.

Judge Morris dismissed the felony charge after listening to Miss Edith Wilson, assistant district attorney.

Miss Wilson said that after reviewing the facts and the law, and after being reliably informed that Murphy has no desire to prosecute, it was clear that a conviction in superior court was impossible and that a trial would only subject the city and county to futile expense.

Accordingly, the district attorney was asking for a dismissal of the felony charge but going ahead with prosecution on charges of violating the gun law.

### COMPLAINT DISMISSED.

Judge Morris asked for a statement from Harold Faulkner, attorney for Murphy. Faulkner said that "very definitely" Murphy does not intend to sign a complaint and never has so intended. Judge Morris shrugged and dismissed the felony complaint.

Whereupon Miss Bellamy's attorney, J. W. Ehrlich, arranged for her bail and then escorted her to a Nob Hill hotel— just across the street from the Pacific Union Club— with the announcement that she had to attend a business conference looking toward a resumption of her career in motion pictures.

Madge's appearance in court.

# COURT DRAMA FIZZLES

RE-ARRESTED—Felony chages against Madge Bellamy were dismissed yesterday. She was charged only with carrying a concealed gun without a license.
—Photo by San Francisco Examiner.

Still, looking back and re-reading the poems that I wrote for him—"When in your arms the world is far/Distant from earth as a star"—I think maybe I did love him after all.

Why was I so unresponsive to Louella, so uncommunicative all the time I worked in Hollywood, so quietly busy on the set reading a book, quiet at parties, silent and unresponsive in tête-à-têtes? The Hollywood crowd thought that I was dumb, but the few who knew me well, respected my mind and scholarship.

I was so inhibited, I think, because I found nearly everyone unsympathetic to my ideas. I was an atheist from the age of twelve. For a time, Mama belonged to the Jehovah's Witnesses, and my father died believing in a hereafter. My mother dominated my life, and my father gave me a prudish attitude towards sex. I must have found it expedient to keep my mouth shut. So now I disappointed Louella. Later, she wrote a kind column about me, urging my continuation in pictures.

After my interview with Louella and the priest, my lawyer and I took the elevator down to the courtroom. In the elevator, I felt that I was surrounded by sympathy as the people looked at me tenderly and then lowered their eyes, as if to hide their warm love for me. I had never before felt so much sympathy from a group of people—and here I was going down to a courtroom where I might be sent to prison, humiliated, soiled, discarded.

At the preliminary hearing held January 29, 1943, I was almost in a coma. Big headlines on January 30th in the *Examiner* read, "Murphy Vanishes at Bellamy Quiz." The other headlines under this one in big print read, "Russ Rip Nazi Lines, Smash 7 Divisions." Then in smaller print:

Disappearing Act by Murphy Stops Bellamy Court Play. Ex-playmate of Miss Madge Bellamy reluctantly made his debut yesterday as her leading man in the courtroom production of "Ambush at the Commonwealth Club"—and stole the show. Not with his lines, which were sparse and pedestrian and read with neither verve nor élan and not with his "business" which consisted chiefly of tapping his foot and staring at some spot which Miss Bellamy did not occupy, did the socialite score—but with his exit.

It was not so much an exit as an evanescence or dissolution into space. A disappearing act that completely fooled not only the audience but also most of the cast and would have gone down in many minds as sheer magic, had not one spectator, seeing through the illusion reported, "He came down the aisle and out the door bounding like an antelope."

On February 6, 1943, the *San Francisco Chronicle* headlined, "Final Rostov Battle is On. Two Rail Cities Fall." Then below:

> The case of Madge Bellamy yesterday started on its inevitable route into limbo. Velocity was provided in absentia by District Attorney Brady, who suddenly developed a blank mind. Dropped was the complaint charging the wistful Miss Bellamy with assault with a fairly innocuous charge, a misdemeanor for carrying a concealed weapon without a license. Murphy was the little man who wasn't there. Jake Ehrlich attained a new record by maintaining silence. Miss Bellamy, herself, attractive in a navy blue frock with a polka-dot collar and matching Queen Anne chapeau, controlled herself until adjournment when she tried to kiss the judge.
>
> "Well, boys," said Judge Morris to the photographers, "are you ready to take pictures?" The boys were and did. Miss Bellamy smiled.
>
> At this point, Assistant District Attorney Edith Wilson rose to address the Court: "After reviewing the legal aspects of this case as well as the factual, and being reliably informed that Mr. Murphy has no intention of prosecuting Miss Bellamy and further would be a reluctant witness in the Superior Court, the District Attorney is of the mind that a conviction would be very unlikely. More than that, a trial would only subject the city to an unnecessary and futile expense, and therefore, the District Attorney has instructed me to ask dismissal of this charge and requests that we proceed to the prosecution of this defendant for violation of the gun law."
>
> Ehrlich looked as if he had swallowed a canary. Judge Morris said, "This complaint is dismissed."
>
> With that, Miss Bellamy was whisked upstairs where she was booked on a midsdemeanor charge, and returned to the Court room.
>
> The new charge was read to her, Miss Bellamy fairly swooned with rapture.
>
> "How do you plead?" asked Morris. "Not guilty," said Ehrlich.
>
> "I want the defendant to do the pleading," he said. "Not guilty," cooed Miss Bellamy.
>
> "Do you want a jury trial?" the court inquired. "I want this matter to go over," Ehrlich interrupted. "We will waive a jury trial." "I didn't ask you," Judge Morris snarled. "We will waive a jury trial," Miss Bellamy repeated, obviously a quick study. "This matter will go over to February 10th," the Court announced. "Bail is set at $100 cash or $200 bail." Judge Morris used his gavel firmly.
>
> The Courtroom emptied, but not until Miss Bellamy had made a flying leap in the general direction of the Judge. Whether she actually succeeded in kissing him remains a military secret.
>
> With this dramatic finale, Miss Bellamy hurried to the Mark Hopkins Hotel to confer with a group of Hollywood moguls about her returning to pictures.

On February 10th, the midsdemeanor charges were dismissed, and I was put on one year's probation.

Two writers offered me $8000 for my life story. They would ghostwrite.

I refused by saying, "If my story is written, *I* will do it myself." I am surprised that I refused this offer in so cavalier a fashion, especially since we were broke—completely broke.

Mama's boyfriend Eddie rented our farmhouse at Perris, California, to someone and joined us in San Francisco, where we found a two-room apartment. He had worked on ships in New York before he came to California. The shipyard at Richmond, California, was doing war work and he got a job there. He was a short, stout, Germanic type and a very hard worker.

Many women were working in the shipyards, he said, so I decided to try out as a welder. About ten women took the test with me, most of them colored. Three of them and I passed.

I got a big pair of overalls, crossed the San Francisco Bay on the ferry, and went to work the next morning. My first job was to team up with a skinny old man working on the floor of one of the great ships. He would fit and set in a floor part, and I would follow, welding in what he had done. This old fellow was simply a bear for work. I was always out of breath keeping up with him. He was so dedicated to the work that he would urge me not to stop when the whistle blew for lunch or quitting time, but to get in a few more licks before we stopped, exhausted.

It was bitterly cold and drafty on the ship's floor. One day when he had been especially industrious, I dragged myself into a deserted corner as the workers rushed by. I tried to find my way to the resting room where there were the lockers and a small stove. I climbed the rickety stairs to this haven and fell to the floor close to the stove. Someone in authority found me there, and I was taken to the emergency hospital where I came to lying on a table. I

Madge and the judge.

saw some men in white coats looking at me. Almost at once, the whistle blew, signifiying that the lunch hour was over. I sat up and asked for my welder's helmet.

"It's the end-of-lunch whistle," I said. "I've got to go back to work." I was hospitalized for four days with pneumonia in the company's hospital.

When I recovered, I went back to work with the industrious old man. I was good at welding; it was like sculpting with fire, so they borrowed me in other sections of the ship if a delicate bit of welding was to be done. Later, I was transferred to a more intricate job than spot welding. I was sent to the deck of a great

ship where I welded the rails to the ship. To do this, one had to lie on one's stomach and lean out over the deck.

I enjoyed this work, but the difficult conditions were overwhelming. When the whistle blew, there was a mad, blind rush to the locker room by a pushing, shouldering, stomping stream of humanity in a frenzy to put away gear and tools, and get their coats. It was a very rude tide of humanity. My locker was at the very bottom row, and the young women with lockers above me would, without a "May I?" get on my shoulders or on my head to reach their lockers.

As I ran with the others to the open ferry for

Richmond, sometimes I wept as I ran, jostled from side to side, my coarse overalls weighing a ton, and the loose tools jangling in the baggy pockets. I felt that this was my punishment for all the mistakes that I had made in life.

Mama decided to go to Nevada to see if she could get a lawyer who could make Murphy pay. She was gone a few days and came back with the news that she had found a wonderful young lawyer who would take the case.

I met him that weekend at the Los Angeles Biltmore Hotel. He was 37 years old, nondescript and intense. On Sunday morning, we met in his room and began our business talk. He said that he would not take the case unless I became his girlfriend and gave him a down payment at once.

I was saved by a telephone call from the house detective. "Get that woman out of there," he said.

I was out and back to my room in the hotel in two seconds. However, later in Nevada, I consented to his business proposition, and he rented a small house for me and his five-year-old, adopted son—an angelic-looking monster who ruled me with an iron fist. His father was not much trouble. Sex with him was so short and simple, so free of emotion or dialogue that it was only a slight inconvenience to me.

This young man was a brilliant lawyer. He got paralyzed with drink every weekend, but on Monday morning, he was furiously back at work. I would go with him to the library to help research his cases.

My grandfather, who was also a lawyer, used to say, "Being a lawyer is not so much knowing, as knowing where to find it." This young fellow would dig and dig until he found an analogous case. In the courtroom, he was vindictive and relentless.

Once he defended the innocent, defenseless Coca-Cola Company against a lawsuit by a former employee who claimed that he had been wrongly fired and arrested for throwing a Coke bottle through a plate glass window.

The employee was reduced to a wilted, worthless piece of humanity by my lawyer's biting words: "This despicable liar says he did not even have a bottle, nor did he throw it. Did the window break of itself? Does he not admit that he was angry at being fired for stealing on the job? Was he not known as one who threw objects when angry?" Of course, the Coca-Cola Company won.

We talked to a judge in Las Vegas, and I filed for divorce from Murphy as his common-law wife. Murphy's lawyers contacted us, and the suit was postponed time after time as the lawyers dickered. I remained in Las Vegas for nine months.

In the meantime, I attended all of my lawyer's courtroom battles. My admiration for his ferocity grew, and I was growing more and more attached to his little son. One night when we had all gone by auto to Elko, Nevada, on a case, I noticed the boy's forehead was hot, and two very frantic people got the child to a hospital.

After nine months, the lawyers came to an agreement. Neither Murphy nor I had to appear in court. The judge found and stated that I was not legally married to Murphy. I stated that I would not further pursue the case. My lawyer and I settled for $100,000 from Murphy.

Of course, it was in all the newspapers, and I got a call from Louella Parsons, who said, "You should have gotten a million." Half of the settlement went to my lawyer.

Instead of going back to Mama at the farm, I went with "T," my lawyer, to Los Angeles. He wanted me to marry him and invest in an apartment building using our two $50,000 as a down payment. I looked at the property and didn't think too much of it.

Living in Vegas was amusing, and I had learned to care for my lawyer's little boy, who always sat on my lap on trips and put his arms around me, whispering, "I love you."

Despite all of this, I told "T" that I would not marry him. This sent him into a towering rage, and he locked me in the hotel room and went out to get drunk. He had not cut off the telephone, however, and I phoned Mama to come and get me. She and Eddie came after me. Mama was, as usual, miffed with me—this time because I had not come home to her at once as soon as the Murphy case was settled.

While I was away, Mama had started a "throw-away" newspaper and made a living for herself. I think that this was pretty clever of her. She drove up and down collecting ads at the small stores on the highway and asked famous people whom she knew for short articles on the law, politics, and sports. Sometimes she included a lecture by my father about California and Perris, San Bernardino, and Riverside. Then she took the material to a printer in Elsinore, and we took completed newspapers to March Field where she had officers and enlisted men help her distribute the papers.

My lawyer from Las Vegas came to the farm urging me once more to marry him. He brought his little son with him.

The child took me aside and said, "Make up your mind; do you love him? Or don't you love him?" I decided that I didn't love him.

Then a wonderful thing happened to me that turned out to be even more wonderful. I received an invitation from Mary Howard, my beautiful blind friend, to visit her in San Francisco to attend the opening of the first session of the United Nations. Of course, I accepted with delight, although looking back, I think I had a lot of gall to return to the social scene where my recent escapade had taken place. I was still on my one-year probation. Mary lived at the Fairmont Hotel where, I learned, Mr. Murphy had established his new wife in the hotel's penthouse.

Mary and I gave a series of dinner parties at the hotel. At a cocktail party, I met a tall handsome youth, one of Murphy's sons, whom I had not seen for some time. Ironically, he seemed to feel an affection for me, and once we double-dated.

The opening of the United Nations at the Opera House in June, 1945, was the most euphoric experience of my life. I felt a new era of goodwill and the expectation of a comradely world order. I heard Harry Truman, Edward R. Stettinius, and Andrei Gromyko foretell a wonderful new era.

In the lobby of the Fairmont, a familiar figure emerged from the cocktail lounge. It was Neil Vanderbilt, in San Francisco to do a column for the *New York Post*. We had met in Hollywood years before, but I had not seen him for years. He took me by the arm, and we marched right back into the cocktail bar. Later, we went to dinner at the Mark Hopkins Hotel. It was not until I felt his hand rubbing my back as we sat close together that I realized he had amorous designs. We saw each other quite often during the next four years and through two of his marriages.

He explained to me, "I never marry anybody I like." However, at this time, I did not succumb to his manly charms; I thought it wise for me to be extremely cautious and subdued so short a time after my "episode." Also, I had learned that men pursued me only until I went to bed with them.

In his column, "The Roving Eye," Neil wrote, "Lovely, blonde cinestar Madge Bellamy, cynosure of all female eyes in the Fairmont's Cirque room, chatting gayly with bridge expert Ely Culbertson, Berkeley columnist Hal Johnson, M.P. Colonel J. Hennessey, Marine Major Bob Ryland. . . . Nearby, Colonel Loring J. Pickering and his new wife sipping Martinis. . . ." (These last two were the Murphy friends who disliked me so much.)

Little did we dream that in two months, Truman would drop the bombs on Hiroshima and Nagasaki; that Churchill, in his "Iron Curtain" speech, and Cardinal Spellman would declare war on communism. That Mary Howard would die of cancer and that Neil Vanderbilt would drag my heart around like an old sock.

I loved him most of all for his name; second, because our politics were the same (we worked together for the election of Henry Wallace); and third, because he gave great parties.

In his column on June 6, 1945, he wrote, "Madge Bellamy's mother was hurriedly operated on for gallstones at the Cottage Hospital in Santa Barbara yesterday." Of course, I was with Mama and remained there with her for the three months that she was ill.

Christmas 1987: Frank Bresee (husband of actress Bobby Bresee); Madge; and Professor David Bradley of UCLA, film historian.

She went to the hospital a vital, youthful woman with dark hair; she came out a thin, old woman with white hair.

Since I was with my mother, I could only read what Neil wrote on the last day of the UNCIO meeting: "Yesterday, June 26th, 1945, the fifty of us became one world."

During the final speech, tears streamed down the cheeks of many around me as Truman ended with his request for a "world-wide rule of reason under the everlasting guidance of God."

Mary Howard had introduced me to a wealthy, elderly man in San Francisco who said that he was going to produce a motion picture with a part in it for me. I accepted his offer and drove with the director, James Tinling, to Mammoth Lakes.

I had made two films previously with him: *Soft Living* with Johnny Mack Brown, and *Very Confidential*. He was clever at organizing a picture and making sense out of poor material. This picture, called *Northwest Mounted*, with John Litel, was very good considering the small amount of time and money spent on it. It still appears frequently on early morning television.

Mama saw it in Palm Springs soon after it was released. I asked her, "Should I see it?"

"I wouldn't if I were you," was her disappointing reply.

I have re-examined my life story as well as I could and hope that it was worth telling. In the years after this story ended, I have become independent, self-sufficient, and straightlaced. I still believe that a more just society will be found in our world's future.

I discovered during the ten years that I have spent writing this book that I have repeated a certain pattern of behavior over and over again. Perhaps if I had recognized this earlier, I could have broken the mold that held me so fast.

I found that I loved only those whom I feared because I thought them to be superior to me, but I did not think them so for long.

My love was the fleeting kind,
Born in a fragile hour,
Delicate and as easily crushed as a flow'r.
I worshipped at a glance, I did not tell,
And at a second look, I became an infidel.

I had profound feelings of inadequacy that kept me from humbly accepting gifts or affection for fear of losing my precarious self-confidence. I maintained my independence, but in the process, lost many of the rewards of life. I did not comprehend all of this; it took me eighty years to know the stranger within.

I can recognize the first example of my pattern of behavior in an incident that took place when I was about six years old. I was visiting a friend and her mother saw me look longingly at a pretty doll's comb.

"Do you want the comb? You can have it," she said. "Take it."

I shook my head. "I don't want it," I said. But before I left and when no one was looking, I took the comb.

Perhaps if the Armageddon partisans do not succeed in blowing us all to smithereens, science will find a way to produce less testosterone in some babies and more in others, thus eliminating the extremes of timidity and belligerence in human nature, and putting an end to "sturm und drang."

If I could live my life again, I would not want to have such an idealistic father who believed that everything was either black or white—a woman was either an angel or a wicked temptress; men were noble, white, Jeffersonian Democrats or demons lost to the devil. All of my life, I have tried to live up to his ideals and found myself lacking. Nor would I want to have a mother so beautiful and charming, but who made me feel inferior. I have competed all of my life not with others, but with my mother.

# EPILOGUE

My editors have asked me to write a short synopsis of my next book (which will never be written) so that our would-be readers will know what happened in the next forty-five years of my life. So here it is. In a few words, I lived in abject poverty for thirty-five years. This is how it happened:

My mother sold what was left of our big farm and bought two pieces of property—one in Glendora, California; and a house, store, and acreage on the main street of Ontario, California—both in the name of her boyfriend and me.

Back in Ontario, my kidneys stopped functioning. I had to have a hysterectomy, wherewith I lost my last boyfriend, C. V., and my remaining beauty.

My mother took ill with an aneurysm. After her many hospital stays, I took care of her for four years. With my mother's boyfriend, we lived by selling the tools from Fairview Farms in the building next to the house.

I was not unhappy; I learned that I was a good salesperson. I learned the name of every known wrench and succeeded in keeping my stage and screen identity undisclosed.

Eddie, my mother's friend, had a terrible accident. A truck backed over his leg. He recovered so that he could still walk a little. I had to tie a rope around his waist and pull him out of bed. This was hard because he was extremely heavy and fat. At last, I had to send him to a nursing home where he died in

Madge showing an advertisement for Fox Studio's first talking film to Marion Roehl, a guest visiting her home in Ontario, California.

Miss Bellamy in her home, September, 1989.

Well! About eight years ago, at the height of the real estate boom, the people who owned the big store and business next door to my house offered me twice as much for my property as I had earned in many years in pictures—a fortune. Naturally, I took it. In the last eight years, I wrote two novels—*Seeds in the Wind* and *Sparks* (about Texas)—one play—*The Last Straw*—and many short stories—all unsold. I wish I could say I lived happily ever after. But my ninetieth birthday was last week, and it now seems I just may do that.

Madge

Publisher's note: Miss Bellamy died on Wednesday, January 24, 1990 in Upland, California of a long-standing heart condition.

a fairly short time of a stroke after being kept alive for nine days in the hospital in a coma.

He was not a bad man. He received a Congressional Medal for valor when he was young. I have the medal in my hand now, but I cannot read it. It was for saving lives at sea, but it is *not* the medal for military action. He was partly blind from birth. He had been a realtor and had sold my mother many properties. All would have turned out well if I had been able to hold onto them. Wealth really is accrued by land held for many years, but you have to begin wealthy in order to do this!

I do not blame my mother for anything; it would be like blaming the unfortunate for their misfortune, the poor for being poor, the unlucky for their bad luck.

My father seems to have been a poor businessman. However, smarter men than he have been ruined by our various depressions.

# Letters

During preparation of this volume, a collection of letters written to Miss Bellamy during the 1920's was made available to the publisher. Since the letters support Miss Bellamy's narrative and seem likely to be of interest to the book's readers, it was decided to include them, with Miss Bellamy's permission.

The writers include
- Norbert Lusk, a journalist for motion picture magazines and publicist;
- Herbert Brenon, a successful film director in the Silent Era;
- C. W. Thomas, General Manager for Thomas H. Ince Studios;
- Keith B. Lewis, a devoted fan;
- Eugene A. Tucker, Miss Bellamy's attorney;
- Ingle Carpenter, attorney for the Thomas H. Ince Corporation;
- William B. Philpott, Miss Bellamy's father;
- Louis Stevens, whom Miss Bellamy remembers as a prolific screen writer and interesting conversationalist who visited at her house and read scripts; Miss Bellamy considered this to be "better than the ordinary recipe swapping;"
- David Swing Ricker, whom Miss Bellamy does not remember at all;
- and someone else who is completely unknown.

This section concludes with a letter to the editor of *The New York Times* written by Miss Bellamy.

Wherever possible, original spelling and punctuation have been retained.

American Releasing Corporation
15 West 44th Street, New York City

Vanderbilt 9080

Thursday

Dear Midgetina:

I'm overwhelmed by the fact that you are here at last: Bensonhurst's fair flower returned to her own!

But I am appalled by the program planned for you and have a sinking feeling when I fear that I shall only see you on the wing.

I realize that it all rests with you and the Queen Regent, so I shall hold myself in readiness to be summoned at any time. My telephone number is at the head of this page, and the number where I can be reached at home is Schuyler 6121.

This is just a stiffly written line to let you know that I am very happy.

/s/Norbert____

———◦≫◦———

106 West Seventy-seventh Street
New York, January twenty-seventh [ca. 1921]

My Poor Little Star:

Just at the moment I was phrasing most bitter denunciations of all stars, and with great gusto was about to begin work on an especially frightful one aimed at YOU: at this moment, I say, came your letter and promptly put a stop to such nonsense. Now I'm all penitence and sympathy because I gather you aren't any too happy. . . But to go back to your letter. I can always dramatize the getting of one, you know, for it isn't a casual occurrence or, as you well know, an everyday happening!

It felt very *thin*. That was bad. I opened it and found it *short*. Worse still. Nor did it "sound" quite like you. At once I jumped to the worst conclusion. Milady's secretary was trying her skill on me.

You see how incorrigibly fault-finding I am. "Never satisfied," my father used to say in the long ago. (My mother never said anything so reproachful in all my life, which may be why I am what I am today.) At any rate, two lines of yours in the reading can change my mood and when I think you need the least I can give—a letter—then it is begun at once.

It is a problem for you to know which way to turn. I have talked about you to several people, without, however, even hinting that I had any opinion of my own but merely as a "case." I mean your starring venture, your professional status and your future as clearly as it can be seen.

To one not in the know it seems to me that Mr. Ince's arrangement with Associated Exhibitors is largely a money-making venture with you as the excuse. By this I mean that everybody will profit without doubt and you will profit perhaps. Every picture, unless the story is in flagrant violation of what is popular, makes money: that is, some money. But you, as the star, may receive only your salary and at the end of the series find yourself lowered in standing because of the stories, the photography, the direction and general tone of production.

From the little I know and what I guess, it seems to me that some sort of shrewd bargain was back of this Associated Exhibitors deal. A bargain with the least possible risk for the magnates—even Clark Thomas I understand is making a little as "production manager"—and considerable risk for you. Especially as you tell me the stories so far are not to your liking and the photography, easiest of all obstacles to conquer, is not what you wish.

[Hand-written in margin] and remember the public never sees a picture's shortcomings as fully as a player does.

At the same time I don't want to seem a kill-joy. It may be that you are over-critical: that the pictures will be charming and act as real stepping-stones to something better. One never knows, my dear little eager star. Miss Vidor, to all intents and purposes, has made out rather well. Her pictures get into some of the first-run houses and she hasn't altogether lost caste as a screen personality. So don't take initial misgivings too much to heart.

As for your remaining or not remaining with Mr. Ince there is this to say. In the two years and five months you have been with him you have had few real opportunities. Goodness knows you have been kept at work but has it been important or advantageous work? I need not answer this.

At the same time I cannot but feel that all this is the formative period of your work and that nothing has been lost or failed to bring you valuable experience. Many, many players have remained on the screen much longer, with fewer appearances, only to achieve a big success suddenly. And in the period of waiting they have wanted for much that you have had from the first . . . Sir Tutsie and now the Italian villa . . .

Leaving Mr. Ince at the end of the year to free lance may or may not bring you those opportunities we think you should have had long ago. While you are under his supervision I do think he keeps more or less of a lookout on the sort of people he "farms you out" to, even though he makes money every time he does lend you to another producer.

I see scores of pictures produced by independent people, the company with which I am identified releasing only such. Therefore I have a chance to study pictures I'd never go to see in a theatre. All sorts of surprising people are found in the casts, some of them really important and "expensive"; yet in few cases have I found such a player in a production that could possibly do him any kind of good. Apparently he has gone into it for the money and without knowing what it was all about; consequently he has given his time and

ability to a mediocre production and received nothing like careful attention from director or cameraman.

I argue that if you could remain with Mr. Ince and play in Ince productions you might fare better than if you free lanced, judging what I have said in the preceding paragraph. If it could be understood that you had the right to refuse any engagement coming from another producer through him you might be protected to a certain extent. I do think there is much to be said in favor of remaining with the same producer. Mr. Ince has the respect of exhibitors and they know his pictures have a better chance of being box-office successes than those of some producers. His name has dignity; it means something, and while others come and go his studio continues to uphold a standard.

All this need not come under the head of advice from me unless you see some good in it. At least it is my opinion and, unlike most movie people, I admit that I am not infallible.

The fact remains, and I subscribe to it most heartily, yours is too delicate and precious a gift to be placed in the hands of those who do not appreciate it. No picture in which I have seen has given you the least chance to project that elusive, fairy-like quality that does so much to make you a girl apart. I have hopes of Ten Ton Love, in spite of its dull, imaginative title, from what I have seen of the stills. It has amazed me that so far you have not been cast for a part that even suggested the Dream Daughter. Instead, they have asked you to play a girl of the streets ("Hail the Woman") and that is about as far from your true métier as they'll ever get.

The foregoing remarks don't begin to touch the case, I admit. It is a serious business this matter of knowing how best to bestow one's ability and I confess if I were in your place I'd not have done so well.

I want so much to see you where you belong, to hear everybody say what I and some others say and think and feel, yet you must always remember, if I may repeat: You have not lost anything you've gained in the work, and you can't see yourself declining.

You are simply at that period which comes to us all, my dear. It's the cross-roads and we must know that God will lead you straight. That's my conviction. . . .

Now for something in lighter vein. It's about a man who likes you passing well. Oh, not myself. *That's* not in lighter vein and it might bring too sudden a drop in your interest. Somebody else. This is the story:

Not long ago on a visit to one of the trade papers a young man very agreeably introduced himself to me by means of pleasant remarks about something I'd written. Needless to say he knew how susceptible I am to praise. In short order he asked me to come and see him some evening. I did. Greenwich Village. Rather quaint quarters. On the mantelpiece I spied a framed photograph of you, autographed, sad to say, by somebody else—probably in the publicity department. Tactfully I refrained from exposing the fraud. But very soon my host mentioned your name. He was going over to Brooklyn, it seemed, to see "Lorna Doone." Now, really, when someone connected with the movies goes to darkest Brooklyn to see a picture . . . My senses worked quickly, my intuitions quicker still. My friend discussed your work, your business connections and your appearances with Mr. Gillette with unusual knowledge and intelligence. I was rather amazed but kept my own counsel. So much for that.

On a later visit, made shortly afterward, I said without warning: "By the way, there is something more to be said of Miss Bellamy. I think you want to say it." Thereupon the man blushed—*terra cotta*!

"Come now," I said, "this is all very well but why should a man show embarrassment when he hears the name of a friend of mine?" Do you know I felt that I had stumbled on a "situation", that it was a moment which should yield something more than evasions.

I may as well confess that I got nowhere. He admitted he's never met you and didn't know anybody who had except myself, and I must say he asked no questions though seemed politely willing to absorb what I chose to tell him. What is significant, though, is the man's efforts to get to California.

He is rather prepossessing and very intelligent though given to much talk about himself, not vaingloriously, but self-centeredly. He knows this, however, which is to his credit, and he knows that I think so. These "faults", so called, developed rather suddenly after I made the discovery of his interest in you, meaning, of course, that I couldn't stamp him a perfect person in the face of what his blush admitted. His name is Larry C. Moen. I tell you this for what it may mean to you, or for all I know what it already means. I don't trust people whose blood pressure betrays so much. Already you may know him and the joke is entirely on me.

By the way, did you receive a box sent you early in December, probably just when you were moving to Villa Italiano? I ask, not to wring an acknowledgement but only that I may destroy a post-office receipt which I hold and which must be used to trace it if the thing did not reach you.

I'd like to have read something you thought of my Picture-Play stories, if you've read them, and also to know if there's any chance of your helping me out with matter similar to that in the Farrar beauty story. Must I do it unaided? Will you authorize me to do so? In the April Picture-Play, out late in February, you will find something about yourself under my name, and I dare say that will urge you to be polite. I am to do another series, along somewhat different lines, as soon as I find the time to write it.

There is much, much more, that I might say in this letter but I've an idea the call of the studio is sounding or you are otherwise on the wing; and so, considerately, I write au revoir.

/s/Norbert

P.S. I know less of that promised trip to California than ever before. I hate to mention it. It is hard not to think of it. I should never have believed it was my luck, but it is, *it is* my luck in having you remember it, and we shall meet— before Sir T. is too old to bark me away.

———◦∞◦———

110 West Sixty-ninth Street
New York, April fifteenth**[1922]

My dear Madge, or better, my favorite name, Margaret:

Today came your letter from Boulder Creek, where I am sending this in the hope that it will not go astray. On location is the logical place from which to write letters, it seems to me, but rarely, in my experience, is the opportunity taken advantage of. You did, which is nice for me.

Too bad it is cold and rainy, for this jaunt is in the nature of a holiday for you and your mother, or should be; but inclement or uncertain weather can spoil the country, especially if one has work to do which depends on favorabe conditions. I dare say you are restless when work lags, but patience you've learned is one of the virtues the eager artists must cultivate. And I am sure you have cultivated it or are giving a beautiful example of acting as if you had!

I'm most interested to know that Cullen Landis is playing opposite you. Why? Because he was a fellow-worker at Goldwyn's and three years ago I thought highly of him. He was modest, cheerful, uncomplaining and really interesting. I have reason to remember him above everyone else there for a single unusual act of his. When suddenly I was missed from the studio he alone came to the hotel to inquire. I wonder if the years have changed him. Recall me to him, if you think it best. He is an excellent actor, in my opinion.

Last night in going through a number of magazines I read that recent "interview" with you in the Motion Picture Mag. Mingled amusement and interest was mine, for honestly the story was good and bad at once. Rather strained, I thought, in places, especially when the writer termed you "the soul of a saint with the spirit of a Hollywood flapper", and "a mother-of-pearl miniature in a brass frame.["] Really, really, what utter rot, and despite the strain on Miss Gebhart, rather unflattering if she only knew it. Nevertheless there were points to the story and I liked reading it. Besides, you're too much of a philosopher not to value all that's printed about you, irrespective of its merits or truthfulness. I liked the pictures, particularly that by Hesser, full face with lifted eyes.

I'm glad you're reading as much as time allows for whether one greatly admires a book or not, a writer of reputation is likely to give something in his books. Usually I like Hergesheimer for his style, and to a certain extent I enjoyed "Cytherea" because it was very stylized although, naturally, the story was not calculated to rouse my sympathies any more than it did yours. Yet I think the story important because, you see, he successfully reflects the spirit of the times: the restlessness often found among married people, the temptations of careless living, and what yielding to restlessness usually brings. Naturally "Cytherea" is scarcely the book for you, but you must not consider as wasted the time you gave it.

"If Winter Come" I have not read in its entirety. I began it but, unusual for me, laid it aside because I felt not in the mood for it. I've no doubt it is as finely wrought as everybody says. F. Scott Fitzgerald is no favorite of mine so I did not bother with "The Beautiful and Damned." The author is too young for my taste and therefore too uneasy in his storytelling. Besides, I am not greatly interested in the people he writes about unless, like Hergesheimer, they are described by a mature writer. "Java Head" in my opinion is Hergesheimer's best. I imagine you would like it better than this latest creation of his.

"Nocturne" I believe is better than you are inclined to grant. Far better, for my part, than Swinnerton's succeeding books. As I may have told you, Leonard Merrick is my favorite modern and I have never failed to find a great deal in any novel of his although at first I did not like him, and still think "When Love Flies Out o' The Window" (which you read on the California train) inferior to his others. "Conrad in Quest of His Youth" — an exquisite trifle. I am reading Arnold Bennett's "Mr. Prohack" which I don't imagine you would greatly like, and I much fear if you ever get an opportunity to read "Grown Under Glass", it would please you no more. That ironic trifle is, I am sorry to say, still in a state of "consideration." More than one reputable editor has praised it, but to date no one has thought it wise to risk bringing it out. This, however, is always the tale of a first novel till finally someone decides to take a chance. Often they gamble to win, and often lose because, you see, publishing a first novel involves a great deal of chance, and in the case of "Grown Under Glass" the chance is rather emphasized. Be that as it may, I have heard enough about it not to think that I had wasted my time, nor to cease believing that another undertaking will be of greater merit. It is said to be "very promising." Meanwhile, waiting for something to eventuate, I am in anything but merry spirits and am, in fact, rather at a standstill, awful as that is to confess to ambitious you. Perhaps my next letter will indicate a change for the better. Things do change, always, for little lasts.

In response to your invitation, I'm afraid there's nothing at all to write about. I'm not at all active just now either in seeking enjoyment or in working. Theatregoing is a form of diversion I slight, yet I can remember the time when the prospect of a play made my heart sing. Pictures that interest me seem fewer and fewer, although when I *approve* my enjoyment is really keen. "The Loves of Pharaoh" I liked without reservation, but I can recall no other that so appealed except, of course, "Hail the Woman" which, as a play, would have annoyed me had it not been for other interests in it. Oh yes, a great deal seems missing from my life nowadays.

The other night I saw an especially noteworthy performance of "Tosca" at the opera, with Farrar making her last appearance in that opera at the Metropolitan. She was superb, really, and her operatic self would have astonished you as much as it did me, knowing her better, as we do, on the films. There was a tremendous demonstration from the audience, with stacks of flowers, and white doves bursting out of a basket passed across the footlights. Perhaps the birds were symbolic of Peace. Monday I shall see her farewell to "Carmen."

Beyond these diversions, and seeing a few friends, life in New York (for me at least) is as uneventful as seclusion in the country. But it is just a phase. Expecting so much of life in the way of surprises, thrills and triumphs, it always goes hard with me, I've discovered, when it is made clear to me that life has to be endured during long periods without surprises, thrills and triumphs. A childish conception, you'll agree.

With your letter came one from Mrs. Williamson recording a stormy voyage and a safe arrival in London before proceeding to Bath, where she lives. I'm glad you found her book entertaining and promise that all the travel romances have the same elements of freshness and romance and beauty. She's a remarkable worker and a very, very generous friend. Even the death of her husband, whom she wildly adored, could not cause her to relax or slight the smallest obligation to her friends or herself.

What about your own literary toilings? You used to say that you were writing plays, and Mr. Blackwood said he'd look over what you'd done and help you. Have you found other work too exacting? Please tell me this and also if your good friends Mr. Frohman and Mr. Gillette are still on your letter list.

Tomorrow is Easter so it will be if not cold, chilly. It always is. Yet people will be garbed for summer, according to immemorial custom. Often I wonder when it will be your good fortune to get a glimpse of the New York you say you love and which I won't admit I care for at all. Your work may bring you here as the same work brings so many for a picture or even a few scenes, and for all we know it may be this summer when it's hottest and you will be happiest. For my part I feel that we shall soon meet again either here or elsewhere. Meanwhile a figure of patience on a monument should be our common altarpiece!

Perhaps someone is calling you now, so you mustn't give more time to this letter. Another, and I hope a better one, will soon come to you. Before time brings that about please know that I am grateful for yours and sincerely appreciative of every work in it. Even your exclamation points delighted me.

Always your devoted,
/s/NL

P.S. The change of address is nothing unusual to a New Yorker. Within a week I shall be in new quarters, so have given you the address to get your next letter the quicker.

Western Union Telegram

Los Angeles SS H F Alexander 820P
May 30 1924
Miss Madge Bellamy
519 Beverly Drive Los Angeles ( Calif )

Off for the north and trying so hard to be as dignified as you would wish please wire me to StFrancis Hotel SanFrancisco and will keep in constant touch with you

Herbert

Telegram

Banff Springs Hotel Alta 10
1924 Jun 10 PM 10 38
Miss Madge Bellamy
519 Beverley Drive Beverly Hills Calif

I really hoped for more than good wishes read like a telegram you had telephoned in presence of witnesses

Herbert Brenon.

THOS. H. INCE STUDIOS
CULVER CITY, CAL.

Apr.
12th
1922

Miss Madge Bellamy,
Thomas Ince Motion Picture
Company,
Boulder Creek,
California.

My dear Madge:

We have just been requested by the manager of the Santa Cruz Theatre to ask you to make a personal appearance during the run of "HAIL THE WOMAN" on the 17th, 18th and 19th of this month.

We would like to have you do this if it is possible for Mr. Wray to arrange his schedule.

I realize that personal appearances are not always very agreeable, but on the other hand, the company is operating so far away from headquarters that it places us under obligations to many people in Santa Cruz and in Boulder Creek. I cannot help but feel that your appearing personally before this audience, would very greatly tend to offset our present indebtedness.

As I have already stated, personal appearances are not always pleasant, but I do believe that the manager of the theatre will see that you are very well entertained in Santa Cruz and I should imagine that a couple of meals in a really good hotel such as the St. George, as well as a nice comfortable room, would be a welcome break in the monotony of your stay at Boulder Creek.

I wish you would talk with Mr. Wray about his being able to spare you and if it can be done, I believe I would at least make an effort to co-operate with them. If you want to do this, I wish you would wire us at our expense and I will personally put it up to the manager of the Santa Cruz Theatre to see that both you and your charming mother are entertained as you should be.

I was very sorry that I could not spend more time with you on my last trip to Santa Cruz, but it was imperative that I make time. I looked for you just before I left, but did not see you and it was necessary that I be at the studio in the morning. However, I am looking forward to seeing you when the company is with the circus.

I remain, with the kindest of good wishes to you all,

Most sincerely,
/s/C.W. Thomas

CWThomas/w

———❧———

THOS. H. INCE STUDIOS
CULVER CITY, CAL.

Apr.
19th
1922

Miss Madge Bellamy
Alphine Hotel,
Boulder Creek, Calif.

Dear Miss Bellamy:

I enclose copy of a letter received this date and our reply to same.

I do not like the tone of Mr. Lewis' letter, as it seems to me he writes like a fit subject of an insane asylum.

I trust that you will take my advice in the spirit of friendship in which it is offered; this advice being to enter into no correspondence with the man if he annoys you with letters or telegrams.

In times past we have had trouble with characters of this type.

With best wishes, as ever, I remain,

Yours most truly,
/s/C. W. Thomas

CWThomas/w
encs.

———❧———

COPY FOR MISS BELLAMY

Johannesburg, Mich.
April 13, 1922.

Thomas H. Ince,
Culver City, Calif.

Dear Sir:

Would like to have you let me know at once Madge Bellamy's private address, that is the street and number of her and her mother's home in Hollywood. Also let me know her name in private life.

Would like you to let me know these facts at once as it is of the utmost importance that I do know, be sure it is her private address and name she goes by in private life if that is different than Madge Bellamy.

Also would like to know when you answer this letter if she will be in California for the next few months so that any letters and telegrams will reach her at once and privately.

You see I took the time to write this letter personal, so you see I am very interested in having a satisfactory answer at once.

Do not care to receive any address of her studio or any for that matter which will not come to her privately, understand?

Very sincerely yours,<br>(Signed) Keith B. Lewis.

P.S. Answer at once.

———∞———

COPY FOR MISS BELLAMY

Apr.<br>19th<br>1922

Mr. Keith B. Lewis,
Johannesburg, Mich.

My dear Sir:

We are in receipt of your letter of recent date.

We regret that we cannot grant your request, as it is entirely foreign to Mr. Ince's policy to furnish the home address of any employee of this studio.

Any communication addressed to Miss Bellamy in care of this studio will be delivered to her promptly.

The stamps which you kindly enclosed are returned herewith.

Yours most truly,<br>THOMAS H. INCE CORPORATION<br>/s/C. W. Thomas<br>General Manager

CWThomas/w
enc.

———∞———

June 4th, 1924.

Mr. Thos. H. Ince,
c/o Ince Studios,
Culver City, Calif.

My Dear Sir:-

As the Attorney for Miss Madge Bellamy, I am requested to call your attention to the fact, that in the Los Angeles Examiner of June 4th, appears an announcement from the Universal Studios, in which it appears from the last item of said announcement, that in

*"THE FLOWER OF NAPOLI"*

Herbert Rawlinson is the featured player, with MADGE BELLAMY in a Subordinate role. I enclose herewith the *objectionable* Announcement.

This may, probably, be an oversight, or an error, but the same is in direct conflict with the contract between Miss Bellamy and yourself, and, as you may appreciate, is very injurious to her.

For this reason, she insists upon an *immediate* correction of the Announcement through the press, and otherwise, so that this injurious Announcement, or article, may be corrected as far as you are able to do in this manner.

I have no doubt that you will at once attend to this, and that you will take such measures as you are able to do to correct this error, so as to protect her in the Announcement, and in the matter of other Companies to which you have loaned her.

You can see the great importance to her in having this corrected, and the serious injury that such an announcement, or advertisement, might be to her.

May I hear from you, by return mail, that such correction will be speedily made?

I remain,

Yours very truly,<br>Eugene A. Tucker,

EAT:K.

INGLE CARPENTER
ATTORNEY AT LAW
SUITE 820 DETWILER BLDG.
LOS ANGELES, CALIFORNIA
PHONE 828-125

June 6, 1924.

Mr. Eugene H. Tucker,
Attorney at Law,
Grosse Bldg.,
Los Angeles, Cal.

Dear Sir:

Your letter addressed to Thomas H. Ince, referring to your client, Miss Madge Bellamy, and relating to an announcement which appeared in the Los Angeles Examiner of June 4th, has been turned over to me as a counsel for the Thos. H. Ince Corporation.

We wish to thank you for calling our attention to the form of the announcement in which Miss Bellamy is mentioned and to say that Mr. Newman, Business Manager for the Ince corporation, called up the Universal Company immediately on receipt of your letter and learned that Miss Bellamy had already taken up the matter with them and that they had promised to remedy the mistake immediately and see that the form of the announcement was corrected through the Press. They stated that Miss Bellamy had been entirely satisfied with the result of their talk with her and that they would supply us with a copy of the corrected announcement when it should appear.

We wish to do everything in our power to aid in Miss Bellamy's value before the public, although we cannot entirely agree with you that the announcement referred to is of such serious consequence inasmuch as Miss Bellamy is so well established at the present time that an erroneous statement such as appeared in the paper if followed up by a correction is not apt, in our opinion, to hurt her professional reputation in any way whatsoever.

Yours very truly,
/s/Ingle Carpenter

IC/FM

———❈———

January 20, 1925.

Mr. Martin J. Quigley,
Pub. Exhibitor's Herald,
407 S. Dearborn St.,
Chicago, Ill.

Dear Sir:

When the enclosed Christmas Greetings appeared in your December 27th issue, I immediately wrote a special delivery letter to your Los Angeles representative, H. H. Beall, calling attention to the insult to Miss Bellamy, and demanding satisfaction.

Several days later, I received a very brief letter from Mr. Beall, stating that the New York office was to blame, and suggesting that I call at his office and "talk it over". To-day, I received the enclosed letter from Mr. Beall, and I hand you herewith copy of my reply to him. It is hardly necessary to say more, except that I ask you to compare the photograph used by the Herald with that used in Liberty, also enclosed. There is a big difference between the joy of a Christmas inspiration, and the humiliation of the niggardly, belittling thing in the Herald, especially to a sensitive, ambitious girl.

Please let me hear from you.

Very truly,
Miss Bellamy's father

WBP:G
Encl.

———❈———

January 20, 1925.

Mr. Harry Hammond Beall,
5528 Santa Monica Blvd.
Los Angeles, California.

Dear Sir:

Replying to your letter of yesterday, would say that while I think it very appropriate that some announcement regarding Miss Bellamy's new contract should be made in the Exhibitor's Herald, the details concerning the deal should be given out by the Fox office. I am sure the Fox people would appreciate it, and I thank you for the suggestion.

I did not reply to your former letter because you placed the blame for this dirty trick perpetrated on Miss Bellamy to the credit of the New York office, and I could not see that anything would be gained by calling at your office as you suggested, and "talking it over". There was nothing to "talk over". The facts spoke for themselves.

I contracted for certain space in the Christmas issue of the Exhibitor's Herald, and indicated certain copy, and a certain photograph to be used in that space. I brought to your office a two page advertisement published in the New York Telegraph, by Fox, so that you could be sure of the photograph, and informed of the source from which it could be obtained, since you said it was too late to take the chance of sending photograph from Los Angeles.

The copy was changed from "Starring in" the Iron Horse, etc., and made to read, "Stellar lead in", and instead of using photograph as indicated, a recent attractive photograph, any number of which could have been secured from Fox, an old photograph, three years out of date, used in a tie-up with a ninety-cent Lorna Doone hat, was dug up out of some rubbish pile, and used in a Christmas Greeting.

I can't think there is any boob connected with the New York office of the Herald, who would not know that this was not a suitable photograph for a boost effect, and the changing of the copy could not have been *accidental.*

No, Mr. Beall, there is a "nigger in the woodpile somewhere". The more I think of it, the more certain I am that somebody for personal spite, used the space I was to pay for, to stab Miss Bellamy with a nasty insult in your Christmas Herald.

In my former letter I mentioned Colvin Brown, because I knew he had already been guilty of some contemptible little meannesses, and because I could not imagine from what other source you could have secured that old photograph.

Miss Bellamy has been a subscriber to the Herald; she never misses carefully reading every number; I express to you my appreciation of it, as the foremost trade publication, and wish to cultivate closer relations by buying a little space for Christmas, and more later.

My attorneys advise me that the proper way to settle this matter is to bring suit for $10,000.00, and have the matter thoroughly sifted in the courts. But, frankly, I do not believe the publisher of the Herald is unfriendly, or that he personally sanctioned such a contemptible trick. On the contrary I imagine Mr. Quigley, if he knew the facts, would be anxious to punish the culprit, and to make amends for the insult to Miss Bellamy. It is reasonable to believe this, for certainly he would not tolerate someone connected with his publication, using the Herald, bought space at that, to belittle and humiliate his patron.

Another reason I did not answer your letter was because I expected you *to do something*, not just "talk it over", and I wanted to give you time.

Again thanking you for the sugggestion regarding the "flash". I am,

Very truly,
[William B. Philpott]

WBP:G

———∽≪∂≫∽———

Dec. 8, '20
11:15P.M.

Dear Madge:-

(Not knowing my status—at the present moment—I was almost going to address this letter as "Miss Bellamy"; such an overwhelming difference a few days make). When I wrote you a letter this morning, I little thought I would write another this evening; nor would I had I not phoned. But I have been so unhappy because of your attitude, stunned with surprise that your regard has changed because of something for which I was not in any way responsible, and for which you evidently blame me. In extenuation I can only say I am deeply sorry; it is something which I cannot explain because there is no explanation. Something weirdly stange posseses me tonight—loneliness. It came over me suddenly after I had got through talking with Mrs. Phillpott. You have taken hold of me as I never knew could be done, and your spell is something I cannot cast off. Like tonight, for instance, I tried to fight it off—to foolish avail ! I brought the typewriter home early tonight so I could work on my story, but it's been a d____ hard thing. I wanted so much to talk to you, to hear your voice; and when I got up from the phone, I felt so unhappy; it's a strange thing to be young and yet lonely, to be filled with the essence of dreaming and yet without companionship. I remember that I said in this morning's letter something about love coming in a "blinding pain"—how much more I realize it this hour. It has come to me now with a sort of rushing worship, with the strangest tension, in it a cry more sad than sane. Madge, Madge, wonder-girl, I love you, I love you. I have not done the work I had planned for tonight—instead, I have been acting "nervous" as someone in the house has told me. You know, wonder-girl, you have made me think like no one else. Since I've known you, but especially the last four weeks you are responsible, you have filled me with a sort of driving unrest (for SUCCESS); a gnawing for something I feel

that I can never attain (YOU). And I know, if the gods are kind and you can still countenance me, my heart shall always have this void in it, growing wider and deeper with the days. Really when I am talking to you, I feel dumb, silent, reticent; such words as I can think of seem so pitifully inadequate for what I feel, to compare to what I think of you. Looking back this moment over the days we have known each other from the very day we met, I feel dumbly unable to tell you what it has all meant to me. Really. After I had first come to know you, I know, that each day (or night) was occupied with the joy of seeing you that instant to think of the next day. Such things as sex, such things as marriage (which, of course, every man thinks of) I never thought of in connection with you, because it seemed a little distasteful. It—our acquaintance—had grown into a sort of little romance; I, for one, certainly feel genuinely happy; more so, because you felt to be so happy in little things. And secretly I thought in the past weeks—all along—that, no matter what chanced to me in later years, I could always cherish this one memory. Something was preparing for me——this was the way I had felt. I felt the influence of you. All the wonder and the magic of you——such as I had dreamt could ever exist. From untouched depths something was rising to consciousness. There is no name for such a thing; but it is something better than love. Madge, Madge, wonder-girl, I love you with all my heart——for always. I feel so much *larger* for having known you. Please believe me, please do not smile flippantly at what I am writing. I learned to love you, Madge, wonder-girl, knowing all the time that it was silly of me to do so because you are so far away. But in the recognition a sterner note has struck for me——the future in which there is work to be done. Lord, lord, how I want to do it, how much of a success I want to be. And this thought coming to me tonight, now as I write, is so terribly poignant, so crushing. You know I feel so sorry for having come to know you so intimately as I have, it was wrong for me to have done so. I have found out that I loved you only in time to feel the wrench of the futility (that is, of losing you) all the more keenly. No matter how I may show it, how crudely I may express it, I can never make you feel how dear you are to me; even now I feel so *weak, so pitiful,* telling you that I love you, because, in virtue, I should keep it silent. It seems such a folly that I should always tell you; but you have given me strength and I had to say it, as I say it now……. And so, after all this, I feel so unhappy—— especially after failing to speak to you on the phone. The whole thing…. why it's just like a picture of a young kid closing his eyes and putting his hands over them and valiantly imaging as *reality* the most impossible, daring adventures and achievements and realities in the world; only to see a stark room of unromantic face when he takes his hands off his eyes and opens them! Knowing the lie of the vision he has conjured, the untruthfulness of it, and that it is always going to be this. And so this is the case with me.

L.S.

P.S. And now having come to this conclusion, I ought to be satisfied with my verdict; but I am not for I want ever so much to call you on the telephone tomorrow, to hear your voice.

———⚬———

a Bord de SAVOIE

Jan 6 1922

Most Intriguing Person:--

Tomorrow night at 5 o'clock I'll be in Paris———

At the moment of writing this French steamer is plowing thru some heavy seas— rocking from side to side like an egg shell in turbulent water—but we arrive on schedule at noon tomorrow at Harve.

I'm scheduled to stay away from the States for two months—two continuities for an English company. I shall, however, take quarters in Paris where I'll do the writing. I'll probably stay for some time in N.Y. upon my return with the Lasky company for whom I had just finished a continuity …. the European trip was too good to give up, so I took it on the jump.

But this letter is chiefly to offer my belated congratulations—something I had intended doing since the time I read in a trade journal that you were heading your own company. I wish you—truly and sincerely—all the success in the world; success, and the splendid, sweet blossoming of womanhood that I know will be yours—heaped in a golden glory over your person of the dust that makes stars.

And I hope you have the financial success you deserve. I know how much you have wanted to star in your own productions— how you have dreamed of doing just the kind of things that would be worthwhile—to play roles of which you could create living images. I know you will.

Please remember me to your dear mother and your very noble and human dad. I figure that even if I be an evanescent sun-flower in your horizon I might still be able to cut up with your mother and father, and give myself a sort of halo. No?—

By-the-by you know that my aim is someday to write a play—since coming to N.Y. and seeing the shows it has been an incessant prod. Well, if I play the cards right with Al Woods the thing might be done—not now, but in due time, perhaps a year— maybe a little longer…..I want to finish this letter now, before the boat keels over.

Very sincerely— /s/Louis Stevens

———⚬———

David Swing Ricker
Hollywood
California

June 3rd, 1924.

Dear Madge:

If you have any faith in me, or want me to continue to have any interest in you, please do not pay one particle of attention to the biggest hot air shooter in Hollywood, Edwin Bower Hesser. Not only does he talk too much, but he makes promises that are impossible of fulfillment and says things that are utterly absurd. I do not know anyone that can get you in any more wrong with the picture world in general than Mr. Hesser.

He is a very fine photographer, but that says everything. Beyond his photography, I regard him as a very perfect nut—most excellent squirrel food. So please do not enter into any arrangment with him until you have seen me tomorrow night, at which time I can explain in detail exactly what I mean.

I do not object to saying above my signature that Mr. Hesser invariably makes the claim that he put your pictures across because of particular devotion to you, and prevails upon his clients to permit him to have exclusive rights for the distribution of their pictures, after he has charged them an exhorbitant figure in the first place; whereas, as a matter of fact, he receives pay from the magazines for every picture he sends in, just like any other photographer, and he has an agent in New York to represent him.

Naturally, he cannot sell a picture to a magazine, if it has been offered to them free by your own publicity representative, or by me. It is very plain that if Mr. Hesser was not receiving pay for placing pictures, but merely securing publicity for himself by having his pictures used, he would not be so particular from what source they reached the magazine. I think you can see that it is perfectly obvious that he must receive pay for them, both from you and the magazines, or else he would not be so insistent in the matter of exclusive rights. Do not believe him if he has ever told you that he can prevent the publication of any picture in any magazine, because all that would be necessary for me to do would be to notify the magazine that he had made this statement and he would never get a photograph in any one of them again as long as he lives.

Furthermore, he has no money of his own to speak of—I am sure he has not as much as I have, which is very little—and I would not undertake to offer to create Madge Bellamy Productions unless I were perfectly willing to tell you the identity of all the principals back of me and just how I expected to raise the money.

Furthermore, unless I can succeed in getting behind you some big, well known producer, such as Goldwyn, I would not advocate the organization just yet of Madge Bellamy Productions, because the most important consideration is not the making of the pictures, but the release of them, and if you remember what happened to Betty Compson Productions, I think you will take the advice of your manager-free-gratis-for-nothing.

I am sending this letter out to you by messenger, because I am afraid you might be misled before I can see you again Wednesday night.

I know at least a dozen girls to whom Hesser in the past has made the same gilded promises that he has made to you. One of them is Derelys Perdue. He was going to star her and do everything under the sun for her, but what he really did for her was to stand in her way, because she held off from other things while she waited for him to accomplish something.

Hesser has had a hard struggle upward; he deserves all credit for his success as a photographer, but I do not believe he could take a motion picture on a bet, and I do not believe he can raise enough money to safely finance you in anything. Capitalists are not putting any money in with photographers and I do not believe a photographer could possibly influence any producer, familiar with the game, to put in any money on his say-so. Therefore, if Hesser did get any money from outside sources, it would be from those unacquainted with motion picture production and all technical knowledge would have to be gained through Hesser, who has none. Hesser is butting in on Howe, who has the right connections for you and is the right man for you. His excuse for doing this is because he stands "so intimately with the family." He is also inspired, possibly, because Mr. Howe does not use Hesser pictures exclusively, because the magazines will not permit the exclusive use of any one-man pictures, nor will the news papers.

In other words, I am very frank to say that Mr. Hesser sees a chance to use you to glorify and advertise himself and wants to make the most of it, and if my advice is worth giving, or worth taking I cannot urge you too strongly to confine your relations to Mr. Hesser in his photographic capacity.

Lastly, the association of Derelys Perdue with Mr. Hesse almost wrecked her reputation. Of course, you will regard this letter as confidential, but I think that if it is going to happen that while I am dickering with a producer of international reputation, and while I am also dickering with Cosmopolitan, it will be well for us to have some sort of memorandum from you, giving me some sort of authority, so that it will not be said to me by any of these men: "How do you happen to be interested in Miss Bellamy? I thought Mr. Hesser was handling her."

This letter may sound pretty straight-from-the-shoulder and rough, but I feel that way—not toward you, but toward this Edwin Bower person. Of course, I love you just as much as ever.

Hastily,
/s/Swing

P.S.—Do you realize, dear, that it cheapens you terribly to have it appear that your services have to be "hocked" on the market by a photographer? It detracts from *your* dignity.

———— ⁓ ————

[previous page missing] and artistic understanding.

Howe will get busy laying the groundwork at once for both of these stories.

I want him also to get a story on "When My Dreams Come True". The dear old public believes that your dreams came true when you were lifted to stardom and received your first big check. In my story I want to convince the public that stardom means to you only the chance to make your dreams come true. And then I want your dream to be a homely dream, an intensely human dream. You must want a piece of land, a house standing on a hill, a stream, horses and dogs to love—a great place in the country to which you may invite crippled little children from Arthur Pedic's hospital to come and play with you in the sunbeams etc etc. In that story I shall reveal your whole sweet character and erect an ideal that the public will not forget. There is fine crowd psychology in that. This one, too, I may try to write myself.

I want to use "Unmarried Stars" for a dual purpose. When it is known that a star has a husband, she loses much of her public following, but I want also to use this story to bring out the fact that never in your sweet life have you been touched by the breath of scandal. This must be carefully handled because we cannot offend the industry, but if this idea can be put over and the public mind saturated with it, you will have an idolizing following such as no actress that has ever lived has had, not even Maude Adams.

Milt Howe is going to find out on what evening Jim Tully will be free. Then if you will invite him to the house and talk, talk, talk—talk as naturally, sweetly and brilliantly as you can talk when you are unafraid—Tully will write a story that will completely destroy the impression, created by jealous women, that our little Madge is a beautiful dumb-bell!

We must also arrange a lot of interviews with you by distinguished persons in which you discuss big, serious questions with a brilliant wit. Do not be frightened. You will have no trouble. I shall give you a recipe.

Tonight I had an inspiration.

Robert Vonnoh, who ranks with Sargent,

as one of the two greatest living American portrait painters, is now in Los Angeles. His most famous portraits have been of red-haired women. He has been known the world over for his passion for your type. Now, I do not known Vonnoh. But his wife is Bessie Potter Vonnoh, sculptor. I knew her well. So I am going to hunt up Vonnoh, who is now almost as old as I am, having been born in 1858, and I am going to invite him to meet you and say that you are the most beautiful girl he has ever seen. Vonnoh as an artist ranks as much higher than men like Stanlaws, Fisher, Christy etc as Booth, Barrett, Irving, Terry, Bernhardt, Duse and Marlowe rank above Herbert Rawlinson and Mary Miles Minter. Not only is Vonnoh in Who's Who, but he is in the Encyclopedia Brittanica. So let us pray that I will be able to land him.

Going to bed now.

/s/Swing
M.F.G.
Please preserve Howe's note.

S.
Howe will get for me today a list of all of the contemplated layout of Preview, so we may decide what ones you will fit into appropriately and without loss of caste.

———❦———

David Swing Ricker
Hollywood
California

Title:
Same Night.
Midnight.

Dear Madge:

I just performed my first official act as your unofficial and unpaid, but devoted private and sub-rosa manager without title.

Drove from 519 down to the corner and bought an Examiner. Got home, opened it up and went into an unholy rage. Found a story containing your picture printed alongside a lot of BABY STARS. Imagine my indignation after I have insisted on publishing you only alongside the most brilliant in the whole firmament! There you were surrounded by Alberta Vaughn, Ann May, Ruth Clifford and Marian Nixon! I saw red, foamed at the gills, grabbed the phone, called the editor and told him that my Madge was being printed alongside a bunch of nothings and I wouldn't stand for it. I told him to take it right out of the paper. Not let it get into another edition.

"All right, old man, all right, all right, I will. It should never have happened etc etc etc."

So it's out and we're saved!

It got into only 22,000 out of 184,000 copies, so no cause for worry.

[2 pages missing]

We do not want to quarrel with him.

We need him for awhile at least, *until we get his brother to put over some stuff for you.*

Do not feel, Madge, that it will hurt me any if you do not accept this suggestion.

I am merely offering my services as an advisor in publicity, but since we agree that we must all have "ego" I shall frankly tell you that I rank quite high in my profession.

I feel that I need not add that I am not trying, in this letter, to *sell myself to you,* though it does sound a bit like a sales talk.

Wanted merely to be sure to "get across" my point of view.

I sincerly, earnestly feel that while you need not change your publicity man, his output should be censored by some one who thinks of your good first and above all.

So let me seek the job of unpaid censor and assure you that I shall be very glad to look over all Howe's stories and picture layouts and give him the best of my 68 years' experience——if you want me to.

Nor shall I be hurt if you do not, but shall hunt out the gold-fish in his bowl just the same.

I enclose the story that outraged me to the extent of causing me to present to you my services—"free gratis", as they say in Yiddish.

Affectionately,
/s/Swing

———◇———

The Lambs
130 West 44th Street
New York

Tuesday midnight

My darling

Your letter came—strange—like you—moments of deep affection—contradicted a paragraph later by burning doubts.

I try so hard to understand you—You do me, too, don't you, dear. Yet the only thing that ever stopped my continuing to try—is the ridiculous position your father placed me in.

However, that's all over. Such a thing could only have happened in Hollywood—and—that's one—if not the principal reason I never want to go there again.

You are so strange—you awaken all my love for you—that slumbered—just until one gentle touch came from you—and then—you revert to your unkind or "proud" self. Is it not time for us to cast that aside.

I always hoped for a call from you—to try me—I did not want you to suffer—God knows!—but I wanted you to need me—and you did—and now I'd do anything in the world for you—You are so extraordinarily sweet—yet at times—like me—a little mad. You do the most glorious generous act—and then wipe it out as if you were a piece of rubber eraser—and—it—a light pencil mark.

Just like that morning to telephone (though I asked you for a number to phone you—for it is silly for you to be paying charges when I make three times what you do—(now get

angry—but Peter Pan did that!) then you wire that you don't want to kerb me "away from home." Do you lie awake at night, [nocturnal?]thinking up bitter things to write or say???

Yet if you were not *You*—I should not be content to win your love—so that's that.

After reading your letter countless times—and trying to forget the last unkind sentence—I went over to the Picadilly to see your lovely face and pretty smile—

Oh, dear, oh dear—it is a bad picture. Is Flynn drinking It was like "the morning after"—incoherent or stupid. But for your dear pretty self I would have walked out. As I viewed you it is just plain DRIVEL!

Your hair looked so sweet Madge

[remainder of letter missing]

———◇———

(Wisconsin Center for Film and Theater Research).

[March 22, 1931]

### ART VS. GOLD

Los Angeles

To the Editor of The New York Times:

It is time for the motion-picture producers to begin to think of their responsibilities. It is time for them to eliminate the crudities of the motion-picture ideology. The education of the masses is in their hands.

The great motion-picture houses are schools of thought, whether the producers think merely of box office and entertainment or not. The premise of art for art's sake or amusement for amusement's sake is a false theory.

The constant repetition of the Cinderella theme with its ideas of monetary success based on the exploitation of sex appeal, the themes aggrandizing banditry and cunning, bring on a reaction of futility and disappointment.

It is the producers who are at fault. They fear to lead the way, for they know that leadership in the domain of ethics has rarely been profitable, but they should look back upon their own pioneering careers and gather courage for a new leadership. As yet, they still have both eyes on the box office. However, to the pioneers has gone the glory and now is the time for this great industry that has made so many fortunes to garner glory to itself.

The producers have shown themselves masters at knowing what the people have wanted. The people have wanted mostly to forget their troubles, to hope, to believe in some chance that will bring them their heart's desire, but now is the time for the producers to show their audiences what they should want, what they really are and what they should hope for.

The tremendous technical advances, the marvelous technic of action, cutting and photography should be relied upon to furnish the thrills and variations that are more often left in the domain of lingerie, or sex, or situations that appeal only to the credulity of a 10-year-old. In the tendency to ape the limitations of the stage and in the natural tendency to exploit such a new thing as sound and dialogue, the producers have for the time being forgotten the springs that make the whole thing move.

From the general run of pictures and imagining them as a school of thought, I should say that they are instilling a doctrine of opportunism, of salesmanship and of personality without inculcating the moral necessity of having something fine to offer. The cinema for the most part is teaching in its themes and subjects the salesmanship of a pretty low order.

The education of the masses is to some extent in the hands of producers of pictures. Youngsters that patronize the cinemas should be taught that crime is a disease and not a short cut to success. We may teach them that success is motor cars or we can teach them the romance of achievement. Which is it to be?

Madge Bellamy

# MADGE BELLAMY: FILMOGRAPHY

prepared by William M. Drew

### The Riddle: Woman

Associated Exhibitors, Incorporated-Pathé Exchange, Incorporated. 6 reels. Released on October 3, 1920.
Director: Edward José. Scenario: John B. Clymer. Based on the play of the same name by Carl Jacobi as adapted by Charlotte E. Wells and Dorothy Donnelly. Photography: Max Schneider. Titles and special effects: Stewart B. Moss.
Cast: Geraldine Farrar, Montague Love, Adele Blood, William P.Carleton, Frank Losee, Madge Bellamy, Louis Stern.

### The Cup of Life

Thomas H. Ince Productions-Associated Producers. 6 reels. Released on August 7, 1921.
Director: Rowland V. Lee. Scenario: Joseph Franklin Poland. From a story by Carey Wilson. Photography: J. O. Taylor.
Cast: Hobart Bosworth, Madge Bellamy, Niles Welch, Tully Marshall, Monte Collins, May Wallace.

### Passing Thru

Thomas H. Ince Productions-Paramount Pictures. 5 reels. Released on August 14, 1921.
Director: William A. Seiter. Scenario: Joseph Franklin Poland. From a story by Agnes Christine Johnston. Photography: Bert Cann.
Cast: Douglas MacLean, Madge Bellamy, Otto Hoffman, Cameron Coffey, Willard Robards, Edith Yorke, Fred Gambould, Margaret Livingston, Louis Natheaux, Bert Hadley.

### Blind Hearts

Hobart Bosworth Productions-Associated Producers. 6 reels. Released on October 3, 1921.
Director: Rowland V. Lee. Scenario: Joseph Franklin Poland. From the story of the same name by Emilie Johnson. Photography: J. O. Taylor.
Cast: Hobart Bosworth, Madge Bellamy, Wade Boteler, Irene Blackwell, Colette Forbes, Raymond McKee, William Conklin, Lule Warrenton, Henry Hebert.

### Love Never Dies

King W. Vidor Productions-Associated Producers. 7 reels. Released on November 14, 1921.
Director: King Vidor. Scenario: King Vidor. Based on the novel *The Cottage of Delight* by William Nathaniel Harben. Photography: Max Dupont.
Cast: Lloyd Hughes, Madge Bellamy, Joe Bennett, Lillian Leighton, Fred Gambould, Julia Brown, Frank Brownlee, Winifred Greenwood, Claire McDowell.

## The Call of the North

Famous Players-Lasky-Paramount Pictures. 5 reels. Released on November 27, 1921.
Director: Joseph Henabery. Scenario: Jack Cunningham. Based on the novel *Conjuror's House* by Stewart Edward White. Photography: Faxon Dean.
Cast: Jack Holt, Madge Bellamy, Noah Beery, Francis McDonald, Edward Martindel, Helen Ferguson, Jack Herbert.

## Hail the Woman

Thomas H. Ince Productions-Associated Producers. 8 reels. Released on November 28, 1921.
Director: John Griffith Wray. Story and scenario: C. Gardner Sullivan. Photography: Henry Sharp.
Cast: Florence Vidor, Lloyd Hughes, Madge Bellamy, Theodore Roberts, Tully Marshall, Gertrude Claire, Vernon Dent, Edward Martindel, Charles Meredith, Mathilde Brundage, Eugene Hoffman, Muriel Frances Dana.

## Lorna Doone

Thomas H. Ince Corp.-Associated First National Pictures. 7 reels. Released on October 4, 1922.
Director: Maurice Tourneur. Scenario: Katherine Reed, Cecil G.Mumford, Wyndham Gittens, Maurice Tourneur. Based on the novel of the same name by Richard Doddridge Blackmore. Photography: Henry Sharp. Set design and costumes: Milton Menasco.
Cast: Madge Bellamy, John Bowers, Frank Keenan, Jack McDonald, Donald MacDonald, Norris Johnson, May Giraci, Charles Hatton.

## The Hottentot

Thomas H. Ince Productions-Associated First National Pictures. 6 reels. Released on December 25, 1922.
Director: James W. Horne. Additional direction and scenario: Del Andrews. Based on the play of the same name by William Collier and Victor Mapes. Photography: Henry Sharp.
Cast: Douglas MacLean, Madge Bellamy, Lila Leslie, Martin Best, Truly Shattuck, Raymond Hatton, Dwight Crittenden, Harry Booker, Bert Lindley, Stanhope Wheatcroft.

## Garrison's Finish

Jack Pickford Productions-Allied Producers and Distributors. 8 reels. Released on January 15, 1923.
Director: Arthur Rosson. Scenario: Elmer Harris. Based on the novel of the same name by William Blair Morton Ferguson. Titles: Mary Pickford. Photography: Harold Rosson.
Cast: Jack Pickford, Madge Bellamy, Charles A. Stevenson, Tom Guise, Frank Elliott, Ethel Grey Terry, Clarence Burton, Audrey Chapman, Dorothy Manners, Herbert Prior, Charles Ogle, Lydia Knott.

## Are You a Failure?

Preferred Pictures (B. P. Schulberg)-Al Lichtman Corp. 6 reels. Released on March 15, 1923.
Director: Tom Forman. Scenario: Eve Unsell. From a story by Larry Evans. Photography: Harry Perry.
Cast: Madge Bellamy, Lloyd Hughes, Tom Santschi, Hardee Kirkland, Jane Keckley, Hallam Cooley, Sam Allen, Myrtle Vane, Sport the dog.

## Soul of the Beast

Thomas H. Ince Corp.-Metro Pictures. 5 reels. Released on May 7, 1923.
Director: John Griffith Wray. Scenario: Ralph H. Dixon. From a story by C. Gardner Sullivan. Photography: Henry Sharp.
Cast: Madge Bellamy, Oscar the elephant, Cullen Landis, Noah Berry, Vola Vale, Bert Sprotte, Harry Rattenberry, Carrie Clark Ward, Lincoln Stedman, Larry Steers, Vernon Dent.

## Do It Now

Phil Goldstone Productions-Renown Pictures. 6 reels. Released on February 1, 1924.
Director: Duke Worne. Story: Malcolm S. White. Photography: Roland Price, Edgar Lyons.
Cast: Madge Bellamy, William Fairbanks, Alec B. Francis, Arthur Hoyt, John Fox, Jr., G. Raymond Nye, Dorothy Revier.

## No More Women

Associated Authors-Allied Producers and Distributors. 6 reels. Released on February 15, 1924.
Director: Lloyd Ingraham. Presented by Frank E. Woods, Thompson Buchanan, Elmer Harris, Clark W. Thomas. Story and scenario: Elmer Harris. Music: James C. Bradford. Casting director: Horace Williams.
Cast: Matt Moore, Madge Bellamy, Kathleen Clifford, Clarence Burton, George Cooper, H. Reeves-Smith, Stanhope Wheatcroft, Don the dog.

## The White Sin

Palmer Photoplay Corporation-Film Booking Offices of America (FBO). 6 reels. Released on February 24, 1924.
Director: William A. Seiter. Scenario: Del Andrews, Julian La Mothe. From a story by Harold Shumate. Photography: MaxDupont.
Cast: Madge Bellamy, John Bowers, Francelia Billington, Hal Cooley, James Corrigan, Billy Bevan, Norris Johnson, Ethel Wales, Otis Harlan, Myrtle Vane, Arthur Millett, James Gordon.

## Love's Whirlpool

Regal Pictures-W. W. Hodkinson Corporation. 6 reels. Released on February 29, 1924.
Director: Bruce Mitchell. Scenario: Elliott Clawson, Bruce Mitchell. From a story by Martha Lord. Photography: Stephen Norton. Film editing: Jack Dennis.
Cast: James Kirkwood, Lila Lee, Madge Bellamy, Robert Agnew, Matthew Betz, Edward Martindel, Margaret Livingston, Clarence Geldert, Joseph Mills.

## His Forgotten Wife

Palmer Photoplay Corp.-Film Booking Offices of America (FBO). 6 reels. Released on April 14, 1924.
Director: William A. Seiter. Story and screenplay: Will Lambert. Adaptation: Will Lambert, Del Andrews. Photography: Max Dupont, Abe Fried.
Cast: Madge Bellamy, Warner Baxter, Maude Wayne, Hazel Keener, Tom Guise, Willis Marks, Eric Mayne.

## The Fire Patrol

Hunt Stromberg Productions-Chadwick Pictures. 7 reels. Released on August 15, 1924.
Director: Hunt Stromberg. Scenario: Garrett Elsden Fort. Based on the play of the same name by James W. Harkins, Jr., and Edwin Barbour. Photography: Silvano Balboni.
Cast: Anna Q. Nilsson, Madge Bellamy, William Jeffries, Spottiswoode Aitken, Helen Jerome Eddy, Jack Richardson, Dicky

Brandon, Johnny Harron, Gale Henry, Frances Ross, Chester Conklin, Bull Montana, Charlie Murray.

## The Iron Horse

Fox Film Corporation. 12 reels. Released on October 4, 1924.
Director: John Ford. Scenario: Charles Kenyon. From a story by Charles Kenyon and John Russell. Titles: Charles Darnton. Photography: George Schneiderman. Additional photography: Burnett Guffey. Musical score: Erno Rapee. Assistant director: Edward O'Fearna.
Cast: George O'Brien, Madge Bellamy, Cyril Chadwick, Fred Kohler, Gladys Hulette, James Marcus, J. Farrell MacDonald, James Welch, Walter Rogers, George Waggner, Jack Padjan, Charles O'Malley, Charles Newton, Charles Edward Bull, Colin Chase, Delbert Mann, Chief Big Tree, Chief White Spear, Edward Piel, James Gordon, Winston Miller, Peggy Cartwright, Thomas Durant, Stanhope Wheatcroft, Frances Teague, Will Walling.

## On the Stroke of Three

Associated Arts Corp.-Film Booking Offices of America (FBO). 7 reels. Released on November 30, 1924.
Director: F. Harmon Weight. Scenario: O. E. Goebel, Philip Lonergan. Based on the novel *The Man From Ashaluna* by Henry Payson Dowst. Photography: Victor Milner, Paul Perry. Assistant director: Thornton Freeland.
Cast: Madge Bellamy, Kenneth Harlan, Mary Carr, John Miljan, Robert Dudley, Leonore Matre, Edwards Davis, Edward Phillips, Dorothy Dahm.

## Love and Glory

(Universal-Jewel) Universal Pictures. 7 reels. Released on December 7, 1924.
Director: Rupert Julian. Scenario: Elliott

Clawson, Rupert Julian. Based on the novel *We Are French!* by Perley Poore Sheehan and Robert Hobart Davis. Photography: Gilbert Warrenton.
Cast: Madge Bellamy, Charles De Roche, Wallace MacDonald, Ford Sterling, Gibson Gowland, Priscilla Moran, Charles De Ravenne, André Lancy, Madame De Bodamere.

## A Fool and His Money

Columbia Pictures. 6 reels. Released on January 1, 1925.
Director: Erle C. Kenton. Continuity: Dorothy Howell. Titles: Walter Anthony. Adaptation: Douglas Z. Doty. Based on the novel of the same name by George Barr McCutcheon. Film editing: Jack Kelly.
Cast: Madge Bellamy, William Haines, Stuart Holmes, Alma Bennett, Charles Conklin, Lon Poff, Carrie Clark Ward, Eugenie Besserer, Edwards Davis, Baby Billie Jean Phyllis.

## The Dancer

Fox Film Corp. 7 reels. Released on January 4, 1925.
Director: Emmett J. Flynn. Scenario: Edmund Goulding. Based on the novel of the same name by Hubert Parsons. Photography: Ernest G. Palmer, Paul Ivano.
Cast: Madge Bellamy, George O'Brien, Alma Rubens, Templar Saxe, Joan Standing, Alice Hollister, Freeman Wood, Walter McGrail, Noble Johnson, Tippy Grey.

## The Parasite

B. P. Schulberg Productions. 6 reels. Released on January 20, 1925.
Director: Louis Gasnier. Scenario: Eve Unsell. Based on the novel of the same name by Helen Reimensnyder Martin. Photography: Joseph Goodrich.
Cast: Madge Bellamy, Owen Moore, Bryant

Washburn, Lilyan Tashman, Mary Carr,
Bruce Guerin.

## The Reckless Sex

Phil Goldstone Productions-Truart Film Corp.
6 reels. Released on February 5, 1925.
Director: Alvin J. Neitz. Story: Travers Wells.
Photography: Bert Baldridge. Additional
photography: Edgar Lyons.
Cast: Madge Bellamy, William Collier, Jr.,
Johnnie Walker, Wyndham Standing, Claire
McDowell, Gertrude Astor, Alec B. Francis,
Gladys Brockwell, David Torrence, Helen
Dunbar, Walter Long.

## Secrets of the Night

(Universal-Jewel) Universal Pictures. 7 reels.
Released on February 15, 1925.
Director: Herbert Blaché. Scenario and
adaptation: Edward J. Montagne. Based on
the play *The Nightcap* by Guy Bolton and Max
Marcin. Photography: Gilbert Warrenton.
Cast: Madge Bellamy, James Kirkwood, Tom
Ricketts, ZaSu Pitts, Tom S. Guise, Arthur
Stuart Hull, Edward Cecil, Frederick Cole,
Rosemary Theby, Tom Wilson, Joe Singleton,
Bull Montana, Tyrone Brereton, Otto
Hoffman, Arthur Thalasso, Anton Vaverka.

## Wings of Youth

Fox Film Corporation. 6 reels. Released on
May 21, 1925.
Director: Emmett J. Flynn. Scenario: Bernard
McConville. Based on the story "Sisters of
Jezebel" by Harold P. Montayne.
Photography: Ernest G. Palmer.
Cast: Ethel Clayton, Madge Bellamy, Charles
Farrell, Freeman Wood, Robert Cain,
Katherine Perry, Marion Harlan, George
Stewart, Douglas Gerrard.

## The Man in Blue

(Universal-Jewel) Universal Pictures. 6 reels.
Released on June 21, 1925.
Director: Edward Laemmle. Scenario: E.
Richard Schayer. Based on the story "The
Flower of Napoli" by Gerald Beaumont.
Photography: Clyde De Vinna.
Cast: Madge Bellamy, Herbert Rawlinson,
Nick De Ruiz, André de Beranger, Cesare
Gravina, Jackie Morgan, Dorothy Brock, D. J.
Mitsoras, Carrie Clark Ward, C. F. Roark,
Martha Mattox.

## Lightnin'

Fox Film Corp. 8 reels. Released on August
23, 1925.
Director: John Ford. Scenario: Frances
Marion. Based on the play of the same name
by Winchell Smith and Frank Bacon.
Photography: Joseph August. Assistant
director: Edward O'Fearna.
Cast: Jay Hunt, Madge Bellamy, Wallace
MacDonald, J. Farrell MacDonald, Ethel
Clayton, James Marcus, Edythe Chapman,
Otis Harlan, Brandon Hurst, Richard Travers,
Peter Mazutis.

## Havoc

Fox Film Corp. 9 reels. Released on
September 27, 1925.
Director: Rowland V. Lee. Scenario: Edmund
Goulding. From the story of the same name
by Henry Wall. Photography: G. O. Post.
Assistant director: Daniel Keefe.
Cast: Madge Bellamy, George O'Brien, Walter
McGrail, Eulalie Jensen, Margaret Livingston,
Leslie Fenton, David Butler, Harvey Clark,
Wade Boteler, Edythe Chapman, Captain E.
H. Calvert, Bertram Grassby.

## Thunder Mountain

Fox Film Corporation. 8 reels. Released on October 11, 1925.
Director: Victor Schertzinger. Scenario: Eve Unsell. From the play *Thunder* or *Howdy Folks* by Pearl Franklin, based on a story by Elia W. Peattie. Photography: Glen MacWilliams.
Cast: Madge Bellamy, Leslie Fenton, Alec B. Francis, Paul Panzer, Arthur Houseman, ZaSu Pitts, Emily Fitzroy, Dan Mason, Otis Harlan, Russell Simpson, Natalie Warfield.

## Lazybones

Fox Film Corp. 8 reels. Released on November 6, 1925.
Director: Frank Borzage. Scenario: Frances Marion. Based on the play of the same name by Owen Davis. Photography: Glen MacWilliams, George Schneiderman. Assistant director: Orville O. Dull.
Cast: Buck Jones, Madge Bellamy, Virginia Marshall, Edythe Chapman, Leslie Fenton, Jane Novak, Emily Fitzroy, ZaSu Pitts, William Norton Bailey.

## The Golden Strain

Fox Film Corp. 6 reels. Released on December 27, 1925.
Director: Victor Schertzinger. Scenario: Eve Unsell. Based on the story "Thoroughbreds" by Peter B. Kyne. Photography: Glen MacWilliams. Assistant director: William Tummel.
Cast: Madge Bellamy, Hobart Bosworth, Kenneth Harlan, Ann Pennington, Lawford Davidson, Frank Beal, Frankie Lee, Coy Watson, Robert Frazer, Oscar Smith, George Reed, Grace Morse, Frank McGlynn, Jr., Larry Fisher, Lola Mackey.

## The Dixie Merchant

Fox Film Corp. 6 reels. Released on March 7, 1926.
Director: Frank Borzage. Scenario: Kenneth B. Clarke. Based on the novel *The Chicken-Wagon Family* by John Barry Benefield. Photography: Frank B. Good. Assistant director: Bunny Dull.
Cast: J. Farrell MacDonald, Madge Bellamy, Jack Mulhall, Claire McDowell, Harvey Clark, Edward Martindel, Evelyn Arden, Onest Conly, Paul Panzer.

## Sandy

Fox Film Corp. 8 reels. Beleased on April 11, 1926.
Director: Harry Beaumont. Scenario: Eve Unsell. Based on the novel of the same name by Elenore Meherin. Photography: Rudolph Bergquist. Assistant director: J. Malcolm Dunn.
Cast: Madge Bellamy, Leslie Fenton, Harrison Ford, Gloria Hope, Bardson Bard, David Torrence, Lillian Leighton, Charles Farrell, Charles Coleman, Joan Standing.

## Black Paradise

Fox Film Corp. 5 reels. Released on May 30, 1926.
Director: R. William Neill. Story and scenario: L. G. Rigby. Photography: George Schneiderman. Assistant director: Edward O'Fearna.
Cast: Madge Bellamy, Edmund Lowe, Leslie Fenton, Edward Piel, Harvey Clark, Paul Panzer, Marcella Daly, Samuel Blum, Doris Lloyd, Patrick Kelly, Mary Gordon.

## Summer Bachelors

Fox Film Corp. 7 reels. Released on December 18, 1926.
Director: Allan Dwan. Scenario: James Shelley

Hamilton. Based on the novel of the same name by Warner Fabian. Photography: Joseph Ruttenberg. Art direction: Sam Corso. Scenic direction: Al Panci. Interior decorator: Miss S. Baxter. Assistant director: Barton Adams. Costumes: Emery J. Herrett. Draperies: J. G. Horton.

Cast: Madge Bellamy, Allan Forrest, Matt Moore, Hale Hamilton, Leila Hyams, Charles Winninger, Clifford Holland, Olive Tell, Walter Catlett, James F. Cullen, Cosmo Kyrle Bellew, Charles Esdale.

## *Bertha, The Sewing Machine Girl*

Fox Film Corp. 6 reels. Released on December 19, 1926.
Director: Irving Cummings. Scenario: Gertrude Orr. Based on the play of the same name by Theodore Kremer. Photography: Abe Fried. Assistant director: Charles Woolstenhulme.
Cast: Madge Bellamy, Allan Simpson, Sally Phipps, Paul Nicholson, Anita Garvin, J. Farrell MacDonald, Ethel Wales, Arthur Houseman, Harry Baily.

## *Ankles Preferred*

Fox Film Corp. 6 reels. Released on February 27, 1927.
Director: John G. Blystone. Scenario: James Shelley Hamilton. From a story by Kenneth Hawks, John G. Blystone, and Philip Klein. Photography: Glen MacWilliams. Assistant director: Jasper Blystone.
Cast: Madge Bellamy, Lawrence Gray, Barry Norton, Allan Forrest, Marjorie Beebe, J. Farrell MacDonald, Joyce Compton, William Strauss, Lillian Elliott, Mary Foy.

## *The Telephone Girl*

Famous Players-Lasky-Paramount Pictures. 6 reels. Released on March 26, 1927.
Director: Herbert Brenon. Scenario: Elizabeth

Meehan. Based on the play *The Women* by William C. deMille. Photography: Leo Tover.
Cast: Madge Bellamy, Holbrook Blinn, Warner Baxter, May Allison, Lawrence Gray, Hale Hamilton, Hamilton Revelle, W. E. Shay, Karen Hansen.

## *Colleen*

Fox Film Corp. 6 reels. Released on July 3, 1927.
Director: Frank O'Connor. Story and scenario: Randall H. Faye. Photography; George Schneiderman. Assistant director: A. F. Erickson.
Cast: Madge Bellamy, Charles Morton, J. Farrell MacDonald, Tom Maguire, Sammy Cohen, Marjorie Beebe, Ted McNamara, Tom McGuire, Sarah Padden, Sidney Franklin, Carl Stockdale.

## *Very Confidential*

Fox Film Corp. 6 reels. Released on November 6, 1927.
Director: James Tinling. Scenario: Randall H. Faye. From a story by James Kevin McGuiness and Randall H. Faye. Photography: Joseph August.
Cast: Madge Bellamy, Patrick Cunning, Mary Duncan, Joseph Cawthorn, Marjorie Beebe, Isabelle Keith, Carl von Haartmann.

## *Silk Legs*

Fox Film Corp. 6 reels. Released on December 18, 1927.
Director: Arthur Rosson. Supervisor: William Conselman. Scenario: Frances Agnew. From a story by Frederica Sagor. Titles: Delos Sutherland. Photography: Rudolph Bergquist. Assistant director: S. Hanberry.
Cast: Madge Bellamy, James Hall, Joseph Cawthorn, Maude Fulton, Margaret Seddon.

## Soft Living

Fox Film Corp. 6 reels. Released on February 5, 1928.
Director: James Tinling. Scenario: Frances Agnew. From a story by Grace Mack. Titles: Malcolm S. Boylan. Photography: Joseph August. Film editing: J. Edwin Robbins. Assistant director: Leslie Selander.
Cast: Madge Bellamy, Johnny Mack Brown, Mary Duncan, Joyce Compton, Thomas Jefferson, Henry Kolker, Olive Tell, Maine Geary, Tom Dugan, David Wengren.

## The Play Girl

Fox Film Corp. 6 reels. Released on April 22, 1928.
Director: Arthur Rosson. Story and scenario: John Stone. Titles: Norman Z. McLeod. Photography: Rudolph Bergquist. Film editing: Ralph Dietrich. Assisant director: William Tummel.
Cast: Madge Bellamy, Johnny Mack Brown, Walter McGrail, Lionel Belmore, Anita Garvin, Thelma Hill, Harry Tenbrook.

## Mother Knows Best

Fox Film Corp. 110 minutes (part-talking). Released on October 28, 1928.
Director: John G. Blystone. Dialogue supervision: Charles Judels, Dave Stamper. Scenario: Marion Orth. Based on the story of the same name by Edna Ferber. Dialogue: Eugene Walter. Titles: William Kernell, Edith Bristol. Music: Erno Rapee, S. L. Rothafel. Song "Sally of My Dreams": William Kernell. Photography: Gilbert Warrenton. Film editing: Margaret V. Clancey. Recording engineer: Joseph Aiken. Assistant director: Jasper Blystone.
Cast: Madge Bellamy, Louise Dresser, Barry Norton, Albert Gran, Joy Auburn, Annette De Kirby, Stuart Erwin, Ivor De Kirby, Lucien Littlefield, Dawn O'Day (Anne Shirley).

## Fugitives

Fox Film Corp. 6 reels (silent with synchronized musical score by Movietone). Released on January 27, 1929.
Director: William Beaudine. Supervisor: Kenneth Hawks. Scenario: John Stone. Based on a story by Richard Harding Davis. Titles: Malcolm Stuart Boylan. Photography: Chester Lyons. Assistant director: Thomas Held.
Cast: Madge Bellamy, Don Terry, Arthur Stone, Earle Foxe, Matthew Betz, Lumsden Hare, Edith Yorke, Jean Laverty, Hap Ward.

## Tonight at Twelve

Universal Pictures. 78 minutes (all-talking). Released on September 29, 1929.
Director: Harry A. Polland. Scenario: Matt Taylor. Adaptation and dialogue: Harry A. Pollard, Matt Taylor. Based on the play of the same name by Owen Davis. Titles (for the silent version): Owen Davis. Photography: Jerome Ash. Film editing: Maurice Pivar.
Cast: Madge Bellamy, Robert Ellis, Margaret Livingston, Vera Reynolds, Norman Trevor, Hallam Cooley, Mary Doran, George Lewis, Madeline Seymour, Josephine Brown, Donald Douglas, Louise Carver, Nick Thompson.

## White Zombie

Amusement Securities Corporation-United Artists. 73 minutes. Released on August 4, 1932.
Director: Victor Hugo Halperin. Producer: Edward Halperin. Screenplay: Garnett Weston. Based on the novel *The Magic Island* by William Seabrook. Photography: Arthur Martinelli. Music: Guy Bevier Williams, Xavier Cugat, Nathaniel Dett, Gaston Borch, Hugo Riesenfeld, Leo Kempenski, H. Herkan, H. Maurice Jacquet. Film editing: Harold MacLernon. Set designs: Ralph Berger, Conrad Tritschler. Special effects: Howard Anderson. Makeup: Jack P. Pierce, Carol Axcelle.

Cast: Bela Lugosi, Madge Bellamy, John Harron, Joseph Cawthorn, Robert Frazer, Clarence Muse, Brandon Hurst, Dan Crimmins, John Peters, George Burr McAnnan, John Printz, Claude Morgan, John Fergusson, Annette Stone, Velma Gresham.

## Gigolettes of Paris

Equitable Pictures. 64 minutes. Released on March 15, 1933.
Director: Alphonse Martel. Story and screenplay: Alphonse Martel. Photography: Henry Cronjager, Herman Schopp. Music: Darby St. John. Film editing: Tom Parsons, Otis Garrett.
Cast: Madge Bellamy, Gilbert Roland, Natalie Moorhead, Theodore von Eltz, Molly O'Day, Henry Kolker, Paul Porcasi, Albert Conti, P. Schumann-Heink.

## Riot Squad

Mayfair Pictures Corporation. 64 minutes. Released on June 15, 1933.
Director: Harry Webb. Story and continuity: Jack Natteford, Barney Sarecky. Photography: Roy Overbaugh. Film editing: Fred Bain.
Cast: Madge Bellamy, Pat O'Malley, James Flavin, Addison Richards, Harrison Greene.

## Gordon of Ghost City

Universal Pictures. A serial in twelve chapters. Ch. 1: "A Lone Hand." Ch. 2: "The Stampede." Ch. 3: "Trapped." Ch. 4: "The Man of Mystery." Ch. 5: "Riding for Life." Ch. 6: "Blazing Prairies." Ch. 7: "Entombed in the Tunnel." Ch. 8: "Stampede." Ch. 9: "Flames of Fury." Ch. 10: "Swimming the Torrent." Ch. 11: "A Wild Ride." Ch. 12: "Mystery of Ghost City." First chapter released on July 26, 1933; final chapter released on October 20, 1933.
Director: Ray Taylor. Screenplay: Ella O'Neill, Basil Dickey, George Plympton, Het

Manheim, Harry Hoyt. Suggested by a story by Peter B. Kyne.
Cast: Buck Jones, Madge Bellamy, Walter Miller, Tom Ricketts, William Desmond, Francis Ford, Edmund Cobb, Hugh Enfield, Bud Osborne, Silver the horse.

## Charlie Chan in London

Fox Film Corp. 79 minutes. Released on September 14, 1934.
Director: Eugene Forde. Producer: John Stone. Screenplay: Philip MacDonald. Based on the character created by Earl Derr Biggers. Photography: L. W. O'Connell. Musical director: Samuel Kaylin.
Cast: Warner Oland, Drue Leyton, Douglas Walton, Alan Mowbray, Mona Barrie, Ray Milland, George Barraud, Paul England, Madge Bellamy, Walter Johnson, Murray Kinnell, E. E. Clive, Elsa Buchanan, Reginald Sheffield, Perry Ivins, John Rogers, Helena Grant, Montague Shaw, Phyllis Coughlan, Margaret Mann, David Torrence, Claude King.

## The Great Hotel Murder

Fox Film Corp. 70 minutes. Released on March 8, 1935.
Director: Eugene Forde. Producer: John Stone. Screenplay: Arthur Kober. Based on a story from *Receipe for Murder* by Vincent Starrett. Photography: Ernest Palmer. Music: Samuel Kaylin.
Cast: Edmund Lowe, Victor McLaglen, Rosemary Ames, Mary Carlisle, Henry O'Neill, C. Henry Gordon, William Janney, Charles C. Wilson, John Wray, John Qualen, Herman Bing, Madge Bellamy, Robert Gleckler, Clarence H. Wilson.

## The Daring Young Man

Fox Film Corp. 76 minutes. Released on May 24, 1935.
Director: William A. Seiter. Producer: Robert T. Kane. Screenplay: William Hurlbut, Sam Hellman, Glenn Tryon. From a story by Bia Claude Binyoh and Sidney Skolsky.
Photography: Merritt Gerstad.
Cast: James Dunn, Mae Clarke, Neil Hamilton, Sidney Toler, Warren Hymer, Stanley Fields, Madge Bellamy, Frank Melton, Raymond Hatton, Jack LaRue, Arthur Treacher, Dorothy Christy, Robert Gleckler, William Pawley, James Donlan, Phil Tead, DeWitt Jennings, Del Henderson.

## Under Your Spell

20th Century-Fox Film Corp. 62 minutes. Released on November 6, 1936.
Director: Otto Preminger. Producer: John Stone. Screenplay: Frances Hyland, Saul Elkins. From a story by Bernice Mason and Sy Bartlett. Photography: Sidney Wagner. Film editing: Fred Allen. Musical director: Arthur Lange. Costumes: Herschel. Choreography: Sammy Lee.
Cast: Lawrence Tibbett, Wendy Barrie, Gregory Ratoff, Arthur Treacher, Gregory Gaye, Berton Churchill, Jed Prouty, Claudia Coleman, Charles Richman, Madge Bellamy, Nora Cecil, Bobby Samarzich, Joyce Compton, June Gittelson, Clyde Dilson, Boyd Irwin, John Dilson, Lloyd Whitlock, Frank Sheridan, Edward Mortimer, Sam Blum, Jay Eaton, Scott Mattraw, Harry Stafford, Edward Gargan, Frank Fanning, Cedric Stevens, Creighton Hale, Harry Harvey, Charles Sherlock, Edward Cooper, Lee Phelps, Bruce Mitchell, Pierre Watkin, Theodore von Eltz, Sherry Hall, Jack Mulhall, Dink Trout, Kate Murray, Mariska Aldrich, Frank Arthur Swales, Troy Brown, Florence Wix, George Magrill, Josef Swickard, Ann Gillis, Robert Dalton, Muriel Evans, Alan Davis.

## Northwest Trail

Action Pictures-Screen Guild. 66 minutes. Released on November 30, 1945.
Director: Derwin Abrahams. Producers: William B. David, Max M. King. Screenplay: Harvey Gates, L. J. Swabacher. Based on the novel of the same name by James Oliver Curwood. Photography (in Cinecolor): Marcel Le Picard. Music: Frank Sanucci. Film editing: Thomas Neff.
Cast: Bob Steele, John Litel, Joan Woodbury, Madge Bellamy, George Meeker, Ian Keith, Raymond Hatton, Poodles Hanneford, John Hamilton, Charles Middleton, Grace Hanneford, Bill Hammond, Bud Osborne, Al Ferguson, Bob Duncan, Josh (John) Carpenter.

# *INDEX*

This index includes only photographs and text material. Photographs are indicated by page numbers in parentheses.

A Darling of the Twenties
Typeset in 11 point Palatino, 13 point leaded.
Composed by Eastern Graphics.
Cover design by Joseph Mastrantuono.
Edited by Margaret D. Lemke.
Printed by Johnson City Publishing, Inc.,
Binghamton, New York,
on Sterling Litho Satin.